The In-House Providing in European Law

Mario Comba & Steen Treumer (Eds.)

The In-House Providing in European Law

DJØF Publishing
2010

The In-House Providing
in European Law
European Procurement Law Series vol. 1

First Edition 2010

DJØF Publishing is a company of the Association of Danish Lawyers and Economists

Print: Scandinavian Book, Århus
Printed in Denmark 2010
ISBN 978-87-574-2168-2

Sold and distributed in North America by:
International Specialized Book Services (ISBS)
Portland, OR 97213, USA
www.isbs.com

Sold in all other countries by:
DJØF Publishing
Lyngbyvej 17, P.O.Box 2702
DK 2100 Copenhagen
Denmark
www.djoef-forlag.dk

Contents

Foreword by the Editors of the European Procurement Law Series

The distinction between in-house and ex-house providing is fundamental and well-known in practice and theory. It is of utmost importance as the consequence of the categorization of an arrangement as "in-house" is, that it falls outside of the scope of the EC public procurement rules. However, for various reasons it is often very difficult to establish whether an arrangement is in-house or not. The case law from the European Court of Justice on this subject-matter is highly complex whereas the case law at national level is sparse. Furthermore, the legal literature both at national and international level has been relatively limited and mainly focuses on the Teckal case law which concerns in-house arrangements with a separate legal entity, cf. C-107/98, Teckal. The present publication deals with in-house in a broader perspective and looks into the interpretation, implementation and practice at national level in a range of member states.

The above-mentioned characteristics should be enough to fuel interest in the topic of this publication but recent case law from the European Court of Justice makes the topic not only fundamental but also "hot". During our writing process the European Court of Justice has developed the state of law in this area in a very dynamic way which has made it necessary to make fundamental adjustments to this publication on the way. The Court has fundamentally modified its case law on the socalled external in-house rule based on the decision in the above-mentioned Teckal ruling. Furthermore, it has introduced what appears to be an entirely new exception to the public procurement rules with the ruling in C-480/06, Commission v Germany in a case where the in-house argumentation was invoked but rejected.

This publication will be the first in the new European Procurement Law Series. Publications in this series are the result of the collaboration in a European research group founded at the University of Turin. The group consists of academics specialized in procurement law that consider a comparative approach both valuable and necessary. The starting point is that European institutions have developed common principles and rules which are applicable all over the European Union. However, uniform application all over Europe cannot be taken for granted. European principles and rules superimpose themselves unto the pre-existing (and at times divergent) national provisions. Once they penetrate the domestic legal orders, the sources of European law interact with national law. They are there to alter domestic law, but they risk being read as to minimise their innovative impact on the national legal order if not to be misunderstood by practitioners and academics alike whose frame of mind was cast in the moulds of national law.

The Commission and the Court of Justice are out there to redress false readings and misunderstandings. Comparative knowledge may however help in avoiding mistakes as well, exposing domestic courts and other actors to possibly different approaches to what are in the end the same principles and rules. Comparative information and analysis of the procurement law and practice in the various Member States is therefore an important tool for the development of procurement regulation and practice in the EU. More into the details, it is valuable for practitioners in the Member States to be aware of practices, regulation, case law and interpretations of procurement law throughout the European Union as this can assist them in understanding the rules applicable and in developing best practices. Likewise, such knowledge can be important for national courts and review bodies as a source of inspiration in their interpretation of the law. As the European Court of Justice reminds us on its official website, the courts of the Member States are the 'ordinary courts in matters of Community law'. National courts may, and in some cases must, refer questions to the Court of Justice. With more and more member states leading to increased delays in the preliminary reference procedures, national courts will more often have to look for answers elsewhere. Precedents from other national courts giving application to the common European rules and principles, are a precious source of inspiration. Finally, it should not be overlooked that the Court of Justice too is aware of the value of the comparative approach and its rulings are from time to time clearly influenced by a development or a trend in regulation or practice at national level. Increased comparative knowledge of the case law of different Member States may alert the Court of Justice to the difficulties national courts are facing in giving full effect to European law. In some cases, it may make Community institutions aware of common trends developing at national level, a spontaneous *jus commune* which it is better to follow than just to oppose or even worse: to ignore.

It is our hope that the European Procurement Law Series will contribute to a strengthened dialogue between the various legal cultures in the field of procurement and that it will become a well-known source of inspiration.

Roberto Caranta
Professor
University of Turin

Steen Treumer
Professor
University of Copenhagen

15th November 2009

The In-House Providing: The Law as It Stands in the EU

*Professor Roberto Caranta, University of Torino, Italy**

To accept that is possible for contracting authorities to have recourse, for the supply of goods, to separate entities over which they maintain either absolute or relative control, in breach of the relevant Community legislation, would open the floodgates for forms of evasion contrary to the objective of ensuring free and undistorted competition which the Community legislature seeks to achieve through the coordination of procedures for the award of public supply contracts [Cosmas AG, Case C-107/98 *Teckal* [1999] ECR I-8121, para 65].

1. Introduction

This paper will assess the present state of European law with reference to in-house providing and public procurement law. Public procurement law is applicable in case procuring entities decide to externalise some activity, production or other tasks. It is not applicable when the procuring entity builds the works, or provides the goods and the services needed with its own means according to the freedom of organisation granted by the Treaty.[1] This is referred to as in-house providing. The notion of in-house providing is therefore an element in the demarcation of the province of application of public procurement law.[2] In given situations, procuring entities, while not strictly

* Professor in Administrative Law, Università degli Studi di Torino.

1. See the conclusions by AG Geelhoed in Case 295/05 *Asemfo* [2007] ECR I-2999, para 49.
2. As such, the 'in-house' doctrine is not strictly speaking an exception to the applicability of procurement rules, rather a limit to its application and more generally to the application of free movements; as a limit, however, it deserves the same restrictive reading as an exception: see J.J. Pernas Garcías *Las operaciones in-house y el Derecho comunitario de contratos públicos* (Madrid: Justel, 2008) 38 ff.; R.

speaking producing themselves the works, goods and services they need, have recourse to entities which cannot be said to be completely district from than the procuring entities themselves. In these cases, it cannot be said that the procuring entities are procuring from the market what they need. As such, public procurement rules do not apply. The problem is to find out exactly when this happens.[3]

The starting point will necessarily be the rather scant legislative texts. The attention will then turn to the case law, which have brought about a difficult evolution leading to some clarification of the essential requisites of in-house providing. The restrictive approach followed by the European Court of justice has quite limited the scope for institutional public-private partnerships. The recent Interpretative Communication by the Commission on the application of Community law on Public Procurement and Concessions to Institutionalised Public-Private Partnership lays down the conditions for this sort of arrangements and will have to be examined.[4] Some more general issues will be referred to in the conclusions.

2. Art. 6 of Directive 92/50/EEC on the procurement of public service contracts and Teckal

According to Art. 6 of Council Directive 92/50/EEC of 18 June 1992 relating to the coordination of procedures for the award of public service contracts "This Directive shall not apply to public service contracts awarded to an entity which is itself a contracting authority within the meaning of Article 1 (b)

Cavallo Perin and D. Casalini *'Control over in-house Providing Organisations'* in Public Procurement Law Rev., 2009, 239.

3. To those quoted in the previous note add F. Avarkioti *'The Application of EU Public Procurement Rules to "in-house" Arrangements'* Public Procurement Law Rev., 2007, 22; K. Weltzein *'Avoiding the Procurement Rules by Awarding Contracts to in-house Entity: The Scope of the Procurement Directives in the Classical Sector'* Public Procurement Law Rev., 2005, 252; C. Lecuyer-Thieffry et P. Thieffry *'Les prestations effectuées in-house sans mise en concurrence'* Act. Jur. Dr. Adm., 2005, 927; D. Casalini, L'organismo di diritto pubblico e l'organizzazione *in-house,* Napoli, Jovene, 2003.
4. COM (2007) 6661; see Ch.D. Tvarnø *'A Critique of the Commission's Interpretative Communication on Institutionalised Public-Private Partnership'* Public Procurement Law. Rev., 2009, NA11; R. Williams *'The Commission Interpretative Communication on the Application of Community law on Public Procurement and Concessions to Institutionalised Public-Private Partnerships (IPPs)'* Public Procurement Law. Rev., 2008, NA115.

on the basis of an exclusive right which it enjoys pursuant to a published law, regulation or administrative provision which is compatible with the Treaty". This clause passed with only minor alterations in Article 18 of the new Directive 2004/18/EC of the European Parliament and of the Council of 31 March 2004 on the coordination of procedures for the award of public works contracts, public supply contracts and public service contracts, devoted to "Service contracts awarded on the basis of an exclusive right"; under the new provision "This Directive shall not apply to public service contracts awarded by a contracting authority to another contracting authority or to an association of contracting authorities on the basis of an exclusive right which they enjoy pursuant to a published law, regulation or administrative provision which is compatible with the Treaty".[5]

Direct award is possible only when the procuring entity beneficiary of the award enjoys legitimate exclusive rights. On this basis, one could also say that competitive award procedure is not just unnecessary; rather, it is impossible, because of the exclusive right making the procuring entity beneficiary of the award the only contractor available. Indeed, exclusive rights exclude the market, which is a condition for competitive procurement procedures.[6]

The leading case is *Teckal*, decided in 1999.7 The Municipality of Viano had directly awarded a contract for the management of the heating services for the municipal buildings, including the provision of fuel, to Azienda Gas-Acqua Consorziale (AGAC) di Reggio Emilia, a consortium set up by several municipalities – that of Viano among them – to manage energy and environmental services. Teckal, a private company operating in the area of heating services brought proceedings before the Tribunale Amministrativo Regionale per l'Emilia-Romagna, in which it argued that the Municipality of Viano should have followed the tendering procedures for public contracts required under Community legislation. The national court was uncertain as to either Directive 92/50/EC or Directive 93/36/EC, on public procurements for goods, were applicable, but asked the Court of justice questions as to the interpretation of Art. 6 of Directive 92/50/EC. The Court of justice, following the conclusions of Advocate general Cosmas, qualified the contract as one of supplies rather than services, and ruled out the applicability of Directive 92/50/EC.[8]

5. See also Art. 23 of Directive 2004/17/EC.
6. See below, Case C-220/06, *Asociación Profesional de Empresas de Reparto y Manipulado de Correspondencia* [2007] ECR I- , para 60.
7. Case C-107/98 *Teckal* [1999] ECR I-8121.
8. Para. 38.

The question then became whether Art. 6 of the procurement of services directive could also be applied by analogy to procurement for goods. Advocate general Cosmas remarked that "the party entering into the contract with the contracting authority, namely the supplier, must have real third-party status *vis-à-vis* that authority, that is to say the supplier must be a separate person from the contracting authority". Indeed, "the directive does not apply where the contracting authority has recourse to its own resources for the supply of the products it wants. Community law does not require contracting authorities to observe the procedure ensuring effective competition between interested parties where those authorities wish to take on themselves the supply of the products they need".[9] However, in his opinion, the consortium was a distinct entity from the municipality. Given the very limited participation the municipality of Viano had in the consortium, less than one per cent, the Advocate general thought unlikely that it "exercises over that consortium the kind of control which an entity exercises over an internal body".[10]

The Court of Justice considered that Directive 93/36/EC did not contain any provision comparable to Art. 6 of Directive 92/50/EC. Moving from the notion of contract as an agreement between two separate persons, the Court held that "in accordance with Article 1(a) of Directive 93/36, it is, in principle, sufficient if the contract was concluded between, on the one hand, a local authority and, on the other, a person legally distinct from that local authority. The position can be otherwise only in the case where the local authority exercises over the person concerned a control which is similar to that which it exercises over its own departments and, at the same time, that person carries out the essential part of its activities with the controlling local authority or authorities".[11]

This way, the Court both affirmed the quite exceptional nature of the provision of Art. 6 of the Directive 92/50/EC and, moving from the notion of contract common to all the public procurement directives, gave vent to the possibility of directly awarding contracts to entities formally, but not substantially distinct from the procuring entities.[12]

9. Paras 53 f.
10. Para 61; in point 62 Cosmas AG also remarks that the consortium could also provide its services on the market.
11. Para 50.
12. The case law of the French Conseil d'Etat has indeed for a long time reasoned along the same lines: for references see F. Rolin *'Les étrangers dans la maison ou l'économie mixte exclue des contrats in-house'* Act. *Jur. Dr. Adm.*, 2005, 899; this has led to divergent opinions on the question whether in-house relationships may

The special provision of Art. 6 of then Directive 92/50/EC was applied in *Asociación Profesional de Empresas de Reparto y Manipulado de Correspondencia.*[13] A reference was made to the Court of justice, concerning the decision of the Administración General del Estado, Ministerio de Educación, Cultura y Deporte to award to the Sociedad Estatal Correos y Telégrafos SA ('Correos'), without a public call for tenders, a contract covering both reserved and non reserved postal services for the State. Correos is the provider of the universal postal service in Spain. Directive 97/67/EC of the European Parliament and of the Council on common rules for the development of the internal market of Community postal services and the improvement of quality of service establishes common rules concerning, inter alia, the provision of a universal postal service within the Community and the criteria defining the services which may be reserved for universal service providers. The directive allows Member States to reserve given postal services to the entities charged with the provision of the universal service. All other postal services may be provided on the competitive market. The award was challenged by a potential competitor and the *Audiencia Nacional* decided to stay the proceedings and to ask the Court whether "Articles 43 [EC] and 49 [...] EC, in conjunction with Article 86 thereof, as applied within the framework of the liberalisation of the postal services established by Directives 1997/67/EC and 2002/39/EC and within the framework of the rules governing public procurement introduced by the ad hoc directives, to be interpreted as precluding an agreement whose subject-matter includes the provision of postal services, both reserved and non-reserved and, therefore, liberalised, concluded between a department of the State Administration and a state company whose capital is wholly state-owned and which is furthermore, the universal postal service provider?"

The reference allowed the Court to discuss all the possible aspects of the in-house providing. Both the exception under Art. 6 of then Directive 92/50/EC, and the definition of contract under Art. 1 of the same directive, and the applicability of the *Teckal* doctrine outside the scope of application of

have contractual nature: for the negative K. Weltzein *'Avoiding the Procurement Rules by Awarding Contracts to in-house Entity'*, above fn 3, 338 ff.; on the contrary, according to J.V. González García *'Medios propios de la administración, colaboración interadministrativa y sometimiento a la normativa comunitaria de contratación'* Revista Admin. Pública, 2007, n° 173, 224 ff., »nos nos encontramos ante un verdadero contracto«.

13. Case C-220/06, Asociación Profesional de Empresas de Reparto y Manipulado de Correspondencia [2007] ECR-I; see D. McGowan 'A Contract or Not? A Note on Asociación Profesional de Empresas de Reparto y Manipulado de Correspondencia (Case C-220/06)' Public Procurement Law. Rev., 2008, NA204.

the procurement directive were examined. Finally, both the *Teckal* requirements were analysed. At this point of the discussion we will concentrate on the aspects concerning the provision in the Directive, while the other profiles will be discussed in a following section of this article.

Indeed, the Court of justice distinguished between reserved and no reserved postal services. As to the former, it held "that Article 7 of Directive 97/67 permits Member States to reserve some postal services for the provider(s) of the universal postal service to the extent necessary to ensure the maintenance of that service. Consequently, in so far as postal services are, in a manner consistent with that directive, reserved for a single universal service provider, such services are by necessity not subject to competition, given that no other economic operator is authorised to offer those services".[14]

The Court of justice then went on to consider whether the direct award of non-priority services was consistent with the provision of Art. 6 of Directive 92/50/EC. The answer was negative, since Member States do not have the power of extending the services reserved for the universal postal service provider pursuant to Article 7 of Directive 97/67/EC, as such extension goes against the purpose of the Directive, which, according to recital 8, aims to establish gradual and controlled liberalisation in the postal sector.[15]

This way, the Court of justice confirms that the special provision is applicable only under very exceptional circumstances. At the same time, it clarifies the relations between what has now become Art. 18 of Directive 2004/18/EC, and the *Teckal* doctrine, which will be analysed in its details in the next paragraphs. Indeed, the legality of direct award follows quite diverging conditions in the two cases. The directive requires both that the beneficiary of the award is itself a procuring entity and that the exclusive right conferred on the provider of the general service is consistent with Community law (which is not always the case). The former condition is less then the two *Teckal* requirements, since there may very well be no "similar control" nor "near exclusivity", so much so that one could well wonder whether Art. 18

14. Para 39; see also para 40: "The fact remains that, as regards such reserved services, Community rules in the field of public procurement, which have as their principal objective the free movement of services and the opening-up to undistorted competition in all the Member States, cannot be applied (Case C-26/03 *Stadt Halle and RPL Lochau* [2005] ECR I-1, paragraph 44, and Case C-340/04 *Carbotermo and Consorzio Alisei* [2006] ECR I-4137, paragraph 58)".

15. Para 67; the Court quotes here Case C-240/02 Asemfo and Asociación Nacional de Empresas de Externalización y Gestión de Envíos y Pequeña Paquetería [2004] ECR I-2461, para 24

has anything to do with in-house providing. The latter condition is something more, with no reference to the *Teckal* requirements.

3. Stadt Halle, Coname, Parking Brixen and Mödling

Two requirements characterise from the onset the notion of in-house providing expounded in *Teckal*: *a*) a control which is similar to that which the contracting authority exercises over its own departments, and *b*) the in-house entity must carry out the essential part of its activities with the controlling public authority or authorities.

Thanks to the case law, a second life independent from Art. 6 of Directive 92/50/EC had begun for the in-house providing, so much so that some Member States tried, unsuccessfully, to have it incorporated into the new 2004 Directives. To no avail.[16]

Years of uncertainty followed *Teckal*.[17] Even if both the Advocate general and the Court of justice had been quite restrained, in more than a few countries the *Teckal* decision was read as a green light to multifarious arrangements, quite often taking the form of institutional public-private partnership, aimed at awarding contracts to entities distinct from the procuring entity without any recourse to competitive procedures.[18]

In 2005, an icy cold shower came in the form of four judgements by the Court of justice, mostly following preliminary references under Art. 234 EC Treaty. The first case in which the Court was called to more precisely define the limits of in-house providing was *Stadt Halle*. Under discussion was the

16. See K. Weltzein *'Avoiding the Procurement Rules by Awarding Contracts to in-house Entity: The Scope of the Procurement Directives in the Classical Sector'* Public Procurement Law Rev., 2005, 252; according to F. Avarkioti *'The Application of EU Public Procurement Rules to "in-house" Arrangements'* above fn 3, 25, "This reveals that the 'in-house' concept constitutes an unclear or rather sensitive issue for the Member States to agree upon due to their different legal and perception of the notion of State".
17. Indeed, *Teckal* "cried out for judicial clarification": A. Brown *'The Treatment of a Contract Which is Awarded by a Public Authority to a Wholly Owned Subsidiary are Sold to a Third Party: a Note on C-29/04, Commission v. Austria'* Public Procurement Law Rev., 2006, NA53,
18. The popularity of the in-house was due to the fact that it was seen by many procuring entities as one of the few avenues left to avoid competitive procedures: see C. Lecuyer-Thieffry et P. Thieffry *'Les prestations effectuées in-house sans mise en concurrence' above*, fn 3, 927.
20. Case C-26/03 *Stadt Halle and RPL Lochau* [2005] ECR I-1.

lawfulness of the award without a public tender procedure of a contract for services concerning the treatment of waste by the municipality of Halle to RPL Lochau, a majority of whose capital was held by the same municipality and a minority by a private company.[20]

Advocate general Stix-Hackl discussed the case referring to quasi-in-house procurement, which differs "from in-house procurement (self-supply), in that it involves awards to an entity separate from the contracting authority, and having legal personality. If the entity responsible for the supply lacks legal personality, no contract could exist. One of the preconditions for a contract within the meaning of the procurement directives would then be missing".[21] Then she distinguished three hypothesis: entities fully owned by one procuring entity; entities jointly owned by a number of procuring entities; entities jointly owned by one or more procuring entities and private parties, but limited her analysis to the latter hypothesis, the only one relevant on the facts of the case.[22]

As to the first requirement set up in *Teckal*, that of a "control which is similar to that which it exercises over its own departments" (in short, similar control), the Advocate general remarked that "any appraisal of the legal position of a majority shareholder must be governed in part by the relevant provisions of national law [...]. One must also consider the provisions – normally the company's statutes – which shape the specific relationship in question. Accordingly, it is not enough to make a purely abstract assessment based on the legal form (the type of legal personality, say) selected for the entity over which the control is exercised".[23] In her opinion, similar control cannot depend on a brute number such as the amount of shares in the hands of the procuring entity.[24] Rather, the point is what powers the controlling body has on the distinct entity.[25]

Concerning the second *Teckal* requirement, that the in-house entity must carry out the "essential part of its activities with the controlling public authority or authorities", the Advocate general was rather non-committal, concluding that the national court should start from the actual activities and take account in particular of both quantitative and qualitative factors.[26]

21. Para 49.
22. Paras 58 ff.
23. Para 65.
24. Para 69.
25. Para 76.
26. Para 96.

The Court of justice began its analysis of the legality of direct contracting remarking that the principal objective of the Community rules in the field of public procurement is "the free movement of services and the opening-up to undistorted competition in all the Member States. That involves an obligation on all contracting authorities to apply the relevant Community rules where the conditions for such application are satisfied".[27] In this light, "Any exception to the application of that obligation must consequently be interpreted strictly".[28]

This does not translate into a positive obligation upon procuring entities to contract out their activities. Indeed, "A public authority which is a contracting authority has the possibility of performing the tasks conferred on it in the public interest by using its own administrative, technical and other resources, without being obliged to call on outside entities not forming part of its own departments. In such a case, there can be no question of a contract for pecuniary interest concluded with an entity legally distinct from the contracting authority. There is therefore no need to apply the Community rules in the field of public procurement".[29]

The Court then recalls the *Teckal* formula to distinguish the case at hand from the precedent: "It should be noted that, in the case cited, the distinct entity was wholly owned by public authorities. By contrast, the participation, even as a minority, of a private undertaking in the capital of a company in which the contracting authority in question is also a participant excludes in any event the possibility of that contracting authority exercising over that company a control similar to that which it exercises over its own departments".[30] In the Community court's view, private participation is incompatible with the idea of control by the procuring entity. Public authorities and private companies pursue different and incompatible goals; moreover, "the award of a public contract to a semi-public company without calling for tenders would interfere with the objective of free and undistorted competition and the principle of equal treatment of the persons concerned [...], in particu-

27. Para 44.
28. Para 46.
29. Para 48; the freedom of choice between self-production and outsourcing is strongly affirmed by the French case law: Conseil d'Etat, 29 avril 1970, *Société Unipain*, Act. Jur. Dr. Adm., 1970, 430, with the conclusions by G. Braibant; see also F. Avarkioti *'The Application of EU Public Procurement Rules to "in-house" Arrangements', above* fn 3, 22.
30. Para 49.

lar in that such a procedure would offer a private undertaking with a capital presence in that undertaking an advantage over its competitors".[31]

In front of the rising tide of public-private initiatives, public-private partnerships and other forms of cooperation between public authorities and private firms one could well think the Court of justice to be out of tune with modern developments in administrative law.[32] The second argument raised, however, has clear merits.[33] More generally, and considering that the 'in house' doctrine has been developed to rule out the necessity of following public award procedures when a procuring entity is having recourse to its own resources instead than to the market, it is indeed difficult to see how private participation would be compatible with this doctrine. Private participation, even when limited – as in the case of public-private partnerships – necessarily involves some measure of outsourcing. As such, award procedure must be followed. Any other position would amount to an elusion of the principles of transparency and open and fair competition embedded in the EC Treaty and spelt out in the procurement directives.[34]

Having found wanting the first requirement for in-house providing, the Court did not feel it necessary to go into the second ("essential part").

The next case was *Coname*.[35] The facts are close to those in *Teckal*. A preliminary reference was referred by an Italian administrative court in a proceeding opposing Consorzio Aziende Metano (Coname) and the municipality of Cingia de' Botti and concerning the direct award by the latter to Padania Acque, a company in which it had a very small participation, of service covering the management, distribution and maintenance of methane gas distribution installations. As in *Teckal*, there were doubts as to the true qualification of the contract at issue. This led to discuss the issue of the direct award on the basis of the general principles of Community law. Maybe because of this, the issue was tackled from an angle different from the usual ones in-house providing cases. The main question was felt to be whether direct award might be justified on the basis of the general interest justifications provided in the rules

31. Para 51.
32. Among the many critics C. Lecuyer-Thieffry et P. Thieffry *'Les prestations effectuées in-house sans mise en concurrence' above* fn 3, 932.
33. See also F. Avarkioti *'The Application of EU Public Procurement Rules to "in-house" Arrangements', above* fn ., at 33, and T. Kaarresalo *'Procuring in-house: The Impact of the EC Procurement Regime'* Public Procurement Law Rev., 2008, 250.
34. See J.J. Pernas Garcías *Las operaciones in-house*, above fn 2, 19 f, 46 and, but not without some wavering, 126 ff.
35. Case C-231/03 *Coname* [2005] ECR I-7287.

on free movement of services. In other terms, the question was whether direct award to a company in which the municipality had a share could be justified by the interest of the same municipality in controlling the provision of services to the general public for which it is responsible. This was excluded by both the Advocate general Stix-Hackl and the Court of justice.

The reasoning of the Court was quite terse. It remarked that "al though the need for a municipality to exercise control over a concessionaire managing a public service may constitute an objective circumstance capable of justifying a possible difference in treatment, it must be pointed out that the 0.97% holding is so small as to preclude any such control, as the referring court itself observes". The Italian Government argued that most municipalities lack the resources to provide, through in-house structures, public services such as that of gas distribution within their territory, and are therefore obliged to resort to structures in the share capital of which several municipalities have holdings.[36] But the Court, without quoting *Stadt Halle*, was fast in retorting that the capital of the company at issue was "open, at least in part, to private capital, which precludes it from being regarded as a structure for the 'in-house' management of a public service on behalf of the municipalities which form part of it".[37]

In *Parking Brixen* the Court elaborated again in some depth, and in a further restrictive way, the first requirement of the in-house providing.[38] The Municipality of Brixen had awarded the management of two pay car parks to its wholly owned subsidiary Stadtwerke Brixen AG without first carrying out an award procedure. The private company Parking Brixen GmbH challenged that award and the local administrative court referred to the Court questions relating to the distinction between service contracts and concessions and to the distinction between external awards subject to a compulsory call for tenders and in-house operations not subject to a compulsory call for tenders.

Advocate general Kokott begins her discussion by recalling the case law according to which "contracting authorities are subject, even outside the prevailing scope of the procurement directives, to the requirements of Community law arising from the fundamental rules of the EC Treaty, in particular the fundamental freedoms and the prohibition of discrimination contained in them",[39] the latter carrying with it an obligation of transparency.[40] Therefore,

36. Para 24.
37. Para 26.
38. Case C-458/03 *Parking Brixen* [2005] ECR I-8585.
39. Para 35.
40. Para 36.

these rules apply both to service contracts and concessions, even if the latter fall outside the provision of Directive 92/50/EC, then applicable.

The case is then analysed along the *Teckal* formula. The difficulty is to pin down what degree of control is actually required to allow direct award. According to the Advocate general, "The control which a public body exercises over its own departments is usually characterised in law by rights to give instructions and supervisory powers. Within a single authority, for example, the authority's management usually has the right to give instructions to the departments under its responsibility. In relation to subordinate authorities, it also has a right to give instructions, or at least the possibility, under its supervisory powers, of reviewing and correcting the decisions they take".[41] Similar control cannot, in the Advocate general's views, require as much. Considering the second *Teckal* criterion, the view expressed is that what is relevant is with whom the entity does business, not with whom it could do.[42]

The Court of justice's attitude is much more severe. It follows the Advocate general conclusions both as to the applicability to service concessions of the principles of equal treatment and non-discrimination on grounds of nationality and the duty of transparency linked to them,[43] and as to the conclusion that the in-house providing exception also applies outside the scope of application of the EU directives, thus covering service concessions.[44]

The analysis of the conditions laid down in *Teckal*, however, moves from the consideration that the in-house providing constitutes an exception to those principles. Accordingly, it must be read narrowly.[45] On this basis, the Court goes into the details of the legal situation of Stadtwerke Brixen AG to rule out the existence of sufficient control powers of the contracting authority over its subsidiary and consequently of the possibility of direct award: "[...] Stadtwerke Brixen AG became market-oriented, which renders the municipality's control tenuous. Militating in that direction are: (a) the conversion of

41. Para 67.
42. Para 85.
43. Paras 48 f.
44. Paras 61 f.; see also A. Brown *'The Application of the EC Treaty to a Services Concession Awarded by a Public Authority to a Wholly Owned Subsidiary: Case C-458/03, Parking Brixen'* Public Procurement Law Rev., 2006, NA40
45. Para 63 "Since it is a matter of a derogation from the general rules of Community law, the two conditions stated in the preceding paragraph must be interpreted strictly and the burden of proving the existence of exceptional circumstances justifying the derogation to those rules lies on the person seeking to rely on those circumstances"; the Court refers here to Case C-26/03 *Stadt Halle and RPL Lochau* [2005] ECR I-1, para 46)

Stadtwerke Brixen – a special undertaking of the Gemeinde Brixen – into a company limited by shares (Stadtwerke Brixen AG) and the nature of that type of company; (b) the broadening of its objects, the company having started to work in significant new fields, particularly those of the carriage of persons and goods, as well as information technology and telecommunications. It must be noted that the company retained the wide range of activities previously carried on by the special undertaking, particularly those of water supply and waste water treatment, the supply of heating and energy, waste disposal and road building; (c) the obligatory opening of the company, in the short term, to other capital; (d) the expansion of the geographical area of the company's activities, to the whole of Italy and abroad; (e) the considerable powers conferred on its Administrative Board, with in practice no management control by the municipality".[46]

The last 2005 judgement came from an infringement procedure against Austria.[47] The municipality of Mödling had decided to create a legally independent body, Stadtgemeinde Mödling Abfallwirtschafts GmbH (in short Abfall GmbH), to supply services in the ecological waste management sector and to engage in related commercial transactions, primarily in the waste disposal sector. These tasks were then transferred to the company by means of a contract concluded for an unlimited period; the contract also stipulated the amount of the remuneration, namely a fixed sum per dustbin or container, which the town of Mödling was to pay to AbfallgmbH. A couple of weeks later, the Mödling municipal council decided to transfer 49% of the shares in AbfallgmbH to the company Saubermacher Dienstleistungs AG, a private company. After a waste transfer centre was put into operation, AbfallgmbH started to provide its services to third parties, mainly to other municipalities in the district.

The difference between this case and *Stadt Halle* was that at the time of the award the municipality owned all the shares of AbfallgmbH. The Court of justice was ready to concede that al though, as a general rule, the legality of the award without tendering is to be established according to the legal and factual situation existing at the time the award was decided, the specific facts of the case led to a different approach. Indeed, privatisation took place shortly after that company was awarded. The municipality had devised an artificial construction comprising several distinct stages; consequently, the award of that contract had to be examined taking into account all those stages as well

46. Para 67; as J.J. Pernas García*s Las operaciones in-house, above* fn 2, at 94, we have here a series of indicators, each one of them would not be decisive if considered in isolation.
47. Case C-29/04, *Commission v. Austria* [2005] ECR I-9705.

as their purpose and not on the basis of their strictly chronological order.[48] From this perspective, it become very easy for the Court to follow closely *Stadt Halle* and to reiterate that any form of private capital participation excludes the same possibility to speak of in-house providing.[49]

The main results of the vintage 2005 case law are that the doctrine of in-house providing constitutes an exception which must correspondingly be read narrowly,[50] and that private involvement is incompatible with it.[51] French authors talk of «*une notion à la portée presque fantomatique*».[52]

48. Paras 39 ff.; see also para 57 of the conclusions by Advocate general Geelhoed: "The fact that the decision to enter into a contract between the municipality of Mödling and AbfallGmbH was adopted while AbfallGmbH was still fully owned by the municipality of Mödling does not alter the finding that the public contract concerned should, under Article 8, in conjunction with Article 11(1) and Article 15(2) of the directive, have been awarded in accordance with the provisions of Titles III to VI thereof. The certainty that Abfall GmbH would gain the contract from the municipality of Mödling made the acquisition of a holding in that undertaking attractive to a private tenderer. However, such forms of external hiving-off in which the hived-off entity is made appealing to private tenderers by means of a contract for an unlimited period acquired in advance by way of a 'dowry' may not undermine the effectiveness of Directive 92/50. The directive is also applicable to such arrangements". Critically A. Brown *'Legality Of a National Law Allowing Public Authorities to Award Services Contracts Directly to Their Subsidiaries: a Note on Case C-410/04, ANAV v Comune di Bari'* Public Procurement Law Rev., 2006, NA220.
49. Paras 45 ff. ; see also T. Kotsonis *'Application of the Teckal Exemption to a Service Concession Contract: Coditel Brabant SA v. Comune d'Uccle, Region de Bruxelles Capitale'* Public Procurement Law Rev. 2009, NA77: "it seems that even the smallest private shareholdings would be sufficient for the purpose of concluding that the exemption is unavailable; contrast Case C-371/95, *Commission* v *Italy* [2008], ECR I-, where (partial) privatisation was possible according to the charter of the company, but not actually envisaged nor in fact decided.
50. T. Kaarresalo *'Procuring in-house: The Impact of the EC Procurement Regime' above* fn 3, 254.
51. For a different take see R. Cavallo Perin and D. Casalini *'Control over in-house Providing Organisations' above* fn 2, 239.
52. C. Pilone *'Réflexions autour de la notion de contrat »in-house«'* in Contrats publics. Mélanges en l'honneur du Professeur Michel Guibal, Montpellier, Université de Montpellier, 2006, 712 ; according to F. Rolin *'Les étrangers dans la maison' above* fn 11, »on a même le sentiment que la notion de prestation *in-house* est finalement réservée à des situations quasiment pathologiques«; in the same vein many Italians: e.g. M. Di donna *'Il caso, chiuso, degli affidamenti in-house'* Urbanistica e appalti, 2006, 377; P. Lotti *'Corte di Giustizia e involuzione dell'in-house providing'* Urbanistica e appalti, 2006, 1054.

4. The evolution of the case law on the "similar control"

In the few years since 2005, the Court of justice has affirmed its previous case law as to the inconsistency between private participation and in-house, while at the same time clarifying a few further points, especially concerning cooperation between procuring entities.

The exceptional character of what is now Art. 18 of Directive 2004/18/EC was at the heart of the *Commune de Roanne* case. The Court reiterated that a contracting authority may only award directly a contract to another procuring entity under the strict conditions laid down in the provision.[53] In principle, contracts falling under the scope of application of the EC Directives are to be passed respecting their provisions (an open question is to what extent is it possible to think of intra-institutional agreements falling outside that scope).[54] At the same time, following *Parking Brixen*, the Court of justice affirmed that the in-house exception issuing from the *Teckal* decision also applies to concessions, including service concessions.[55]

Unsurprisingly, most cases have centred on the tricky notion of "similar" control.

An easy case was the recent *Augusta* infringement proceeding against Italy.[57] The Commission asked the Court to declare that by adopting a procedure, which has been in existence for a long time and was still followed, of directly awarding to Agusta SpA contracts for the purchase of Agusta and Agusta Bell helicopters to meet the requirements of several military and civilian corps of the Italian State, without any competitive tendering procedure and, in particular, without complying with the procedures provided for by Council Directive 93/36/EEC and previously, by Council Directive

53. Case C-220/05, *Commune de Roanne*, [2007] ECR I-389.
54. See Case C-84/03, *Commission v. Spain*; [2005] ECR I-139, paras 39 f.; the issue is worrying countries now in the process to depart with a long tradition of intra-institutional control mechanism to adopt a system of intra-institutional co-operation: see L. Richer '*L'assistance technique de l'Etat aux communes peut-elle réellement s'affranchir de la concurrence?*' *Rev. fr. dr. adm.*, 2002, 1056.
55. Case C-410/04, *Associazione Nazionale Autotrasporto Viaggiatori (ANAV)* [2006] ECR I-3303.
57. Case C-337/05, *Commission* v *Italy* [2008] ECR I-; see B. Heuninckx '*A Note on Case Commission v Italy* (Case C-337/05) (Agusta Helicopters Case)' Public Procurement Law Rev. 2008, NA187.

77/62/EEC, the Italian Republic has failed to fulfil its obligations under those directives. Among its defences the Italian government argued that, until the end of the 1990s, the relations of the Italian State with Agusta could be analysed as 'in-house' relations. Advocate general Mazák was swift in rejecting this argument. Apart for being unsubstantiated, it was enough to recall that under the more recent case law the participation, even as a minority, of a private undertaking in the capital of a company in which the contracting authority in question is also a participant excludes in any event the possibility of that contracting authority exercising over that company a control similar to that which it exercises over its own departments; between the 1970s and the 1990s Agusta was never wholly owned by the Italian State, and that in itself suffices to exclude the existence of an in-house relationship with Agusta; since 2000, when a joint-venture 'Agusta Westland' was created with the British company Westland, the in-house relationship with the Italian State has to be excluded as well.[58] The Court of justice followed the conclusions and ruled out the existence of any in-house situation, without the necessity of examining whether Agusta carries out the essential part of its activities with the Italian government.[59]

In *Carbotermo*, again a case arising from the Italian provisions on local services, the Court of justice quite closely followed *Parking Brixen* in ruling that usual corporate governance rules are not enough to meet the requisite of "similar" control,[60] adding that this is so much more true when the contracting authority' ownership is mediated through an intermediate company, such as a holding.[61]

58. Paras 39 f.
59. Paras 38 ff.
60. Case C-340/04, *Carbotermo S.P.A.* [2006] ECR-I, 4137, para 36. The Court remarks that the statutes "confer on the Board of Directors of each of those companies the broadest possible powers for the ordinary and extraordinary management of the company. Those statutes do not reserve for the Comune di Busto Arsizio any control or specific voting powers for restricting the freedom of action conferred on those Boards of Directors. The control exercised by the Comune di Busto Arsizio over those two companies can be described as consisting essentially of the latitude conferred by company law on the majority of the shareholders, which places considerable limits on its power to influence the decisions of those companies" (para 38).
61. Para 39: "Moreover, any influence which the Comune di Busto Arsizio might have on AGESP's decisions is through a holding company. The intervention of such an intermediary may, depending on the circumstances of the case, weaken any control possibly exercised by the contracting authority over a joint stock company merely because it holds shares in that company"; this approach is criticised by P. Henry

Carbotermo was possibly the high point of the most restrictive case-law, consistently denying the in-house character of the arrangements brought in front of the Court of justice. A new phase, mostly focused on cases where no private involvement was at issue, started with *Asemfo*, a case originating from a preliminary reference from the Spanish *Tribunal Supremo*.[63] This judgement is of major interest because it identified conditions under which direct award is indeed possible instead of – as was the case with the judgments discussed so far – situations in which "similar control" is to be ruled out. The litigation was rooted in competition law rather than in public procurement law. A forestry firm, Asemfo, had lodged a complaint against Tragsa for a declaration that it was abusing its dominant position in the Spanish forestry works, services and projects market. Tragsa was set up in 1977. Its major shareholder is the Spanish State. The *Comunidades Autonomas* have only minor shares. It is 'an instrument and technical service of the Administration' which is required to carry out, either itself or using its subsidiaries, any work entrusted to it by the General Administration of the State, the Autonomous Communities or the public bodies subject to them. It is required to give priority to urgent and exceptional work arising from natural disasters and similar events. It cannot refuse the work entrusted to it or negotiate the deadline for completion, and must execute the works assigned in accordance with the instructions it is given. Its work is paid according to a system of tariffs decided by a joint ministerial committee partly on the basis of information supplied by Tragsa as to its costs. According to ASEMFO, Tragsa's special status enables it to carry out a large number of works at the direct demand of the Administration, in breach of the principles relating to public procurement and to free competition.

The Court of justice considered that the relationships between the State and the *Comunidades Autonomas* on the one hand, and Trasga on the other, fall outside the scope of application of the EC procurement directives. The reasoning is not exempt of some repetition, the same argument recurring again and again. Moving from the definition of procurement contract as a contract for pecuniary interest in writing between, first, a service provider, a supplier or a contractor and, second, a contracting authority, the Court points

'Carbotermo SpA, and Consorzio Alisei v. Comune di Busto Arsizio, AGESAP SpA, Identity crisis: When is a subsidiary part of a contracting authority?' in Public *Procurement Law Rev.*, 2006 NA 153.

63. Case 295/05 Asemfo [2007] ECR I-2999.

65. Paras 49 ff.

out that Tragsa is: *a*) a State company the share capital of which may also be held by the Autonomous Communities; *b*) an instrument and a technical service of the General State Administration and of the administration of each of the Autonomous Communities concerned; *c*) required to carry out the orders given it by the General State Administration, the Autonomous Communities and the public bodies subject to them, in the areas covered by its company objects, and it is not entitled to fix freely the tariff for its actions, and, finally, that "Tragsa's relations with those public bodies, inasmuch as that company is an instrument and a technical service of those bodies, are not contractual, but in every respect internal, dependent and subordinate".[65]

To rebut Asemfo's arguments, the Court of justice referred to a precedent decision concerning Trasga, when, although in a different context, the Court held that being an instrument and technical service of the Spanish Administration, Tragsa is required to implement, itself or using its subsidiaries, only the works entrusted to it.[66] At that point, the Court was ready to conclude that, "if, which it is for the referring court to establish, Tragsa has no choice, either as to the acceptance of a demand made by the competent authorities in question, or as to the tariff for its services, the requirement for the application of the directives concerned relating to the existence of a contract is not met".[67]

Having already disposed of the issue, the Court of justice "in any event" thought it expedient to look into the case law concerning in-house providing. The negative condition as to the first requirement ("similar control") which was established in *Stadt Halle* is turned into its correlated opposite: "As regards the first condition, relating to the public authority's control, it follows from the Court's case-law that the fact that the contracting authority holds, alone or together with other public authorities, all of the share capital in a successful tenderer tends to indicate, generally, that that contracting authority exercises over that company a control similar to that which it exercises over its own departments".[68]

66. Case C-349/97 *Spain* v *Commission* [2003] ECR I-3851.
67. Para 54; see J.J. Pernas Garcías *Las operaciones in-house*, above fn 2, 101 ff.
68. Para 57. There is a subtle difference here with what was held for instance in Case C-340/04, *Carbotermo S.P.A.* [2006] ECR-I, 4137, para 37: "The fact that the contracting authority holds, alone or together with other public authorities, all of the share capital in a successful tenderer tends to indicate, *without being decisive*, that that contracting authority exercises over that company a control similar to that which it exercises over its own departments".

Moreover, rejecting Advocate general Geelhoed conclusions to the effect that "similar control" could be established with reference to the Spanish State only, and not to the *Comunidades Autonomas*, whose stake in Trasga is marginal,[69] the Court of justice held "that Tragsa is required to carry out the orders given it by the public authorities, including the Autonomous Communities. It also seems to follow from that national legislation that, as with the Spanish State, in the context of its activities with those Communities as an instrument and technical service, Tragsa is not free to fix the tariff for its actions and that its relationships with them are not contractual".[70]

This judgement maybe considered a turning point and adds to the previous case law on two important aspects. On the one hand, it distinguishes between private law contracts between different contracting authorities which freely negotiate between them, on the one hand, and instances where one procuring entity has a sort of command power and the other has no choice but complying, on the other hand. Only the latter situation is compatible with the in-house providing.[71] On the other hand, departing from *Coname*, it goes in the way of considering even a minimal stake in a jointly held company as consistent with "similar control", provided not only that all the shareholders are public law entities, a condition not present on the facts of *Coname*, but also that the shareholders concerned, notwithstanding their marginal participation in the capital of the company, may issue orders to – rather than being obliged to negotiate contracts with – the in-house entity.[72]

69. According to the Advocate general, "in cases where an executive service acts as an 'instrument' for various public authorities, the statutory regime that applies to it must ensure that all the contracting public authorities have effective influence over its strategic objectives and significant decisions" (para 97); he excluded the recurrence of this condition with reference to the *Comunidades Autonomas*, not only because of the minimal stake they have in Trasga, but also because the relevant legislation is national and it is the State that determines the tariffs applied by Trasga (paras 98 ff.).
70. Para 60; see M. Dischendorfer *'The Compatibility of Contracts Awarded Directly to "Jointly Executive Services" with the Community Rules on Public Procurement and Fair Competition: A note on Case C-295/05, ASEMFO v. Trasga' Public* Procurement Law Rev., 2007, NA129; another "no contract present" case, albeit not concerning in-house provisions, is Case C-532/03 *Commission v Ireland* [2007] ECR I-; here again, the application of procurement law is ruled out: see also A. Brown *'The Commission Loses another Action against Ireland Owing to Lack of Evidence: A Note on Case C-532/03 Commission v Ireland'* Public Procurement Law Review, 2008, NA94.
71. See also Case C-220/05, *Commune de Roanne* [2007] ECR I-389.
72. It is worth mentioning that the EC Commission seems to think otherwise and as recently as January 31st, 2008, it brought an infringement proceeding under Art. 228 EC Treaty against Italy over the procurement of waste management services

A case of major interest is the already recalled *Asociación Profesional de Empresas de Reparto y Manipulado de Correspondencia.*[73] Advocate general Bot addressed the first *Teckal* requirement paraphrasing *Stadt Halle* and *Parking Brixen.* In his view "that condition implies that the company providing the services has no discretion whatsoever and that, in the end, the public authority is the only one to take decisions concerning that company. Moreover, use of the expression 'in-house' indeed reveals the intention to make a distinction between activities which the authority carries out directly – by means of internal structures 'belonging to the house' – and those that it will entrust to a third-party operator".[74] Since Correos' status is that of limited liability company having the possibility to broaden its company objects and to terminate the contract which binds it to the State administration, the Advocate general concluded that Correos had become market-oriented, which renders the State administration's control tenuous.[75]

The Court of justice started by enquiring whether the agreement between the Ministry and Correos could be considered a contract falling under the provisions of Directive 92/50/EC. The Spanish Government argued that the agreement is not contractual but instrumental, given that Correos is unable to refuse to enter into such an agreement, but is under an obligation to accept. The Court was thus called to examine the situation in the light of the *Asemfo* case, which it qualified to a certain extent. The Court conceded that in *Asemfo* it had held "that the requirement for the application of the directives governing the award of public service contracts relating to the existence of a contract was not met where the State company in issue in the case that gave rise to the judgment had no choice as to the acceptance of a demand made by the com-

by the city of Contigliano. The case concerns the direct award of waste management services by the Municipality of Contigliano in Lazio to a public-owned limited liability company, namely A.M.A. Servizi S.r.l., of which the town of Contigliano owns 0,5% of the capital. The Commission considers that the conditions required by the ECJ case-law for the application of the "in-house" exception are not met in this case *inter alia* because the powers entrusted to the Municipality of Contigliano as a minority owner are insufficient to confer on the latter a control which is similar to the one exercised over its own departments. Secondly, the undertaking is active in the market and it carries out a significant part of its activities with parties other than its controlling entities (IP/08/123).

73. Case C-220/06, *Asociación Profesional de Empresas de Reparto y Manipulado de Correspondencia* [2007] ECR-I

74. Para 75.

75. Para 79.

77. Para 51.

petent authorities in question or as to the tariff for its services, a matter which was for the referring court to establish".[77] However, according to the Court, in that case the State company was "an instrument and a technical service of the General State Administration and of the administration of each of the Autonomous Communities concerned" which "is required to implement only work entrusted to it by the General Administration of that State, the Autonomous Communities or the public bodies subject to them".[78]

The distinction here is traced on the second rather than the first *Teckal* requirement. The Court indeed remarks that Correos' customers consist of any person wishing to use the universal postal service. The reasoning shifts back to the "similar" control requirement when the Court points out that "The mere fact that that company has no choice as to the acceptance of a demand made by the Ministerio or as to the tariff for its services cannot automatically entail that no contract was concluded between the two entities".[79] The distinction between *Asemfo* and *Correos* is very much made to depend on the nature of the legal act binding the contracting authority with the entity providing the services.[80] In the Court's reasoning, the fact that Correos is required to provide the services requested and must do so, if necessary, for a fixed tariff or, in any event, for a price that is transparent and non-discriminatory does not alter the contractual character of the relationship binding it to the Ministry: "It is only if the agreement between Correos and the Ministerio were in actual fact a unilateral administrative measure solely creating obligations for Correos – and as such a measure departing significantly from the normal conditions of a commercial offer made by that company, a matter which is for the *Audiencia Nacional* to establish – that it would have to be held that there is no contract and that, consequently, Directive 92/50 could not apply".[81]

Finally, in *Correos* the Court considered whether the conclusions to which it had arrived also apply to the award of non reserved postal contracts which, because of their limited value, fall below the threshold for the application of

78. Para 52.
79. Para 53.
80. See J.J. Pernas Garcías *Las operaciones in-house, above* fn 2, 115 ff.
81. Para 54; see also para 55 "In the course of that examination, the Audiencia Nacional will have to consider, in particular, whether Correos is able to negotiate with the Ministerio the actual content of the services it has to provide and the tariffs to be applied to those services and whether, as regards non-reserved services, the company can free itself from obligations arising under the Cooperation Agreement, by giving notice as provided for in that agreement"; see also D. McGowan *'A Contract or Not? A Note on Asociación Profesional de Empresas de Reparto y Manipulado de Correspondencia* (Case C-220/06)' *above* fn 14, 297 f.

the procurement directives.[82] A growing line of cases indeed maintains that the general principle of non discrimination on the ground of nationality, along with the ancillary principle of transparency and equal treatment of tenderers, also apply to contracts not or not fully regulated by the procurement directives.[83]

The Court fully followed this trend, reiterating that although "certain contracts are excluded from the scope of Community directives in the field of public procurement, the contracting authorities which conclude them are nevertheless bound to comply with the fundamental rules of the Treaty and the principle of non-discrimination on grounds of nationality in particular".[84] According to the Court, "That is particularly the case in relation to public service contracts whose value does not reach the thresholds fixed by Directive 92/50. The mere fact that the Community legislature considered that the strict special procedures laid down in the directives on public procurement are not ap-

82. Para 67; the Court quotes here Case C-240/02 *Asemfo and Asociación Nacional de Empresas de Externalización y Gestión de Envíos y Pequeña Paquetería* [2004] ECR I-2461, para 24.
84. Concerning in-house providing the most relevant precedent is Case C-458/03 *Parking Brixen* [2005] ECR I-8585, at 48 f.; in the same vein, Case 532/03, *Commission* v *Ireland* [2007] ECR I-; case C-119/06, *Commission v. Italy* [2007] ECR I-; case C-260/04, *Commission* v *Italy* [2007] ECR I-; the two judgments are commented by A. Brown *'The Commission Loses another Action against Ireland Owing to Lack of Evidence: A Note on Case C-532/03 Commission v Ireland'* Public Procurement L. Rev., 2008, NA92; Id. *'Application of the Directives to Contracts to Non-for-profit Organisations and Transparency under the EC Treaty: A Note on Case C-119/06 Commission v Italy' ibid.*, NA96; R. Caranta, *'Attività pubblica, attività no-profit, e disciplina dei contratti pubblici di servizi'* Urbanistica e appalti, 2008, 293; the latter is also reported in *Foro amm. CdS*, 2008, , note M. Mattalia *'Convenzionamento diretto o procedure concorsuali nell'affidamento del servizio di trasporto sanitario?'*; and A. Albanese *'L'affidamento di servizi socio-sanitari alle organizzazioni di volontariato e il diritto comunitario: la Corte di giustizia manda un monito agli enti pubblici italiani'* Riv. it. dir. pubbl. comunitario, 2008, 1453; the Commission adopted an interpretative communication on the Community law applicable to contract awards not or not fully subject to the provisions of the Public Procurement Directives (2006/C 179/02) and the comments by A. Brown *'Seeing Through Transparency: the Requirement to Advertise Public Contracts and Concessions Under the EC Treaty'* Public Procurement Law Rev., 2007, 1; R. Williams *'Contracts Awarded Outside the Scope of the Public Procurement Directives'* Public Procurement Law Rev., 2007, NA1.
84. Para 71; Case C-264/03 *Commission* v *France* [2005] ECR I-8831, para 32 is quoted.

propriate in the case of public contracts of small value does not mean that those contracts are excluded from the scope of Community law".[85]

On this ground, the total lack of any tendering procedure in the instant case could not be considered but in breach of Community law.[86] The conclusions could not be changed because Correos is charged with the provision of a service of general economic interest under Art. 86 of the EC Treaty. At the onset of its discussion of the topic, the Court of justice seems even to be bold enough to impose tendering procedures for the award of any contract for the provision of services,[87] in this way departing from a case law which is more reserved on this point.[88] However, the Court admitted that Art. 86 (1) and (2) of the EC Treaty may justify the grant by a Member State to an undertaking entrusted with the operation of services of general economic interest of special or exclusive rights which are contrary to the provisions of the Treaty,[89] but held that the special regime laid by Directive 97/67/EC excluded the power of Member States of extending the services reserved for the universal postal service provider.[90]

85. Para 72; the Court quotes Order in Case C-59/00 *Vestergaard* [2001] ECR I-9505, para 19, and *Commission* v *France*, para 33.
86. See para 76 "As a rule, a complete lack of any call for competition in the case of the award of a public service contract like that at issue in the main proceedings does not comply with the requirements of Articles 43 EC and 49 EC any more than with the principles of equal treatment, non-discrimination and transparency (see, by analogy, *Parking Brixen*, paragraph 50, and *ANAV*, paragraph 22)".
87. Para 77 "it follows from Article 86(1) EC that the Member States must not maintain in force national legislation which permits the award of public service contracts without a call for tenders since such an award infringes Article 43 EC or 49 EC or the principles of equal treatment, non-discrimination and transparency (see, by analogy, *Parking Brixen*, paragraph 52, and *ANAV*, paragraph 23)".
88. According to Case T-17/02, *Olsen* [2005] ECR II-2031 at 239 "it is not apparent either from the wording of Article 86(2) EC or from the case-law on that provision that a general interest task may be entrusted to an operator only as a result of a tendering procedure".
89. Paras 78 f.
90. Paras 81 ff.; see also the conclusions of Advocate general Bot: "96. Directive 97/67 has established a regulatory framework for the postal sector. In particular, the Directive makes provisions for securing a universal service in this sector by giving Member States the opportunity to reserve certain postal services. The provision of all other services which cannot be reserved must be open to competition. 97. If Member States were able to grant a public contract for non-reserved postal services to a single provider without a prior call for tenders, this would actually go against the purpose of Directive 97/67, which is to liberalise the postal sector".

In 2008, the Court of justice went back to the cooperation between contracting authorities in a number of cases. In an infringement proceeding brought against Italy, the EC Commission lamented that the Municipality of Mantua had directly awarded information services to a company in whose capital it had a majority participation. The action was dismissed. “Similar control” was established because the municipality choose the members of the boards of the company and could give orders to the boards, including as to the costs for the service provided. Further, the municipality could at any time inspect the activities managed by the company and an officer from the same municipality had been named to follow on an everyday basis the activities of the company. The Court, distinguishing the case from *Mödling*, considered irrelevant a clause in the articles of association making it possible to sell stakes to private persons, considering that privatisation was not foreseen at the time of the award (and anyway had never occurred).[91] Finally, concerning the second *Teckal* requirement, the Court followed *Carbotermo* holding that the activities performed to the benefit of all the shareholders are to be considered to see whether the requirement is met.[92] A brief mention is also due to the *Termoraggi* case. An Italian first instance administrative court had asked the Court whether it was consistent with Community law for a municipality (the *Comune di Monza*) to directly award a service contract to a technical unit of the same municipality, which however enjoys some degree of autonomy from it. The Court reply was very short, in the form of and order. Il simply held that from the dossier it appeared as the two *Teckal* requirements were met.[93]

In *Coditel Brabant* a preliminary reference was made in the course of proceedings brought by Coditel Brabant SA against the Commune d'Uccle ‘the (Municipality of Uccle’), the Région de Bruxelles-Capitale and the Société Intercommunale pour la Diffusion de la Télévision (Brutélé), concerning the award of a concession for the management of the municipal cable television network by the Municipality of Uccle to an inter-municipal cooperative soci-

91. Case C-371/05, Commission v Italy [2008] ECR I-; see A. Brown ‘The ECJ Upholds an Italian Municipality's Reliance on the Teckal Exemption for in-house Contracts: A Note on Commission v Italy (C-371/05)’ Public Procurement L. Rev., 2009, NA6, and J.J. Pernas Garcías Las operaciones in-house, above fn. 2, 141 ff.

92. Point 31.

93. Case C-323/07, *Termoraggi* [2008] ECR I-; see A. Brown *‘Award of a Contract for Management of Heating Installations by an Italian Local Authority to a Connected Undertaking without Competition: Termoraggi SpA v Comune di Monza* (C-323/07)’ Public Procurement L. Rev. 20098, NA218.

ety.[94] As Advocate general Verica Trstenjak remarked, the case «concerns the question as to whether procurement law is applicable where a regional authority, in this case a municipality, delegates the management of its cable television network to a body that is purely an inter-municipal cooperative entity with the involvement of that municipality, yet without drawing on any private capital. The present case involves inter-municipal cooperation in the form of a cooperative and the questions submitted by the referring court concern the first of the well-known *Teckal* criteria: control similar to that exercised over an entity's own department».[95]

Private participation is not an issue in *Coditel Brabant* and the Court of justice may focus on the different issue of the cooperation among different procuring entities. The issue is relevant in many Member States, and some governments intervened fiercely in the proceeding to upheld the freedom of public law entities to cooperate among themselves. The conclusions by Advocate general Verica Trstenjak are accordingly much thoughtful and articulated. They usher a major readjustment in the case law. Through a very detailed analysis, she makes the case that in previous cases "various special circumstances came together which led to an overall view being formed", which excluded the "similar control" even in cases where there was no actual private involvement in the in-house entity.[96] Generally speaking, however, and *Asemfo* is here the main authority referred to, «where the awarding authority or concession-awarding authority, either alone or in conjunction with other public authorities, owns the entire share capital in a body that is awarded a contract or concession this as a rule shows that it or they exercise control over that body as over their own departments»; accordingly, «This rule can be displaced, but [...] only by the concurrence of special circumstances».[97] The conclusion reached is reinforced by policy reasons echoing the position defended by the German government. A too strict application of the *Teckal* requirements would make cooperation impossible among procuring entities. Indeed, only one authority could claim to have « similar control». As a consequence, «Inter-municipal cooperating regional authorities would then always have to reckon with the likelihood of having to award their tasks to pri-

94. Case C-324/07, Coditel Brabant [2008] ECR I-; see R. Caranta 'Jurisprudence Telaustria et contrat in-house', Droit adm., 2009, 2, 19; T. Kotsonis 'Application of the Teckal Exemption to a Service Concession Contract: Coditel Brabant SA v. Comune d'Uccle, Ragion de Bruxelles Capitale' Public Procurement L. Rev. 2009, NA73.
95. Point 1 of the conclusions.
96. Point 62.
97. Both quotes are from point 67.

vate third parties making more favourable bids; that would be tantamount to the compulsory privatisation by means of procurement law of public-interest tasks».[98] That would be politically unacceptable: «To construe the first *Teckal* criterion so narrowly would be to attach disproportionate weight to competition-law objectives at the same time as interfering too much with the municipalities' right to self-government and with it in the competences of the Member States».[99]

The Court of justice is somewhat less outspoken. Following *Carbotermo* and *Asemfo*, the Court accepts that « the fact that the concession-granting public authority holds, alone or together with other public authorities, all of the share capital in a concessionaire, tends to indicate – generally, but not conclusively – that that contracting authority exercises over that company a control similar to that which it exercises over its own departments».[100] On the specific facts of the case, this indication is reinforced by other elements, such as: «The fact that Brutélé's decision-making bodies are composed of representatives of the public authorities which are affiliated to Brutélé shows that those bodies are under the control of the public authorities, which are thus able to exert decisive influence over both Brutélé's strategic objectives and significant decisions».[101] While deferring to the national court for a definitive

98. Point 83.
99. Point 84; see also points 86 f.; »86. Municipalities have themselves to decide whether they wish to carry out their general-interest tasks with their own administrative, technical and other means, without being compelled to have recourse to external establishments that do not form part of their own departments, or whether they wish to carry them out with the assistance of an establishment legally distinct from them in their capacity as public entity awarding the contract or concession. If they opt for the second alternative, it is open to them to carry out these tasks of theirs on their own or in 'pure' cooperation with other public authorities 'controlled similarly to their own departments' and with the law on aid and procurement being largely suspended or to tackle them by calling on private capital and/or by increasing market orientation and participating in competition, the latter case entailing a loss of prerogatives. Finally, they have the further alternatives of the classic award to an independent third party or privatisation which in any event do not confer any privilege in regard to competition law. 87. To tackle the many traditional and new tasks of municipalities – and local authorities in general – is, particularly in times of restricted budgets, not always easy, especially for smaller authorities. In addition, many tasks, in particular in the areas of environment and transport are not confined to the municipality. Conversely, intermunicipal cooperation without calling on private capital is owing to its synergistic effects a method used in many Member States for performing public functions in an efficient and cost-effective manner».
100. Point 31.
101. Point 34.

appraisal, the Court is inclined to rule out the possibility that the cooperative company concerned might have «become market-oriented and gained a degree of independence which would render tenuous the control exercised by the public authorities affiliated to it»:[102] «In this regard, it should be pointed out that Brutélé does not take the form of a *société par actions*, or a *société anonyme*, either of which is capable of pursuing objectives independently of its shareholders, but of an inter-municipal cooperative society governed by the Law on inter-municipal cooperatives. Moreover, in accordance with Article 3 of that Law, inter-municipal cooperatives are not to have a commercial character».[103]

But the most innovative new concept developed by *Coditel Brabant* is the idea of «joint similar control».[104] This allows the Court to accept that more than one procuring entity might exercise control over the same company. The reasoning moves from *Carbotermo* and *Asemfo*, which, as it will be shown below, held that «where several public authorities control a concessionaire, the condition relating to the essential part of that entity's activities may be met if account is taken of the activities which that entity carries out with all those authorities».[105] According to the Court, «It would be consistent with the reasoning underlying that case-law to consider that the condition as to the control exercised by the public authorities may also be satisfied if account is taken of the control exercised jointly over the concessionaire by the controlling public authorities».[106] Indeed, «where a number of public authorities elect to carry out their public service tasks by having recourse to a municipal concessionaire, it is usually not possible for one of those authorities, unless it has a majority interest in that entity, to exercise decisive control over the decisions of the latter. To require the control exercised by a public authority in such a case to be individual would have the effect of requiring a call for com-

102. Point 36.
103. Point 37; see also point 38 : »It seems to be apparent from that Law, which is supplemented by Brutélé's statutes, that Brutélé's object under its statutes is the pursuit of the municipal interest – that being the raison d'être for its creation – and that it does not pursue any interest which is distinct from that of the public authorities affiliated to it».
104. According to A. Brown 'The ECJ Upholds an Italian Municipality's Reliance on the Teckal Exemption for in-house Contracts: A Note on Commission v Italy (C-371/05)' in Public Procurement Law Rev., 2009, NA7, it was already established that the two Teckal requirements could be "met collectively"; it is however doubtful that the case law was so clear concerning the first requirement.
105. Point 44.
106. Point 45.

petition in the majority of cases where a public authority seeks to join a grouping composed of other public authorities, such as an inter-municipal cooperative society».[107] This would be inconsistent with the Community rules allowing public authorities to perform the public interest tasks conferred on them by using their own administrative, technical and other resources, «without being obliged to call on outside entities not forming part of its own departments».[108] Therefore, it must be recognised that, «where a number of public authorities own a concessionaire to which they entrust the performance of one of their public service tasks, the control which those public authorities exercise over that entity may be exercised jointly».[109] If this is the case, «the procedure which is used for adopting decisions – such as, inter alia, adoption by majority – is of no importance».[110]

It is to be wondered if, when admitting the possibility of joint similar control, the Court doesn't considerably water down the first *Teckal* requisite? Indeed, for the first time the Court accepts that «the control exercised over the concessionaire by a concession-granting public authority must be similar to that which the authority exercises over its own departments, but not identical in every respect. The control exercised over the concessionaire must be effective, but it is not essential that it be exercised individually».[111]

Summing up the case law on the "similar control", while the more recent judgements affirm the inconsistency between in-house providing and private participation, they also allow considerable room for instances of purely public cooperation. This trend may have been reinforced by the recent judgement concerning the waste disposal arrangement concluded by the city-state of Hamburg and four adjoining *Landkreise*.[112] Hamburg was to build a new incineration facility intended to produce both electricity and heat. It reserved a third of the overall capacity of the facility for the four *Landkreise* in question, for a price calculated using the same formula for each of the parties con-

107. Point 47.
108. Point 48; Case C-26/03 *Stadt Halle and RPL Lochau*, paragraph 48 is referred to here.
109. Point 50.
110. Point 51.
111. Point 46; the Court disposes quite quickly of the contrary indication flowing from Case C-231/03 *Coname*: »Admittedly, the Court considered in that judgment that a 0.97% interest is so small as to preclude a municipality from exercising control over the concessionaire managing a public service. However, in that passage of the judgment, the Court was not concerned with the question whether such control could be exercised jointly».
112. Case C-480/06 *Commission v. Germany* [2009] ECR I-.

cerned. The price was to be paid to the facility's operator. The contract was to run for 20 years. The parties agreed to open negotiations five years at the latest before the end of that contract in order to make a decision as to its extension. The EC Commission brought an infringement procedure against Germany for the failure to have a call for tenders in the context of a formal tendering procedure at European Community for the waste disposal of the four *Landkreise*. Advocate general Mazák ruled out the applicability of the in-house exception since there was nothing to indicate that the *Landkreise* participated «in the City of Hamburg refuse disposal services and thus exercise control over them».[113]

The Court of justice reasoned along different lines. It accepted that the four *Landkreise* concerned did not exercise any 'similar' control neither over the other contracting party, the city Hamburg, nor over the operator of the waste incineration facility, which is a company whose capital consists in part of private funds.[114] Considering however that the infringement procedure only concerned the contract between the city of Hamburg and the four neighbouring *Landkreise* for reciprocal treatment of waste, and not the contract governing the relationship between the city and the operator of the waste treatment facility, it nevertheless considered that the contract at issue established a form of cooperation between local authorities with the aim of ensuring that a public task that they all have to perform, namely waste disposal, is carried out, a task relating to the implementation of Directive 75/442/EEC on waste. On this different basis, the Court remarked that the directive on waste «requires the Member States to draw up plans for waste management providing, in particular for 'appropriate measures to encourage rationalisation of the collection, sorting and treatment of waste', one of the most important of such measures being [...] ensuring that waste be treated in the nearest possible installation».[115] In the Court's view, the contract between the German local authorities had to be analysed «as the culmination of a process of inter-municipal cooperation between the parties thereto and that it contains requirements to ensure that the task of waste disposal is carried out»,[116] the city

113. Para 43.
114. Para 36.
115. Para 37.
116. Para 38; the Court goes on: »The purpose of that contract is to enable the City of Hamburg to build and operate a waste treatment facility under the most favourable economic conditions owing to the waste contributions from the neighbouring *Landkreise*, making it possible for a capacity of 320 000 tonnes per annum to be attained. For that reason, the construction of that facility was decided upon and un-

of Hamburg not assuming, according to the Court, any obligation as to the actual disposal of waste, this being the responsibility of the operator of the facility,[117] which is paid directly by the *Landkreise*.[118]

On this reading of the contractual arrangements between the parties, the Court of justice concluded that the contract in question formed «both the basis and the legal framework for the future construction and operation of a facility intended to perform a public service, namely thermal incineration of waste. That contract was concluded solely by public authorities, without the participation of any private party, and does not provide for or prejudice the award of any contracts that may be necessary in respect of the construction and operation of the waste treatment facility».[119] As such (but the Court is not so explicit as to the legal qualification) the contract arranged a form of centralised procurement of waste service. Contrary to the Commission's view, this did not entail the need to set up a centralised purchasing entity as a formal distinct legal entity: indeed, Community law does not require public authorities to use any particular legal form in order to carry out jointly their public service tasks, and «such cooperation between public authorities does not undermine the principal objective of the Community rules on public procurement, that is, the free movement of services and the opening-up of undistorted competition in all the Member States, where implementation of that cooperation is governed solely by considerations and requirements relating to the pursuit of objectives in the public interest and the principle of equal treatment of the persons concerned, referred to in Directive 92/50, is respected, so that no private undertaking is placed in a position of advantage vis-à-vis competitors».[120]

The agreement in question did not constitute an *in-house* arrangement even if maybe on the facts the arrangement was not too far from the one found in *Asemfo* (a possible difference being that the *Comunidades autonomas* were empowered by law rather than by contract to have recourse to the services of the *in-house* entity). The judgement, however, could be read as leaving the door open for procuring entities to transfer their purchasing powers to one of them, eventually maybe, but that was not the issue in the case just discussed and the conclusion could seriously undermine the all *in-house*

dertaken only after the four *Landkreise* concerned had agreed to use the facility and entered into commitments to that effect».

117. Para 39.

118. Para 43.

119. Para 44.

120. Para 47, referring to *Stadt Halle and RPL Lochau* [2005] ECR I-1, para, 50.

doctrine, benefiting from any 'similar control' exercised by the procuring entity having been chosen as 'centralised' procurer.

5. The essential part of the activities

A few of the cases recalled in the previous paragraph also gave some indications as to the second *Teckal* requirement, the "essential part of the activities".[121] This requirement too was read restrictively – even if it is difficult to ascertain precisely how much – in *Carbotermo*. According to the Court of justice, "An undertaking is not necessarily deprived of freedom of action merely because the decisions concerning it are controlled by the controlling authority, if it can still carry out a large part of its economic activities with other operators. It is still necessary that that undertaking's services be intended mostly for that authority alone".[122] The Court was however ready to somewhat help entities jointly held by a number of contracting authorities. It held – albeit *obiter* since the first *Teckal* requirement was not met – that "Where several authorities control an undertaking, the condition relating to the essential part of its activities may be met if that undertaking carries out the essential part of its activities, not necessarily with one of those authorities, but with all of those authorities together".[123] A more precise indication came from *Asemfo*. The Court held that "as is clear from the case-file, Tragsa carries out more than 55% of its activities with the Autonomous Communities and nearly 35% with the State. It thus appears that the essential part of its activities is carried out with the public authorities and bodies which control it."[124]

What is still uncertain is how much less than 90% could still amount to a large part or – to use the more restrictive formula of *Carbotermo* – most part of the economic activities of the in-house entity. The *Correos* case is not very helpful here. Indeed, Correos operates the universal postal service, whose main recipients are third parties, across the whole of Spain, so that public authorities are neither the only nor the main recipients of its services.[125] The Court of justice rightly rebuffed the quite novel argument by the Spanish

121. See J.J. Pernas Garcías *Las operaciones in-house*, *above* fn. 2, 154 ff.
122. Paras 61 f.
123. Para 70; see also para 71; this conclusion was affirmed in Case C-371/95, *Commission v Italy*, [2008] ECR I-, para 32.
124. Para 63.
125. Paras 85 f. of the conclusions by Advocate general Bot.

Government according to which the relationship between the public authority and a company with exclusive rights would be, by its very nature, exclusive, therefore implying a degree of exclusivity higher than in the case of 'essential activity'. Indeed it is hard to see how this arguments, which concern the 'similar control' requirement, has to do with the beneficiaries of the activities.[126]

6. Communication on the application of Community law on Public Procurement and Concessions to Institutionalised Public-Private Partnership

The case law maintaining a rigid incompatibility between in-house providing and private participation was deemed to be problematic with reference to the growing trend in public-private partnership arrangements for the building of public works and provision of public services.

Beginning in the '80 with the British public private initiative, the relationships of contracting authorities and contractors have been increasingly transformed from a commutative *do ut des* model to one of cooperation.[127] This is due to many factors, including the growing technical knowledge deficit of procuring entities, the paucity of public resources, and the desire to reduce or keep within limits the budget deficit to meet Maastricht standards.[128]

In 2004, the EC Commission published a Green paper on public-private partnerships and Community law on public contracts and concessions.[129] The paper listed the main characteristics of public-private partnerships, namely the relatively long duration of the relationship, involving cooperation between the public partner and the private partner on different aspects of a

126. See para 61.
127. See X. Bezançon *'Le contrat de partenariat : est-ce vraiment nouveau?* Revue du Trésor, 2007, 195; F. Melleray *'Contrat de partenariat et externalisation'* Revue du Trésor, 2007, 246.
128. This point is often stressed in the literature: e.g. F. Bergère *'PPP et comptabilisation des engagements'* Revue du Trésor, 2007, 255 ff.; F. Villar Rojas *'El servicio sanitario y social en España. En particolar, la concesión como modalidad de colaboración privada'* in C. Mignone, G. Pericu and F. Roversi Monaco (edds.), *Le esternalizzazioni*, Bologna, Bonomia University Press, 2007, 178 f. spec. 184 ff.; F. Merusi *'Le esternalizzazioni: tendenze nel diritto amministrativo italiano' ibid.*, spec. 260; the results of a very useful comparative short research may be read in D. de Pretis *'Servizi pubblici locali e società miste: una visione comparativa'* Diritto pubblico comarato ed europeo, 2006, 803 ff.
129. COM(2004) 327 final

planned project, the method of funding the project, in part from the private sector, sometimes by means of complex arrangements among the various players, the important role of the economic operator, who participates at different stages in the project while the public partner concentrates primarily on defining the objectives to be attained, and finally the distribution of risks between the public partner and the private partner, to whom the risks generally borne by the public sector are transferred.[130]

On this basis, the Green paper went on to distinguish between two main types of public-private partnerships: PPPs of a purely contractual nature, in which the partnership between the public and the private sector is based solely on contractual links, and PPPs of an institutional nature, involving co-operation between the public and the private sector within a distinct entity.[131] As to the difference among the two types, it was remarked that "In a PPP the asset or service is entrusted to the private sector, and in the IPPP the asset or service is entrusted of the joint company. By setting up a IPPP instead of a PPP, the public party can retain a relatively high degree of control over the infrastructure project or service".[132]

The Green paper was then mainly devoted to the former. Few paragraphs concerned institutional public-private partnerships; the Commission, which referred to *Teckal*, was mainly worried to stress that "the participation of the contracting body in the mixed entity, which becomes the joint holder of the contract at the end of the selection procedure, does not justify not applying the law on public contracts and concessions when selecting the private partner".[133]

The time before *Stadt Halle* was not ripe for an exhaustive discipline of institutionalised public-private partnerships. The situation has now matured enough for the Commission to issue a Communication on the application of Community law on Public Procurement and Concessions to Institutionalised Public-Private Partnership.[134]

The Communication aims at enhancing legal certainty and, in particular, assuaging repeatedly expressed concerns that applying Community law to the involvement of private partners into IPPP would make these arrangements

130. Point. 2.
131. Point 20.
132. Ch.D. Tvarnø *'A Critique of the Commission's Interpretative Communication on Institutionalised Public-Private Partnership'* in Public Procurement Law. Rev. 2009, NA12.
133. Point 63.
134. COM(2007) 6661.

unattractive or even impossible.[135] It is to be read in the framework of the Commission's commitment to provide legal guidance in the area of services of general interest.[136]

The starting point are the general principles of Community law, foremost among them the prohibition of discrimination on grounds of nationality, transparency, mutual recognition and proportionality. These principles require contracting entities to follow a fair and transparent procedure, either when selecting the private partner, who supplies goods, works or services through its participation in the IPPP, or when granting a public contract or a concession to the public-private entity. The Commission considers unpractical a double tendering procedure (one for selecting the private partner to the IPPP and another one for awarding public contracts or concessions to the public-private entity). To avoid this, the private partner may be selected by means of "a procedure, the subject of which is both the public contract or the concession which is to be awarded to the future public-private entity, and the private partner's operational contribution to perform these tasks and/or his contribution to the management of the public-private entity. The selection of the private partner is accompanied by the founding of the IPPP and the award of the contract or concession to the public-private entity".[137]

When the public procurement directives do not apply, and this is the case with services concessions, "the principles of transparency and equal treatment arising from the EC Treaty require potential bidders to have equal access to suitable information about the intent of a contracting entity to set up a public-private entity and to award it a public contract or a concession".[138] The intention to set up an institutional public-private partnership must therefore be advertised. Moreover, "the contracting entity should include in the contract notice or the contract documents basic information on the following: the public contracts and/or concessions which are to be awarded to the future public-private entity, the statutes and articles of association, the shareholder agreement and all other elements governing the contractual relationship between the contracting entity and the private partner on the one hand, and the contracting entity and the future public-private entity on the other hand".[139] Fi-

135. See the indications in C. Pilone *'Réflexions autour de la notion de contrat »in-house«', above* fn 53, 714 ff.

136. Point 1.

137. Point 2.2.

138. Point 2.3.3.

139. *Ibidem*; moreover, "In the Commission's opinion, the principle of transparency requires the disclosure in the tender documents of optional renewals or modifications

nally, institutional public-private partnership, in application of the case law on *in-house providing*, "must remain within the scope of their initial object and can as a matter of principle not obtain any further public contracts or concessions without a procedure respecting Community law on public contracts and concessions".[140]

The indications in the interpretative communication, if indeed quite useful in laying down a sufficiently precise framework for institutional public-private partnerships, are in the main restrictive. The possibilities to alter the initial configuration and tasks of the joint entity are very limited, and may impose a straightjacket on a co-operation mechanism which normally lasts for a long term and thus needs flexibility.

A specific discipline of institutional public-private partnership is to be found in Regulation 2007/1370/EC of the European Parliament and of the Council of 23 October 2007 on public passenger transport services by rail and by road. One of the reasons for a new legislative framework was that older rules were "considered obsolete while limiting the application of Article 73 of the Treaty without granting an appropriate legal basis for authorising current investment schemes, in particular in relation to investment in transport infrastructure in a public-private partnership".[141]

Art. 5 of the new regulation lays down the rules on the award of public service concessions.[142] As far as Community rules are concerned, "any competent local authority, whether or not it is an individual authority or a group of authorities providing integrated public passenger transport services, may decide to provide public passenger transport services itself or to award public service contracts directly to a legally distinct entity over which the competent local authority, or in the case of a group of authorities at least one competent local authority, exercises control similar to that exercised over its own departments" (Art. 5(2)). The notion of "similar" control diverges from an important aspect from the Stadt Halle doctrine. Under the same provision "(a) for the purposes of determining whether the competent local authority exer-

of the public contract or concession initially awarded to the public-private entity and the disclosure of optional assignments of additional tasks. The tender documents should cover at least the number and conditions of these options. The information thus provided should be sufficiently detailed, in order to ensure fair and effective competition".

140. Point 3.

141. Cons. 37.

142. See G.S. Ølykke *'Regulation 1370/2007 on Public Passenger Transport Services'* Public Procurement Law Review, 2008, NA84.

cises control, factors such as the degree of representation on administrative, management or supervisory bodies, specifications relating thereto in the articles of association, ownership, effective influence and control over strategic decisions and individual management decisions shall be taken into consideration. In accordance with Community law, 100% ownership by the competent public authority, in particular in the case of public-private partnerships, is not a mandatory requirement for establishing control within the meaning of this paragraph, provided that there is a dominant public influence and that control can be established on the basis of other criteria".

The specific provision just examined seems indeed more relaxed that the case law and the interpretative communication. It is however doubtful whether is it now too late to make the overall attitude of both the Commission and the Court of justice less rigid than it has become in the past few years.

7. Conclusions as to the points which are yet to be clarified

We are light years far from the uncertainty as to the boundaries of the in-house providing originated by *Teckal*. A number of problems seems however to be still in need of clarification.

Apart from the question of national law as to whether in-house providing rules need to be specifically enacted in any given legal system or whether the Community authorisation coupled with the freedom of contract eventually recognised to public law entities is sufficient to allow them to set up in-house organisations, a number of doubts still concern the *Teckal* requirements. As was already remarked, most of the cases – and *Asemfo* and *Coditel Brabant* are here the main but not only exceptions – have centred on those situations which are incompatible with in-house providing rather than on its positive conditions.

The most intriguing problem is still to define what constitutes the "control which is similar to that which it exercises over its own departments"?[143] Ordinary corporate governance rules will not do, but what will do? In the more recent case law, particularly in *Asemfo* and *Correos*, the legal act ruling the relationship between the contracting authority and its contractor seems to have been paramount. Is it necessary to conclude that contractual relationships are *per se* exclusive of the in-house providing? If this is the case, but

143. J.J. Pernas Garcías *Las operaciones in-house*, *above* fn 2, at 73 aptly speaks of *depencia decisioria*; see also R. Cavallo Perin and D. Casalini *'Control over in-house Providing Organisations' above*, fn 2, 239.

Coditel Brabant does not confirm such a radical conclusion, which kind of public law instruments (law, regulation, other) may take the place of contracts in ruling the relationships between procuring and other entities and lead to an *in-house* characterisation?[144]

Given that "the relationship between a public authority which is a contracting authority and its own departments is governed by considerations and requirements proper to the pursuit of objectives in the public interest" and that "Any private capital investment in an undertaking, on the other hand, follows considerations proper to private interests and pursues objectives of a different kind", is participation in the capital of an in-house company of private or quasi private law entities pursuing not private but institutional or quasi public interests (e.g. Chambers of commerce, associations of workers, private law foundations or trusts ...) always to be excluded?[145]

In any case, are there other, if any, considerations relevant in establishing the 'similar control'? Last but not least, is it possible following the Hamburg waste case, for procuring entities, to benefit from the 'similar control' exercised by one of them in the framework of a purchase centralisation agreement?

A few questions are also raised by the requirement under which the *in-house* entity must carry out the "essential part of its activities with the controlling public authority or authorities": how is the 'essential part' quantifiable? Is it relevant that the extant part is carried out with procuring entities and following awarding procedures?

Provided we have a genuine in-house situation, the case law has yet to consider whether and under which conditions *in-house* entities may take part in awarding procedures managed by procuring entities different from those with which the *in-house* relationship has been established (at least in so far as

144. In the recent case relating to the waste disposal in the Hamburg area, Case C-480/06 *Commission v. Germany* [2009] ECR I-, Advocate general Mazák put some emphasis on the fact that a purely contractual agreement was in place (see para 44: »the refuse disposal services do not perform their activities for the districts under statute or other public law provisions, but on the basis of a contract. The contract in dispute represents the only legal connection between the districts and the City of Hamburg refuse disposal services and that contract does not make it possible for the districts to exercise control»); the Court however decided the case on other grounds.

145. According to the conclusions by Advocate general Verica Trstenjak in *Coditel Brabant* »It remains unclear how the involvement of private persons or non-profit organisations, for example in the social or cultural fields, is to be regarded« (footnote 31).

the "essential part of the activities" requirement is abided to)? On the one hand, having being awarded a contract without competition may give to the *in-house* entity a competitive advantage which could be leveraged against other competitors. This may be the reason way Art. 5(2) of Regulation 2007/1370/EC on public passenger transport services by rail and by road restricts the possibility for in-house providers of transport services to act outside the territory of their controlling contract authorities.[146] At the same time, forbidding *in-house* entities to take part in tendering procedures restricts competition overall and one could doubt whether national rules forbidding in-house companies to provide goods or services to entities other than their controlling authority would be compatible with the EC Treaty?[147]

This inevitably leads to a more general question concerning the relations between public procurement law on the one hand and the rules on State aids and on services of general economic interest on the other hand.[148] The lead-

146. "(b) the condition for applying this paragraph is that the internal operator and any entity over which this operator exerts even a minimal influence perform their public passenger transport activity within the territory of the competent local authority, notwithstanding any outgoing lines or other ancillary elements of that activity which enter the territory of neighbouring competent local authorities, and do not take part in competitive tenders concerning the provision of public passenger transport services organised outside the territory of the competent local authority; (c) notwithstanding point (b), an internal operator may participate in fair competitive tenders as from two years before the end of its directly awarded public service contract under the condition that a final decision has been taken to submit the public passenger transport services covered by the internal operator contract to fair competitive tender and that the internal operator has not concluded any other directly awarded public service contract"; see also cons. 18 ot the Regulation: "this self-provision option needs to be strictly controlled to ensure a level playing field".

147. See also M. Dischendorfer 'The Compatibility of Contracts Awarded Directly to "Jointly Executive Services"', above fn 71, NA130.

148. See P. Dethlefsen *'Public Services in EU – Between State Aid and Public Procurement Rules'* Public Procurement Law Rev., 2007, NA55. More generally, concerning services, one could question whether the case is one of procurements or subventions; the problem has surfaced in the French case law: CE 6 avril 2007, *Commune Aix-en-Provence,* Contrat et Marchés publics, 2007, comm. 191, note G. Eckert *'Des modalités de dévolution de la gestion d'un service public à un opérateur privé'*; also Droit adm., 2007, comm. 95, note M. Bazex et S. Blazy 'Les voies de l'externalisation des activités de service public'; this case may be contrasted with Tribunal administratif de Melun, 1er décembre 2006, *Dép. de Seine-et-Marne*, Actualité juridique Droit Administratif, 2007, 856, concl. S. Dewailly.

ing case here is *Altmark.*[149] It concerned compensation for the costs incurred by a firm charged with the provision of a service of general economic interest (transport services) because of the universal service obligation imposed on it. The real meaning of the Court of justice's decision has been hotly debated.[150] Here it is sufficient to remark that the Court laid down a number of conditions necessary to make the compensation consistent with Community law. The last one reads: "Fourth, where the undertaking which is to discharge public service obligations, in a specific case, is not chosen pursuant to a public procurement procedure which would allow for the selection of the tenderer capable of providing those services at the least cost to the community, the level of compensation needed must be determined on the basis of an analysis of the costs which a typical undertaking, well run and adequately provided with means of transport so as to be able to meet the necessary public service requirements, would have incurred in discharging those obligations, taking into account the relevant receipts and a reasonable profit for discharging the obligations".[151]

While in *Olsen* the Court of first instance held that Art. 86(2) of the EC Treaty does not by itself impose that general interest tasks may be entrusted to an operator only as a result of a tendering procedure",[152] the decision in *Correos* is ambiguous. The question is whether this obligation (absent specific secondary law rules usually relevant with reference to specific sectors, e.g. Regulation 2007/1370/EC on public passenger transport services by rail and by road) may be deduced from the general principles of Community law made applicable to all contracts passed by public authorities. If this is the case, the *in-house* exception would also be relevant under Art. 86(2).

149. Case C-280/00 *Altmark Trans and Regierungspräsidium Magdeburg* [2003] ECR I-7747. It is fair to say that to this day the fourth *Altmark* condition has not found much of an application in the case law: in Joined Cases T-309/04, T-317/04, T-329/04 and T-336/04, *TV 2/Danmark A/S* [2008] ECR II-, paragraphs 228 ff., the Tribunal of first instance ruled that compliance with the second *Altmark* requirement actually implied compliance with the fourth; in Case T-289/03, *BUPA*, paragraph 246 ff., the Tribunal distinguished *Altmark*, holding that the fourth condition was not "strictly applicable" when the burden for the universal service was shared in a non discriminatory way by all the market participants.

150. See generally J. Vaquero Cruz *'Beyond Competition: Services of General Interest and European Community Law'* in G. de Búrca (ed.), *EU Law and the Welfare State. In search of Solidarity*, Oxford, Oxford University Press, 2005, 205 ff.

151. Para 93.

152. Case T-17/02, *Olsen*, at 239.

Moreover, some doubts still linger as to the possible future of the entity having been awarded an in-house contract. If, as it flows from the judgement concerning the Mantua municipality, the mere abstract possibility of privatisation does not exclude "similar control", what happens when, maybe after a few years, during the validity time of the contract, the procuring authority decides to sell its stake in the in-house entity? Is this a cause for contract termination and shall an award procedure be followed to award the contract anew? This is not a moot question, considering on the one hand that privatising an entity at the same time that you deprive it of its living does not make economic sense; at the same time, the *Stadt Mödling* case is against helping privatisation too much with previous direct award.[153]

Selected bibliography

F. Avarkioti *'The Application of EU Public Procurement Rules to "in-house" Arrangements'* Public Procurement Law Rev., 2007, 22;

D. Casalini, *L'organismo di diritto pubblico e l'organizzazione* in-house, Napoli, Jovene, 2003;

R. Cavallo Perin and D. Casalini *'Control over in-house Providing Organisations'* Public Procurement Law Rev., 2009, 227;

T. Kaarresalo '*Procuring in-house: The Impact of the EC Procurement Regime'* Public Procurement Law Rev., 2008, 242;

C. Lecuyer-Thieffry et P. Thieffry *'Les prestations effectuées in-house sans mise en concurrence'*, Act. Jur. Dr. Adm., 2005, 927;

J.J. Pernas Garcías *Las operaciones in-house y el Derecho comunitario de contratos públicos* (Madrid: Justel, 2008) 38 ff.;

C. Pilone *'Réflexions autour de la notion de contrat »in-house«'* in Contrats publics. Mélanges en l'honneur du Professeur Michel Guibal, Montpellier, Université de Montpellier, 2006, 712;

K. Weltzein *'Avoiding the Procurement Rules by Awarding Contracts to in-house Entity: The Scope of the Procurement Directives in the Classical Sector'* Public Procurement Law Rev., 2005, 252.

153. Case C-29/04, *Commission* v *Austria* [2005] ECR I-9705

In-House Providing – European regulations vs. national systems

Professor Fabrizio Cassella, University of Torino, Italy

1. In-House providing under European law following EU Court of Justice intervention

For research and legal practice, different profiles of interest are emerging from an analysis of the overall EU regulatory framework and regulations in individual EU member countries with regard to in-house providing institutions. One of the first aspects of the survey has to focus on the features of regulations enacted at European level.

On the one hand, in fact, the still very much "open floodgates" approach to community law in this sector means it is impossible to provide an organised reconstruction of the lines of conduct to be followed by parties to the system. in-house regulations are still a tangible example of internal shortcomings in European law.

Called upon to regulate the specific interaction between public organisations and the market, the European Union ordained the general obligation for all public organisations to follow standardised procedures so as to guarantee their implementation in the public interest, safeguarding the basic principles of transparency and competition. Furthermore, in this context EU law did not fully consider the possibility that a public organisation might intend to pursue its own institutional purpose by making use of other public organisations which, as such, do not fully comply with regulations of the market.

It is only in Directive 92/50/EEC that a specific provision can be found on the question of the award of public service contracts. According to art. 6 of the Directive, the articles "*shall not apply to public service contracts awarded to an entity which is itself a contracting authority within the meaning of Article 1 (b), on the basis of an exclusive right which it enjoys pursuant to published law, regulation or administrative provision, provided such provision is compatible with the Treaty*".[1]

The rationale behind this provision, later included in Directive 2004/-18/EC with no particular amendments,[2] lies in the consideration that there is no interaction between a public entity and the market where the national law of an individual EU member country, balanced in a manner compatible with the aim of EU law, decides in general to reserve certain service providing to an entity within a public organisation where such services are considered particularly important to the public interest. In other words, the law safeguards the legitimate decision of each member country not to make use of the free market, but rather of the contribution from entities called upon to act in the public interest, considered 'superior' to the general interest of the community in terms of efficiency and cost performance of the public organisation.

This approach, however, is not only limited merely to the case of awarding public service contracts, but is per se fragmented as it contains no rule to govern all cases in which the balance between the public interest and the market might legitimately encourage public entities to sidestep the tight-knit rules on competition.

It is in this legal framework that the Court of Justice made its contribution in the *Teckal* case. Having ruled out applicability of the directive on public service contracts in the case in question, the court recognised the general obligation of public administrations to follow the standard procedures under EU law in awarding a contract to a third party may not always apply, this being however "*possible only if, and at the same time, ...*" the public organisation "*... exercises similar control over the person concerned to that exercised over*

1. Under Art. 1 (b) of the Directive, these are "'contracting authorities', the State, local authorities, public organisations, associations established by such entities or public organisations.

   'Public organisation' shall mean any organisation:
   – established to specifically satisfy general needs not of an industrial or commercial nature, and
   – a legal person, and
   – whose activities are for the most part financed by the State, by local authorities or public organisations, or whose management is controlled by such entities, or more than half of the membership of whose administrative, management and supervisory bodies qualify as the State, local authorities or other public organisations ..."
2. The wording of Art. 18 of the Directive states that "This Directive shall not apply to public service contracts awarded by a contracting authority to another contracting authority or to an association of contracting authorities on the basis of an exclusive right which they enjoy pursuant to a published law, regulation or administrative provisions, provided such provisions are compatible with the Treaty".

its own services, and most of the business activities of said person are provided to its controlling organisation or local authority".[3]

Though justification in substance was similar, given the impossibility of basing its decision on the exception offered by art. 6 of Directive 92/50/EEC, which only refers to public service contracts "reserved" under general authority ruling to specific public entities, the Court adopts a stricter reading of the free sphere of action granted to procuring entities under EU law. In reference to the meaning of art. 1 (a) of Directive 93/36/CEE,[4] the Court emphasises that European provisions should be followed in a case involving a contract deriving from "*an agreement between two separate persons*".[5]

Essentially, if art. 6, Directive 92/50/EEC recognises in principle that market competition rules need not be followed if the national system, in compliance with European law, gives precedence to other public interests entrusted, in general and abstract terms, to particular public entities, the Court states that, in theory more so than in practice, interaction between public administration and the market cannot be brought into question if the public entity should decide to pursue its institutional purpose by making use of its 'internal' organisations. In such circumstances, in fact, we would have the scenario of a "contract with itself", in that from a logical point of view all minimum subjective prerequisites for the concept of a contract are lacking, where 'contract' is taken to mean an agreement between two separate persons.

In a similar manner to the Directive, however, the Court's decision per se does not appear to clarify the rules that should be followed by public administrations when their conduct affects the market. Far from being a decisive solution to all interpretation problems associated with shortcomings in EU law,

3. Case C-107/98 *Teckal* [1999], paragraph 50.
4. The wording of the provision envisages that the concept of public supply contracts covers "contracts against payment for the purchase, leasing, rental, hire purchase with or without buy-back option of products, concluded in writing between a supplier (natural or legal person) and one of the contracting authorities defined in paragraph b)". Similarly, Directive 92/50/EEC had clarified that public service contracts shall mean "contracts against payment concluded in writing between a service provide and a contracting authority".

   The same clarification is now adopted in art. 1, Directive 2004/18/EC on the coordination of procedures for the award of public works contracts, public supply contracts and public service contracts, which states that "public contracts" are contracts against payment concluded in writing between one or more businesses and one or more contracting authorities for the execution of works, the supply of products or the provision of services pursuant to this directive".
5. Case C-107/98 *Teckal* [1999], paragraph 49.

the aforementioned decision of the ECJ is instead a starting point and constant reference for subsequent 'creative' action, which through a gradual process, not without its instances of suddenly speeding up or braking, the Luxembourg court has so far restricted the sphere of action of institutions regarding in-house providing. Over the years, in fact, the Court has on a number of occasions clarified essential points of the exceptions provided in art. 6 of Directive 92/50/EEC and in the precise scenario of the *Teckal* case.

With regard to the effective scope of the Directive provision, the courts have emphasised that the envisaged exception to the norm must be strictly interpreted. In particular, in the *Asociación Profesional de Empresas de Reparto y Manipulado de Correspondencia*[6] case, the Court stated that exclusive right under national regulations can be recognised in favour of certain public entities for the provision of specific services, but does not legitimise any decision by the contracting authority to disregard EU provisions by directly awarding the provision of services not qualifying as "reserved" to that same entity.

With regard to the *Teckal* exception, the case law has completed a more or less thorough analysis of the first condition, i.e. 'similar control', to be met in order to classify as a legitimate exception to current law. In this respect, the courts have focused on different aspects.

One case law scenario insists on the level of investment required from the contracting authority in order to be classed as having 'similar control' over the provider. Abandoning its initial reading, according to which a public entity with a minority interest in the share capital of the provider is per se unable to exercise actual control over the provider,[7] the courts recently accepted in-house providing as legitimate by entities with a minority interest in the provider. Reconsidering, in effect, the definition adopted in the *Teckal* case, requiring that the entity exercise similar control over the provider, but not identical to the control exercised over its own organisation, it was emphasised

6. Case C-220/06 *Asociación Profesional de Empresas de Reparto y Manipulado de Correspondencia* [2007], cited in R. Caranta, *The in-house Providing: The Law as It Stands in the EU*' in this book, p. 17 f., specifying the different sphere of action granted under art. 6 of Directive 92/50/EEC compared to that outlined in the *Teckal* case.
7. Case C-231/03 *Coname* [2005], cited in R. Caranta, *The in-house Providing*, above fn 6, p. 22 f.

that similar control can be exercised 'jointly' by all entities with an investment in the in-house provider.[8]

Likewise, a second scenario could support development of the legal framework on the matter of opening up the concept of in-house to private entities. In this respect, though the Court was largely reluctant to accept recourse to in-house when the provider acts not only in the public interest, but is also under pressure from private entities,[9] Regulation 2007/1370/EC of the European Parliament and Council expressly stated that recourse to in-house can also apply where the contracting authority does not possess all the shares, it being sufficient that the provider's ownership structure allows the contracting authority control over ordinary and extraordinary management of the provider.[10] More recent decisions of the Court seem to move in a similar direction, in which attention is focused on the need, regardless of any private entity investments, for the provider's ownership structure to allow the contracting authority effective control over the ordinary and extraordinary management of its business activities.[11]

In setting limits on the concept of similar control, the courts, albeit incidentally, also discussed the question of the nature of the relationship on which in-house award is based. On two separate occasions, in fact, the Court

8. Case C-324/07 *Coditel Brabant*, cited in R. Caranta, *The in-house Providing*, above fn 6, 36 ff. A recent decision seems to follow the same direction, confirming that a public entity need not apply EU regulations if its own operations are substantially delegated to another public entity, with subsequent assignment of related public services (Case C-480/06 *Commission vs. Germany* [2009], indicated in R. Caranta, ivi, 40 ff.).
9. Referring to a case of minority interest of private entities in the share capital of the organisation granted direct award see Case C-26/03 *Stadt Halle and RPL Lochau* [2005], cited in R. Caranta, *The in-house Providing*, above fn 6, 19 ff. A conclusion allowing applicability of direct award can also be found in cases in which the articles of association of the provider envisage the option of future extension of the ownership structure to investment by private entities. In this respect, amongst others, see Case C-458/03 *Coname* [2005], cited above fn 7.
10. In effect, the Commission's Green Paper of 2004 in principle confirmed the possibility of an institutional investment in private entities, provided such 'partners' were chosen through procedures complying with EU provisions on the award of public contracts.
11. Case C-371/03 *Coname* [2005], cited above fn 7. Vice versa, equally important would be an analysis not restricted to formal data as found in Case C-29/04, *Commission vs. Austria* [2005], in which the court deemed illegal the decision of a local authority to proceed to directly award a service contract to a company, 100% publicly owned, in which the authority later decided to dispose of 49% of its shares to a private company.

has emphasised that recourse to in-house can also be considered legitimate in a case where the provider's services, whether or not indicated in a formal contract, are the result of controlling power recognised to the contracting authority, even where the authority has a minority interest only.[12] In other words, the circumstance that a public entity stakeholder can place restrictions on the provision of a given service and unilaterally decide the price of such services gives rise to the assumption of a scenario of incisive control over the in-house provider.

Albeit to a lesser extent, the Court's analysis also affected the second criterion established in the *Teckal* case: i.e. 'most of' the business activities. Despite the uncertain meaning of the definition and subsequent need for greater specification, the court nevertheless stated that the requirement must be verified as met on the basis of an aggregate examination of the activities performed by the provider, with due regard to the total services provided to all public entities with an investment in the provider's share capital. From a numeric point of view, far from generally defining a minimum threshold for activities 'reserved' to investors who are public entities, the Court merely clarified that the requirement can be considered satisfied if 90% of the provider's activities are dedicated to satisfying the needs of such entities.[13]

2. In-House providing under European law: the supplementary role of national laws

An analysis of the contribution of EU Court of Justice case law in outlining the essential requirements for institutional in-house configuration shows that many factors which are strictly related to this issue have been covered by EU institutions only "en passant". The exact boundaries of the two requirements defined in the *Teckal* judgement, in fact, were only partly illustrated by the Luxembourg Court, therefore placing the primary role on the shoulders of the laws in individual member Countries, which are called upon not only to adapt

12. Case C-295/05 *Asociación nacional de Empresas Forestales (Asemfo) vs. Transformación Agraria SA (Tragsa),* cited in R. Caranta, *The in-house Providing,* above fn 6, 29 ff. Vice versa, see Case C-220/06 *Asociación Profesional de Empresas de Reparto y Manipulado de Correspondencia* [2007], in which the cost of the service is fixed and pre-established, but essentially freely determined by the service provider.
13. See Case C-295/05 *Asociación nacional de Empresas Forestales (Asemfo) vs. Transformación Agraria SA (Tragsa).*

to EU provisions, but also to integrate and actually implement the principles defined at supranational level.

In this context a wide variety of positions has been adopted. The organisational differences, therefore, can be seen not only between the individual national laws, but also in the arrangements adopted on individual topics.

With regard to the definition of the second *Teckal* requirement, therefore, an analysis of the respective national legal frameworks indicates that, in effect, all EU member Countries have adopted a strict interpretation of the European law. In fact, though, by extension the 80% threshold of activities performed in favour of investors in the contractor could apply, in accordance with EU law, as the minimum percentage acceptable in a case of in-house providing,[14] individual laws that have taken a position on this issue seem to have opted for an even stricter application, albeit undefined, of the limits mentioned in the Court's judgements.

On this point, reference could initially be made to Poland. During the organisation of the 2012 World Cup, albeit in the absence of general legal provisions and notwithstanding silence from the European case law in this regard, the law placed strict limits on the sphere of action of "investee" companies created to execute works and provide services relating to the event, envisaging that such entities cannot perform business activities in addition to and/or other than those under contract, without recourse to public procedures by the public authority investors.[15]

A similar line is taken by the Danish legal system. Unlike the case in Poland, where the law has adopted a definite position, though limited to a specific case, the position in Denmark remains even more faithful to the development path adopted by European law. In the absence of specific legal provisions, in fact, the national case law limited its evaluation of the legitimacy of recourse to in-house to a specific case, accepting that a publicly-owned company designating 3% of its business to third parties is compliant with EU law.[16] It seems perfectly clear that, despite the fact that it refers to a specific case, the decision in question could form the basis for further case law devel-

14. In this respect, see the comments provided in M. Burgi, *"In-House" Providing in Germany*, in the current publication, 84, of the applicability of Art. 23, Directive 2004/17/EC on excluded sectors.
15. On this point, see the M. Spyra report, *"In-House" Providing in Polish Public Procurement Law*, in this book, 163.
16. In this respect, reference should be made to S. Treumer's further study, *In-House providing in Denmark*, in the current publicarion, 169.

opment in Denmark, therefore leading to a further restriction in the already strict margin outlined by EU case law.

Similar results, though taking somewhat different routes, are also seen under German and Italian law. Far from identifying specific percentages, the two systems are implementing the second requirement of the *Teckal* case by recourse to conceptual clarification.

The Italian Council of State, therefore, in providing an organisational reconstruction of the EU and domestic legal framework, replaced the requirement regarding "most of" the business activities with the different condition that in-house can be adopted only if there is a "strong instrumental relationship" between the activities performed under public contract by the in-house provider and the needs of a public authority that is an investor in that provider.[17] In this manner Italian law seemingly loosens the tight-knit EU regulations, distancing itself from a strictly quantitative concept of the interdependence between public authorities and in-house providers. From a more thorough examination, however, it emerges that adoption of the qualitative criterion, i.e. the "instrumental" nature of business activities compared to the institutional needs of the institutional investor, could lead to an even stricter recourse to in-house than that accepted by the EU Court of Justice. In fact, there is the risk that it would appear unlikely (and this from a theoretical even more so than a practical point of view) that a given administrative organisation could include the provision of services to entities external to its own sphere of business, whether private or public, in fulfilling its institutional purpose.

The solution enacted in German law with regard to local authorities seems to be along the same lines. Regardless of the specific nature of regulations adopted in each *Land* on the financial regime for the various municipalities, it is recognised that "institutionalised" local companies (typical of entities operating under an in-house regime) should operate mainly on behalf of their "founding" entities. If in practical terms the case law shows that this solution is linked to the financial liability of the local authorities of reference, responsible for ironing out any deficit in the accounts of the institutionalised companies, from a theoretical point of view it can be seen that the Constitutional Charter, limiting local authority self-governance to affairs of local interest only (art. 28, GG), excludes the option of companies 'dependent' on the local

17. On this point, see the M. E. Comba contribution, *In-House contracts in Italy: the circulation of a model*, published in this book, 107 and 109.

authority from operating in material and territorial spheres outside its geographical boundaries.[18]

A basic propensity towards a restrictive interpretation of the clauses defined by EU case law also transpires from an analysis of the various positions adopted in relation to the first *Teckal* criterion. In this respect, reference can be made to the highly theorising judgment of the Italian Council of State which, given the exceptional nature of the institution in question, generally accepted the opportunity of adopting a restricted interpretation of the two requirements defined by EU case law.

This tendency has in the main led Italian case law and lawmakers to adopt the initial perspectives of the European court, and disregard more recent developments. For example, this is the overall view of solutions adopted on the delicate matter of institutional investments involving both public and private entities. On this point, Italian law widely agrees with the idea that a public authority cannot make recourse to in-house if the ownership structure of the potential provider includes private entities among its investors.

This point of view characterised the Danish system even before the *Teckal* leading case. In a 1996 judgement, in fact, the special Commission for public procurement recognised the legitimacy of awarding public contracts directly to companies 100% owned by a public entity. The absolute lock-down on any scenario involving an institutional partnership between public and private entities was confirmed in more recent case law, which states that the "similar control" requirement as outlined in the *Teckal* case applies only if the public entity owns the entire share capital of the provider.[19]

A similar situation is found in Germany, where investment by private entities in various vertical cooperation formats among the entities is considered incompatible with the concept of similar control regarding the public authorities involved. In more general terms, it is considered that the direct award of public contracts to "mixed" companies would lead to a sidestepping of the principles of fair market competition, offering an unfair advantage to private

18. In this respect, see the contribution by M Burgi, *"In-House" Providing in Germany, above fn 14*, 85, in which is specifically evoked the *Ortlichkeitsprinzip*.

19. *Dansk Byggeri against Vejle Kommune Case* [2005], cited in S. Treumer, *In-House providing in Denmark*, above fn 16, 171. The same author also reported that the stance adopted by Danish case law is even more restrictive. Contrary to EU case law, in fact, the special Commission for public procurement did not consider the requirement of similar control to be automatically guaranteed where the share capital of the provider is divided among several public entities, as controlling power becomes more and more stringent the more investors there are in the share capital of the provider.

entities involved in the ownership structure of the contractor.[20] A restricted exception to this general approach concerns the specific case of the participation of private investors not bound to the tight-knit doctrine on market. In certain cases in fact, though in the absence of full control by the public authority investor, the in-house provider also has private investors completely detached from any specific economic interest, and in these circumstances a public invitation to tender would not be needed. This would apply to a worker cooperative with public authority investors, rather than to chamber organisations (e.g. Chambers of commerce) representing related 'public' interests. In such cases there would be no potential conflict between different types of interest, all in-house provider investors having the same 'overall' interest as the contracting authority.

Moreover, an analysis of Spanish law shows adoption of the same interpretation, where the law on public sector contracts requires that the share capital of companies obtaining a directly-awarded contract is 100% owned by one or more public entities, representing the only possible real guarantee that the contractor acts in the general public interest.[21]

Similar conclusions, albeit with certain slightly different nuances, were drawn in Polish and Italian law. In the first we see a convergence between case law and legislation. In fact, where case law has often stated that 100% holding of the share capital of the contractor by one or more public entities effectively excludes separation of the two parties, national law has recently submitted a draft reform of public procurement law which, in the case of contracts tendered by local authorities, accepts in-house providing only for entities whose share capital is 100% publicly owned.[22] However, unlike the situation encountered in other countries, Polish law has, at least in part, aimed to follow the developments seen in European case law. The recent 2008 law on Private Public Partnership, in fact, permits entities of a "mixed" nature, i.e.

20. See M. Burgi, *"In-House" Providing in Germany*, above fn 14, 75 ff. and 81 ff., who states that even legislation, albeit in the midst of heated debate of uncertain outcome, has presented a draft law on the safeguarding of competition, whereby recourse to in-house is limited to the situation in which the provider does not offer its services on the market, i.e. performs its main business activities in favour of its 'investor' authorities, and whose share capital is not open to investment by private entities.

21. In this respect, see J. González García, *"In-House" Providing in Spanish Public Procurement Law*, in the current publication, 136.

22. See the contribution by M. Spyra, *"In-House" Providing, above fn 15*, 151 f., who comments that, similar to that adopted in Germany, this draft law is currently a matter for lively, heated debate.

where the ownership structure includes both public and private entities. Any in-house providing to such entities does not call for open public procedures, provided that the procedures are applied in the choice of a private partner and the related invitation to tender specifically envisages not only activities to be provided by the future entity, but also the forms of control over the investee by the public authority investor.[23]

A similar scenario can be found in Italy. In effect, though guidelines on in-house defined by the Council of State have essentially excluded the option of direct award of contracts to companies not 100% owned by public entities,[24] the Council did recognise the option of in-house in cases where 'mixed' companies in which the private partner was chosen by open public procedures, provided that the business delegated was not different from that specifically stated in the invitation to tender through which the partner was identified.[25]

A stronger differentiation among national laws can be seen in relation to the delicate matter of ownership structures considered compatible with the requirement of 'similar control' as defined in the *Teckal* case. In this respect, as seen in previous observations, the EU case law did not go on to indicate the different types of commercial entity capable per se of guaranteeing effective control by public authority investors, limiting its statements to repeating that the latter must actually be able to supervise both ordinary and extraordinary decision-making with regard to the potential provider. In this context, far from identifying a specific ownership structure, EU case law considered important the option for the investor authorities to appoint its own representative to the decision-making bodies of the provider.[26]

23. In this respect, however, Spyra, *loc. cit.*, points out that the actual potential of such a provision still has to be evaluated, as to date it has seen no specific application.
24. Note that, unlike the situation in Germany and Spain where only public investment is required as a means of safeguarding free competition and of guaranteeing that action taken is in the public interest, respectively, the Italian Council of State attaches the presence of private entities to the impossibility of public partners meeting the requirement of 'similar control'. On this point, see M. E. Comba, *In-House contracts in Italy*, above fn 17, 108 f.
25. Respectively, opinion 456/07 and Decision 4603/08, cited in M. E. Comba, *In-House contracts in Italy*, above fn 17, 112 f. Nevertheless, it should be noted that the margins of applicability of this hypothesis are still somewhat confused, being unclear whether other contracts may be directly awarded to the 'mixed' company (the negative approach is predominant).
26. In this case, as seen previously, the Court limited its declaration to the illegal nature of solutions that fail to comply with the spirit of EU law, but without specifying in substance the significance of the two requirements. Therefore, in Case C.- 340/04

In the absence of specific EU legal provisions, the individual national laws have generally sought a solution consistent with EU principles with regard to the formats of associations determined under their own corporate laws and, more in general, to the different company formats. In this respect, the analysis conducted in Poland is of prime importance. Reviewing the individual business association formats envisaged under commercial law, it emphasised that the model envisaged for a joint stock company is in clear conflict with any decision open to a public investor to award public contracts without launching a public invitation to tender. On the one hand, the independence of directors with respect to the shareholders' meeting and, on the other hand, their evaluation with respect to the duties performed by the investors, led to the conclusion that such a corporate format does not satisfy the requirements for in-house providing. Relatively softer objections, albeit unable per se to guarantee effective control by the various supervisory bodies of the entity, could emerge with regard to 'limited' company formats, offering a more incisive controlling power to public entities involved in the decision-making bodies concerned.[27]

Similar observations can be made with regard to Italian law, where alongside the *società per azioni* (public limited company) and *società a responsabilità limitata* (limited liability company) there are also the consortiums, believed to best meet the EU requirements in terms of the controlling powers attributed to public authority investors, to which the law additionally recognises the option of asking an investee company to provide services on its behalf. Such a legal framework was recently confirmed in the aforementioned decision of the Council of State, which specifically emphasises that the board of directors of the investee cannot have significant powers, as a higher degree of power has to be reserved to the investor authorities than that normally guaranteed to majority shareholders under traditional commercial law.[28] Spe-

Carbotermo S.P.A. (cited in R. Caranta, *The In-House Providing, above fn 6*, 28 f., the Court declared recourse to in-house as illegal when the provider is not directly governed by a public authority but by a publicly-owned holding. In this case, in fact, the control exercised by the investor would be considerably weakened by the presence of an intermediate and independent company.

27. See M. Spyra, *"In-House" Providing*, above fn 15, 154 ff.
28. On this point see M. E. Comba, *In-House contracts in Italy, above fn 17*, 110 ff. The author nevertheless mentions that the law had foreseen special solutions from the outset for the option of local authorities to assign public services to "special companies" and "institutionalised companies". With an ownership structure unique among other forms of company envisaged under commercial law, complying with what would later be defined in European court case law, such entities were characterised

cifically, the investors would be granted the power to approve major decisions regarding the investee (e.g. approval of the financial statements), and the option of performing inspections and monitoring the quality of ordinary business operations and policies. This, however, in the opinion of the Court, does not automatically exclude the option of structuring the provider in accordance with standard commercial law, more specifically as public limited companies. In fact, though in this company format the management body is somewhat independent of the shareholders' meeting, a recent decision reflected European case law by confirming that control may also be exercised jointly by all the investors.[29] Therefore in cases where the public authority investors are able to 'govern' the investee, in principle the option of structuring the investee along the lines of a traditional public limited company should not be excluded.

Denmark appears to focus more on the specific powers recognised to public authority investors than on the providers' ownership structure. Without automatically excluding any particular corporate format, Danish law emphasises the importance of contractual clauses specifically included in the memorandum of association of the provider. In effect, a recent case recognised as legal the decision of the competent authority to create a cooperative, when the memorandum of association not only specified the power of each investor to appoint its representative on the management board of the company, but also envisaged compulsory unanimous vote by members of the board in order for internal decisions to be adopted. Hence the importance, for the purpose of meeting "similar control" requirements, not so much of the specific ownership structure of the company as of the specific measures, whether envisaged in the memorandum of association or under contract, to ensure real powers of the institutional investor to control the in-house provider.[30]

Likewise focusing on the actual situation rather than on abstract compatibility between a given corporate model and the controlling powers of its investors, UK law has indicated that articles of association attributing an appreciable margin of independence to the management body of the in-house provider, required as a result of the nature of the business activities concerned, lead to the material impossibility of different investors having effective con-

from the time of their setting up by inclusion on the board of directors of members directly appointed by the investors.

29. Council of State decision no. 1365/09, cited in M. E. Comba, *ibidem*.

30. In this respect, see S. Treume, *In-House providing in Denmark, above fn 16*, 170 ff.

trol over the investee.[31] Furthermore, in the opinion of the British courts, reflecting that of the European court,[32] this separation of 'controlling body' from 'controlled body' can derive not only from a strengthening of the investee's management independence, but also from an investor authority's decision to delegate material participation in the everyday business of the investee decision-making bodies to a third party company. In this case, in effect, there would be a weakening of the bond between the contractıng authority and the provider, which would render any control of the former over the latter completely inexistent.

One particular case in Europe is that of the nationwide in-house practice adopted by Spain for the assignment of works or services. Here, in fact, the Government normally opts for in-house assignment to providers legally set up and organised in accordance with formats and parameters quite different from those envisaged under normal commercial and corporate law.[33]

3. Legal contribution to development of the In-House concept in the wider context of regulations on public works contracts

The report has so far highlighted the fundamental role played by the various national laws in setting boundaries around the scope of application of the in-house providing in the area of public works contracts governed by EU law. European rules, however, still only affects a part of the procurement activities in the various EU member countries. Regardless of the more general consideration that the application of European provisions to 'below the threshold' contracts has been ruled out, by way of example it can be stated that, at least from a formal point of view,[34] the in-house concept was developed and governed solely with regard to public service contracts.

31. Risk Management *Partners v Brent LBC* [2008] EWHC and [2009] EWCA, cited in M. Trybus, *From the indivisible Crown to Teckal: the In-House provision of works and services in the United Kingdom*, in this book, 202 ff.
32. Case C-340/03 *Coname* [2006], cited above fn 7.
33. On this point, see J. González García, *"In-House Providing", above fn 21*, 123 ff.
34. In fact, the Court's case law regarding general applicability of the fundamental principles, descending from several regulations to different sectors is well known. In this respect, amongst others, see Case C-458/03 *Parking Brixen* [2005], cited in R. Caranta, *The In-House Providing*, above fn 6, 23 ff.

It is therefore extremely important to assess the position adopted by the various national laws, in relation to areas not covered by the EU provisions, so as to evaluate possible extension of the in-house format.

In this respect, it needs to be verified first of all whether the various national systems envisage compulsory public tenders for contracts beyond the scope of application of European law. Amongst others, Polish and Italian law fall into this category.

In Poland in particular, the law on local authority control envisages the authority option to delegate a number of its services. Both in the case of third party and in-house awards, the Polish system involves compulsory public invitations to tender in its regulations on public finance and public procurement. Traditionally, the public expenditure criterion represented the hub of the entire system, deciding the need for open competition in all cases of provision of services involving recourse to public finance.[35] Recent reforms of public procurement (the 2004 PPL), replacing the public expenditure criterion with the more flexible criterion of an economic agreement between officially-classified third parties, could lead to changes. However, it is important to note that the continuing central nature of the principle of subsidiarity steers legal experts into considering an in-house decision legitimate only if the providers can demonstrate, through a public tender, that they can provide the required services more economically and efficiently than private entities. In fact, the case law has emphasised that the absence of public tender procedures can result not only in the violation of the principles of equality and competition, but also in a sidestepping of the principle of subsidiarity, as it is only through public 'comparison' that the entity best able to perform public duties in the most efficient and economic manner for the community can be discovered.[36]

In a similar manner to the Polish context, Italian law (dating back to the 20th century but still in force) applying to sectors not regulated by EU law, envisages the general obligation to complete public tender procedures in any case where a public authority[37] is required to stipulate a contract involving

35. The only exception was in art. 6 of the Public Procurement Act (PPA) of 1994 for cases of contracts between a public authority and one of its internal departments for standard authority business activities. On this point, see the contribution by M. Spyra, *"In-House" Providing*, above fn 15, 140 f.

36. Municipality of Krasnik Case [2005], cited in M. Spyra, *"In-House" Providing*, above fn 15, 150 f.

37. On this point it should be noted that, as normally occurs in other EU member countries, the rules for contracts not covered by European law apply only to public authority activities, other entities classified under European law as public organisations in the wider sense being excluded from the legal parameters.

outlay from the public coffers. However, unlike Polish law, Italian regulations expressly envisage the option of proceeding without public invitation to tender in special and exceptional circumstances.[38]

A resemblance to the Polish legal framework can also be seen in the policy adopted by the United Kingdom. Since the 1980s, in fact, UK law has attempted to 'steer' the provision of state services towards the market, so towards outsourcing of public services. In this context, albeit in the presence of 'instrumental' public organisations, individual administrations intending to free themselves from the direct provision of certain services have been obliged to verify which entity, public or private, would provide a more efficient service.[39]

Moreover, the British situation becomes significant under the different, more specific profile of discretionary powers and parameters set for performing those evaluations deferred to public authorities. Over the years, the development of UK policy has gradually abandoned the original criterion of the most economic service in favour of the current, though more ambiguous, principle of 'best value' of service.

A more delicate matter is most certainly that regarding the discretionary power of the contracting authority. British case law, in fact, drew attention to the significant power of a public authority to suspend a public tender at any time in order to make in-house arrangements with the investee. It is this recourse to the in-house format, in effect, that in a leading case resulted in the court's conclusion that European rules did not apply, and consequently the contracting authority was free, at its own discretion, to overturn its decision to complete a public tender procedure.[40] This solution also seems to have been adopted in a recent decision, in which the decision of the contracting authority to cancel an invitation to tender already launched was sanctioned only for non compliance with *Teckal* requirements for recourse to in-house, and not

38. See the contribution by M. E. Comba, *In-House contracts in Italy, above fn 17*, 96, commenting that case law has excluded the significance of such circumstances for a legal point of view in cases deriving from the conduct of the public authority acting as the contracting party.
39. See M. Trybus, *From the indivisible Crown to Teckal, above fn 31,* 190, commenting that a similar policy led to a reduction in service costs for the public authorities involved.
40. *R. v Portsmouth City Council Ex p. George Austin (Builders) Ltd.* [1997] 95 LGR 494 (Court of Appeal), cited in M. Trybus, above fn 31, 194 ff.

for failing to comply with the supposed authority obligation to award the contract to the winner of the public tender.[41]

Danish law also seems to have adopted similar positions. An analysis of the Danish system shows that if, during the procedure, the contracting authority considers the bid from possible 'external' contractors to be unsatisfactory, it has the option of deciding instead to appoint an in-house provider.[42] As already indicated, such arrangements put equal treatment and transparency as promoted under European law in serious jeopardy, in that they fail to guarantee treatment of potential private bidders on a par with their public administration in-house competitors.

As with other topics briefly discussed in this analysis, however, in confirmation of a non-systematic "open floodgates" approach to the European regulatory framework, it is important to mention that the topic in question, though extremely significant for effective, across-the-board sector regulations, has still not been clarified by the Court of Justice, and even less so by European law.

41. Case *Risk Management Partners* Case [2008-2009], cited in M. Trybus, above fn 31, 200 ff.
42. *Risk Management Partners* Case [2008-2009], cited in M. Trybus, above fn 31, 200 ff.

"In-House" Providing in Germany

Professor Martin Burgi, University of Bochum, Germany

1. Starting point: The German administrative ("In-House") landscape

Describing and analysing the topic of "in-house" procurement in the *Federal Republic of Germany* equates to finding one's way through a dendritic labyrinth of administrative authorities. The labyrinth in our case exists as a result of *Germany's* federal structure enshrined in article 20 (1) of its constitution, the *so-called Basic Law* (hereinafter referred to as BL). As a result of the federal structure, the organisation of *Germany's* administration can be regarded as extraordinarily pluralistic.

Since the *German Reunification* in 1990, the federation has consisted of sixteen federal states (*Länder*), each of which has its own constitution, parliament and government. Additionally, on the municipal level, there are approximately 12.500 municipalities[1] that enjoy a constitutionally recognised right to self-government (article 28 (2) BL) and are considered a constituent part of the Länder and therefore, in terms of state law, constitute no separate order within the *German* federal system.[2] Thus, in the federal system of *Germany*, the federation (consisting of numerous authorities, Public Foundations, Institutions and Corporations, not to mention the Federal Courts or the Federal Bank), the "*Länder*" and the municipalities share the multifaceted administrative tasks. With the exception of some matters that are dealt with at the federal level, the majority of administrative activities are carried out by the federal states and the districts, cities and communities. Furthermore, a

1. See *German Federal Statistical Office*, Statistical Yearbook 2008 for the Federal Republic of Germany, p. 40.
2. See Hans-Peter Schneider, *The Federal Republic of Germany*, in: Akhtar Majeed/Ronald L Watts/Douglas M. Brown/John Kincaid (Ed.), *A Global Dialogue on Federalism*, Volume II, *Distribution of Powers and Responsibilities in Federal Countries*, 2005, pp.124 (129).

number of independent entities, such as universities, public broadcasting stations and chambers of commerce etc., add to the potpourri of, in total, approximately 35.000 contracting authorities in *Germany*.[3]

The majority of administrative tasks and services are administered at the local level, mostly (although not only) by local authorities.[4] In *Germany*, it has long been a tradition that public tasks are executed by municipal public companies (often called *Stadtwerke*). Furthermore, the *Stadtwerke* are often deeply rooted within the municipal societies; they enjoy a good reputation for being an efficient[5] and responsible medium to fulfil public tasks. Additionally, they are seen as important local employers.[6]

With the expansion of the welfare state the sphere of its responsibilities has been growing continuously over the years. As a consequence, local governments in particular have had to assume increasing responsibilities for providing expensive social welfare services, leaving fewer assets for actual self-government. Not surprisingly, local government resources have become strained and many municipalities are unable to balance their budgets and run huge deficits[7] resulting in finance being their predominant issue. Often, this leads to the unfortunate situation in award procedures that contracting au-

3. Thus, *Germany* provides almost 10% of *Europe's* 500.000 contracting entities; see Horn, *Public Procurement in Germany*, 2001, p. 11. Figures must be handled with caution though since they are from 1997 only.
4. Local authorities are responsible for awarding more than 50% of the total procurement volume, followed by the Länder with 25% and the federal share of 20% (excluding defence procurement). The remainder of 5% pertain to social to contracts awarded by social security authorities, see Horn, *Public Procurement in Germany*, 2001, p. 11.
5. A substantial part of local governments' income is generated through commercial activities. In fact, many municipalities run partly profitable public enterprises, sometimes alone, sometimes jointly with neighbouring municipalities or together with private partners (Public Private-Partnership). Quite regularly, profits made from such services as energy/water supply or waste/sewage disposal are used to cross-subsidise less profitable activities such as public transport. According to all Länder statutes, commercial activity on the part of local authorities is only admissible if it is "in the public interest"; see Burgi, *Kommunalrecht*, 2. Aufl. 2008, § 17 para. 5 *et seq*.
6. It is estimated that there are 2500 municipal public companies in Germany with round about 530 000 employees, see Burgi, *Kommunalrecht*, 2. Aufl. 2008, § 17 para. 7.
7. By the end of 2006, the overall debt burden of German municipalities amounted to roughly 88 billion €; see press release of the Deutscher Städte und Gemeindebund of 21st March 2007, "Lang- und kurzfristige Verschuldung der Gemeinden von 1999 bis 2006 (in Milliarden €)" available at http://www.dstgb.de (10.01.2009).

thorities have no choice but to base the award on the lowest price only instead of choosing the most economically advantageous tender.[8]

Another consequence of the financial difficulties is that especially (but not only) local authorities have been forced to reassess their activities and focus on their core business only. What is more, they have to look for alternative means to cope with the financial crisis. Therefore, they are trying to implement cost-saving measures by means of cooperation in order to maximise resources and enhance service delivery, in particular with regard to such (expensive) activities as water/energy supply, waste/sewage disposal, public transport, IT-infrastructure and maintenance.

However, cooperation is not only to be found at the municipal level but in all spheres of the *German* federal structure. Nevertheless, cooperation between local municipalities (intermunicipal cooperation) is most common and plays an increasingly important role between nearby municipalities as well as within major metropolitan areas. By way of simplified classification, cooperation in *Germany* can be systemised as follows:[9]

First, *vertical* and *horizontal* cooperation must be distinguished. *Vertical* cooperation means that one or more municipalities own or run an undertaking with legal personality. An example might be that the neighbouring cities of Bochum and Dortmund own or run an undertaking responsible for the water supply in these cities. Often these undertakings are run as stock corporations or as joint institutions governed by public law (so-called *Zweckverbände*).[10] *Horizontal* cooperation, on the other hand, means that two or more municipalities enter into a contract in order to delegate[11] or mandate[12] the legal responsibility for a public task to the partner municipality (e.g. *Bochum* and *Dortmund* decide that *Bochum* will take care of the waste disposal in Dortmund which will reimburse the city of *Bochum* for taking over that task) or agree on an ordinary service contract.

8. Although article 53 of Directive 2004/18/EC and article 55 of Directive 2004/17/EC explicitly provide otherwise.
9. Because cooperation takes place predominantly on the local level, for the purpose of this paper, the *Länder* and federal level will be left aside.
10. For a full description of the different forms of cooperation between municipalities see Bernd Jürgen Schneider (Hrsg.), *Handbuch Interkommunale Zusammenarbeit in Nordrhein-Westfalen*, 2005.
11. In the case of a delegation, the *legal responsibility* is completely transferred to the partner municipality.
12. If two entities agree that a task shall be mandated, only the legal responsibility for the *execution* of the task is transferred, but the actual responsibility remains with each municipality.

Second, a distinction must be drawn between cooperation founded on the basis of public and cooperation founded on the basis of private law. For the latter, limited liability companies or stock corporations are common. Under a public law regime, cooperation can either be formed on a contractual basis or as *Zweckverbände*. The latter usually are responsible for a few specific purposes (for example, waste disposal or public transport) and are governed by legislation relating to the administrative structures and organisation only, but *not* by procurement law.

It is important to mention that all variations of this kind of cooperation are conceivable with (Public-Private Partnerships) or without (Public-Public Partnerships) the participation of a private partner in different aspects of a planned project.

2. Legal framework

Although in recent years the importance and necessity of building cooperation to increase efficiency and to respond to public budget constraints has become (more or less) beyond doubt and, accordingly, institutionalised Public-Private Partnerships as well as Public-Public Partnerships have developed in great number in many fields, up until today neither the *German* nor the *European* lawmaker has yet passed specific legislation, neither regulating the conditions for "in-house" providing in accordance with community law nor regulating the selection of the envisaged partner. Thus, practitioners in administration and elsewhere must find their way through the jurisdiction of the *European Court of Justice (ECJ)*.[13] The only relevant *German* legislation to date[14] is more or less a translation of "public contracts" as defined in Art. 1 para. 2 of Directive 2004/18/EC.[15]

13. For a detailed overview see the paper prepared by Roberto Caranta, *The in-house Providing: The law as it stands in the EU*, 2008 (not published yet).
14. § 99 of the Act against Restraints of Competition (Gesetz gegen Wettbewerbsbeschränkungen – GWB) reads:
    (1) Public contracts are contracts for a valuable consideration concluded between contracting authorities and enterprises the subject matter of which is supplies, works or services, and reward procedures (Auslobungsverfahren) intended to lead to service contracts.
    (2) ...
15. Directive 2004/18/EC of the European Parliament and of the Council of 31 March 2004 on the coordination of procedures for the award of public works contracts,

Recently, however, the *German* parliament discussed the implementation of a definition of "in-house" providing in § 99 GWB. The second sentence of the reformed § 99 para. 1 GWB would read:

> It is not a public contract, if a contracting authority in terms of § 98 Nr. 1, 2 or 3 GWB (i.e. the classical, non-sectoral contracting authorities) get supplies, works or services rendered by legal entities which are themselves contracting authorities in whom private capital is not involved, provided that these legal entities do not offer their service on the market or carry out essential parts of its activity for contracting authorities.16

This envisaged amendment has been criticised for various reasons. On the one the hand, it has been assessed as being too broad and therefore in violation of European Community Law.[17] On the other hand, the *Federal Council of Germany* (*Bundesrat*) has criticised the proposed amendment as being a mere codification of the *ECJ* "in-house" case-law and does not take into account the need of local authorities for a clarification that intermunicipal cooperations do not fall within the scope of Community procurement law. Therefore, the *Bundesrat* suggested the following proposition which is aimed at explicitly excluding intermunicipal cooperation from the scope of public procurement law:

It is not a public contract if

- the cooperation is between local authorities,
- the tasks, the performance of which was assigned to these local authorities, are to be considered a matter of administrative reorganisation or if the supervisory powers of the local authorities concerned are similar to those which they exercise with regard to their own departments, and

public supply contracts and public service contracts, OJ EU L134 of 30.4.2004, p. 114.

16. See Gesetzentwurf der Bundesregierung zur Modernisierung des Vergaberechts vom 21.05.2008, available at http://www.bmwi.de/BMWi/Navigation/Presse/pressemitteilungen,did=249454.html (10.01.2009) Translation and remarks in brackets by the author.
17. von dem Bussche, *Das ausschreibungsfreie in-house-Geschäft nach dem Gesetzesentwurf zur Modernisierung des Vergaberechts: Schaffung eines isolierten Verwaltungsmarktes?*, Vergaberecht 2008, 881, 887 et seqq.

– *the activities are essentially performed for the local authorities concerned*[18]

Not surprisingly, this suggestion was strongly supported by the three central local government associations of Germany.[19]

After all, the implementation was stopped last minute[20] for various reasons and although implementation of such legislation would have been the first explicit reference to the possibility of "in-house" providing in *German* legislation so far, it would not alter the current legal situation because public authorities are already free to decide whether they want to involve (public) third parties to execute their tasks. But this option is based solely on the contracting authorities' organisational autonomy and organisational power. Additionally, for local authorities, the opportunity to cooperate derives from the right of local authorities to self-government, as constitutionally enshrined in article 28 (2) of the BL.

Thus, an implementation of the "in-house" option in *German* procurement law would comprise a mere clarification only; it would not do away with the frustration caused by the *EU* (procurement law) interference in what is seen traditionally (especially on municipal level) as an exclusively *affaire nationale*: the power and autonomy to organise and structure the national administration.

Nevertheless, when looking at the remaining legal regime affecting "in-house" providing in *Germany*, one encounters a wide, complex and diverse field of law.

First and above all, of course, stands the *European Community* law set out in the treaties, directives and regulations as defined by the *ECJ*.[21]

Apart from community law, two fields of law are particularly important for the "in-house" issue in Ger*many*. The first area is the law governing the

18. See Stellungnahme des Bundesrates zum Entwurf eines Gesetzes zur Modernisierung des Vergaberechts vom 04.07.2008, BR –Drucksache 349/08. Translation by the author.
19. See Press release of the Deutscher Landkreistag (German County Association) of December 19th 2008, available at http://www.kreise.de/landkreistag/auswahl-presse.htm (10.01.2009).
20. See the new version of the GWB of 23.04.2009, BGBl. I, S. 790, with minor changes in § 99 GWB only.
21. See below 4.

organisation of administrative public bodies.[22] The relevant norms are widespread and can be found, inter alia, in public law norms such as the constitution, the *Länder* constitutions, budget law (*Haushaltsrecht*), *Länder* organisation acts (*Landesorganisationsgesetz*), *Länder* statutes concerning the organisation and powers of the municipalities (*Gemeindeordnungen*), *Länder* municipal economic statutes (*Gemeindewirtschaftsrecht*) and *Länder* statutes regulating intermunicipal cooperation (*Gesetze über kommunale Gemeinschaftsarbeit*).[23] The second field is the body of private law statutes concerning the founding of corporate legal entities governed by private law such as, for example, limited liability companies or stock corporations.

It is important to point out that the mentioned fields of law are concerned with the modalities of cooperation only, i.e. *if and how* public entities may cooperate. They do not contain any legal framework for awarding procedures. What is more, these provisions are not aiming at the prevention of inappropriate restrictions on competition and are not intended to stimulate the spirit of the *European Internal Market*.[24]

The purpose of the third field of law that comes into play is fairly different: *Germany's* public procurement law intends mainly to safeguard the principles of competition, equal treatment and transparency (see § 97 GWB)[25] as envisaged by the *EU* procurement system.

However, it is necessary to realise the systemic difference between these sets of rules: On the one hand are the statutes governing the composition and organisation of the *German* administration, which is a purely national matter. On the other hand, there are the (national) procurement rules that give effect to the *EU* procurement legislation intended to ensure undistorted competition and the functioning of the *European Internal Market*.

22. Additionally, European Community law on state aid (Art. 87 EC *et seq.*) and antitrust law (Art. 81 EC) have to be considered, but are left aside for the purpose of this paper.
23. See for example for North Rhine-Westphalia: Gesetz über kommunale Gemeinschaftsarbeit in der Fassung der Bekanntmachung vom 1. Oktober 1979 (GV. NRW. S. 621) zuletzt geändert durch Artikel V des Gesetzes vom 9. Oktober 2007 (GV. NRW. S. 380).
24. Accordingly, quite recently in Germany a higher administrative court decided that in award review procedures the compliance of successful bidders with municipal economic law cannot be reviewed, see ruling by OVG Münster, 01.04.2008, DVBL 2008, 919 et seqq.
25. For an exhaustive explanation of their meaning see Burgi, *Die Bedeutung der allgemeinen Vergabegrundsätze Wettbewerb, Transparenz und Gleichbehandlung*, NZBau 2008, 29 *et seqq*.

3. Limits of EU competencies

It is essential to accentuate that it falls exclusively within the discretionary power of each member state to determine the composition and organisation of its national institutions and administration. It is a common view of the *ECJ* itself and among *German* scholars that the *EU* lacks competence to determine organisational structures within the member states.[26] To clarify: It is not up to the *EU* to establish rules concerning the internal organisational structures of the member states. The question of how to ensure and to organise the fulfilment of its (*European*) obligations remains solely a matter of the constitutional system of each member state.

In particular, the well-established right to regional and municipal self-government[27] is an important aspect of the member states' organisational sovereignty. This argument was recently emphasised by Advocate-General *Trstenjak.* In her opinion delivered in *Coditel Brabant*[28] she pointed out that "municipalities have themselves to decide whether they wish to carry out their general-interest tasks with their own administrative, technical and other

26. See ECJ, ECR 1971, p. 1107 paras. 3, 4 – *International Fruit*; ECJ, ECR 1987, p. 2141 para. 22 – *Traen*; see also Burgi, in: Erichsen/Ehlers (Hrsg.), *Allgemeines Verwaltungsrecht*, 13. Aufl. 2006, § 6 Rn. 32.
27. The right to municipal self-government is inter alia reflected in the legal provisions of the member states (see e.g. Article 28 para. 2 *Basic Law*) and the European Charter on Local Self-Government (opened for signature by the member states of the Council of Europe on 15 October 1985 in Strasbourg, in force since 1 September 1988), signed by all EU member states and also ratified by most of them. Article 6 (1) of the Charter provides that, without prejudice to more general statutory provisions, local authorities must be able to determine their own internal administrative structures in order to adapt them to local needs and ensure effective management. Furthermore, Article 263 of the *EC* Treaty (Treaty establishing the *European Community*, OJ EU C 325 of 24 December 2002) makes provision for the Committee of the Regions comprising representatives of regional and local authorities. Inherent in this provision is a certain recognition of self-government alongside the possibility of providing institutionalised machinery for bringing to bear regional and municipal perspectives. Finally, the Treaty of Lisbon (Treaty of Lisbon amending the Treaty on *European Union* and the Treaty establishing the *European Community*, [OJ EU C 306 of 17 December 2007, p. 1], Article 3a of the future *EU* Treaty, not yet in force. In the consolidated versions of the Treaty on *European Union* and the Treaty on the Functioning of the *European Union* [OJ C115 of 9 May 2008, p. 1] underlines the role of regional and local self-government, Article 4 of the *EU* Treaty, not yet in force.
28. ECJ Case C-324/07 *Coditel Brabant* (13.11.2008), now confirmed in ECJ Case C-480/06 *Stadtreinigung Hamburg* (09.06.2009), para 45.

means, without being compelled to have recourse to external establishments that do not form part of their own departments, or whether they wish to carry them out with the assistance of an establishment legally distinct from them in their capacity as public entity awarding the contract or concession. If they opt for the second alternative, it is open to them to carry out these tasks of theirs on their own or in 'pure' cooperation with other public authorities 'controlled similarly to their own departments' ..."[29] She warned that an overly narrow interpretation of the "in-house" criteria would "... render virtual impossible even pure inter-municipal cooperation ..." and expressed concern that "... Inter-municipal cooperating regional authorities would then always have to reckon with the likelihood of having to award their tasks to private third parties making more favourable bids; that would be tantamount to the compulsory privatisation by means of procurement law of public-interest tasks."[30] One can agree with the Advocate-General that disproportionate weight might be attached to competition law objectives at the same time as interfering too much with the municipalities' right to self-government and the organisational sovereignty of the member states.[31]

As is often the case, the *ECJ* later in its judgement upheld the opinion of the Advocate General. The court strengthened the right to regional and municipal self-government by affirming that public authorities indeed have the option to perform the public interest tasks conferred on them by using their own resources without being obliged to call on outside entities not forming part of their own departments. Furthermore, the possibility for public authorities to use their own resources to perform the public interest tasks conferred on them may indeed be exercised in cooperation with other public authorities.[32]

Given the above, (*European*) public procurement law must be reduced to its core meaning again: It is about procurement, i.e. public entities buying from or cooperating with the private sector and hence opening up competition. But as long as the public sector does not seek to involve the private sector at all and the (private) market is not affected, cooperation between purely

29. Advocate-General Trstenjak, opinion delivered in ECJ Case C-324/07 *Coditel Brabant* (13.11.2008), para. 86.
30. Advocate-General Trstenjak, opinion delivered in ECJ Case C-324/07 *Coditel Brabant* (13.11.2008), paras. 82 *et seqq*.
31. Advocate-General Trstenjak, opinion delivered in ECJ Case C-324/07 *Coditel Brabant* (13.11.2008), para. 84.
32. ECJ Case C-324/07 *Coditel Brabant* (13.11.2008), paras. 48 *et seq*., now also confirmed in ECJ Case C-480/06 *Stadtreinigung Hamburg* (09.06.2009), para 45.

public entities is a question of the member states' organisational sovereignty only, in which the *EU* lacks competence to interfere. Reorganising a member state's administrative structure has never been and will never be a question of *EU* procurement law.

This should be clarified (on the *European* level). A first step towards such a clarification might be seen in the Protocol on services of general interest to the Treaty of *Lisbon*[33] which stipulates in Article 1

"(...)the essential role and the wide discretion of national, regional and local authorities in providing, commissioning and organising services of general economic interest as closely as possible to the needs of the users; (...)"

4. Conditions of the "In-House" doctrine

The lack of influence on the free competition between private contestants is the main argument for the acceptance of "in-house" providing. It is primarily the decision of the public authority whether to purchase needed goods or services from a part of another administration, a wholly owned subsidiary or from private companies. The *ECJ* has developed different preconditions for the legitimacy of "in-house" providing. It is the ambition of the *ECJ* to limit "in-house" to constellations of internal administrative providing. There are three main preconditions that are very important for procuring entities and courts in the member states of the *EC*. Based on the *Teckal* case,[34] the contract must be concluded between two separate persons: a local authority and a person legally distinct from the local authority. Furthermore, the local authority must exercise over the person concerned a control which is similar to that which it exercises over its own departments and, at the same time, that person carries out the essential part of its activities with the controlling local authority or authorities. The second and the third points must be considered carefully because of their association with difficult questions and they have been the subject of many other decisions of the *ECJ*.[35] This case-law has a major

33. OJ EU C 306 of 17.12.2007, p. 158 and Protocol (No 26) of the consolidated versions of the Treaty on *European Union* and the Treaty on the Functioning of the *European Union* OJ EU C115 of 9.5.2008, p. 308.
34. ECJ C-107/98 – *Teckal* [1999], ECR I-8121.
35. E.g. ECJ, C-26/03 – Stadt Halle [2005], ECR I-1; C-231/03 – Coname [2005], ECR I-7287; C-458/03 – Parking Brixen [2005], ECR I-8585; C-295/05 – Asociación Nacional des Empresas Forestales (Asemfo) v. Transformación Agraria SA (Tragsa)

impact on national solutions to "in-house" providing cases. Therefore, it is presented below in a nutshell.

4.1. The "similar control" criterion

4.1.1.

The *ECJ* has tightened its jurisprudence after the *Teckal* decision insofar that a similar control is only exercised over companies without any private shareholding, which means wholly owned subsidiaries.[36] No private company should derive advantage from contracts concluded without following the tendering procedures for public contracts required under Community legislation. The first *Teckal* criterion is fulfilled even if more than one public authority has a holding in the procuring entity beneficiary and a shareholding of 0.97 % is sufficient for adequate control.[37]

In *Germany*, this case-law is accepted by courts and all parties concerned in the field of vertical cooperation. A private shareholding, even as a minority, in the capital of a company in which the contracting authority is also a participant excludes in any event the possibility of that contracting authority exercising over that company a control similar to that which it exercises over its own departments.[38] Private participation is incompatible with the idea of control by the procuring entity. Furthermore, the award of a public contract to a semi-public company without calling for tenders would offer a private undertaking with capital presence in that undertaking an advantage over its competitors.[39]

The *ECJ* verifies this precondition in every individual case and has developed a wide range of criteria to check whether the first *Teckal* requirement is fulfilled or not. The tendency is to interpret the requirement narrowly.[40] To

[2007], ECR I-2999; ECJ C-324/07 – Coditel Brabant (13.11.2008); ECJ C-480/06 – Stadtreinigung Hamburg (09.06.2009), para 45.

36. ECJ, C-26/03 – *Stadt Halle* [2005], ECR I-1.
37. ECJ, C-231/03 – *Coname* [2005], ECR I-7287.
38. BGH, 03.07.2008, WRP 2008, 1182, 1184 et seq.; Kammergericht, 27.07.2006, Vergaberecht 2006, 904, 906; OLG Düsseldorf, 21.06.2006, Vergaberecht 2006, 777, 782.
39. BGH, 03.07.2008, WRP 2008, 1182, 1185.
40. However, in ECJ Case C-324/07 *Coditel Brabant* (13.11.2008), paras. 54, the court seems to have eased the first *Teckal* criterion in so far that, where a public authority joins an inter-communal cooperative of which all the members are public authorities in order to transfer to that cooperative the management of a public service, it is possible, in order for the control which those member authorities exercise over the cooperative to be regarded as similar to that which they exercise over their

prevent artificial constructions, such as in the *Mödling* case,[41] the court demands consistency of the two *Teckal* criteria.[42] One must agree with this because the guidelines of primary legislation must be followed. But the court takes into account with increasing intensity aspects such as the interests of the shareholders, the legal form of the company, the possible investment of private capital, influence on the appointment of the administrative board and the director of subsidiary companies and sub-subsidiaries, the authority of the administrative board and the possibility of founding branch offices in other states. It seems that especially the legal form of the public limited company is one important indicator for the *ECJ* not to accept the existence of an "in-house" providing.[43] Today's situation is that there are many different aspects to be noted before answering the question whether it is an "in-house" providing or not. These aspects have nothing to do with the actual award because there is nothing to be awarded nor is there a change in matters of competition. Consequently, the choice of the legal form is ruled by aspects of procurement law and not of aspects of the best way to found such an undertaking. It would be a great achievement for legal certainty if the *ECJ* case-law would dispense with all these aspects. A better way would be a clarification in the procurement directives as to which criteria have to be fulfilled for the acceptance of an "in-house" providing – independent from the legal form of the company or other aspects of company law. Two categories should be decisive for the exclusion from the duty to follow the tendering procedures for public contracts: on the one hand the question of private shareholding and on the other hand the question of a participation in the external competition with private companies.[44]

4.1.2.

In two other constellations of shareholding, the existence of the "similar control" criterion is questionable. Considering employees share ownership, it is important to see the difference between an employee of a wholly-owned sub-

own departments, for it to be exercised jointly by those authorities, decisions being taken by a majority and that the control has not to be exercised individually by each of those public authorities.

41. ECJ, C-29/04 – *Commission v. Austria* [2005], ECR I-9705.
42. ECJ, C-29/04 – *Commission v. Austria* [2005], ECR I-9705; C-410/04 – *ANAV* [2006], ECR I-3303.
43. ECJ, C-340/04 – *Carbotermo* [2006], ECR I-4137.
44. *Burgi,* Privatisierung öffentlicher Aufgaben, Gutachten D für den 67. Deutschen Juristentag, München 2008, p. 80.

sidiary and of a private capital participation. At first sight, the situation seems to be quite equal. A public company receives the contract award and, following this, shares are given to a private person. If there is no public contract given to the undertaking before without the accomplishment of a tendering procedure, the *Mödling* case-law[45] is not relevant. Otherwise tendering procedures are not applicable either because an employee is not a contractor according to Art. 1 (8) of Directive 2004/18/EC. He or she does not offer the execution of works and/or a work, products or services. An employee share ownership does not bear relation to the external market and private competitors. There is even no need to apply tendering procedures.

The participation of chambers[46] is the second case in which it seems to be possible that the "similar control" criterion is not fulfilled, e.g. if the city of *Bochum* cooperates with the *Chamber of Industry and Commerce* in order to found a mutual subsidiary to perform a public task. Chambers in *Germany* are part of the self-administration, i.e. they are administrative bodies fulfilling their duties and responsibilities mostly independent from other administrative authorities under inclusion of its members. The attribute of independence from other administrative authorities shows that there cannot be a control similar to the control it exercises over its own departments. From this point of view, the chamber is comparable to a private shareholder. Its participation leads to a lack of control. The difference is that a chamber is part of the public administration. There is no relationship to external competitors because the public contracting authority decides to award a contract to a public undertaking. If it performs the services on its own, it would be the same and no private interests would be affected. There is no right of private undertakings that administrative bodies award contracts to private competitors. Only when a public authority has decided to do so must the tendering procedures be followed.[47] Finally, it can be said that a tendering procedure is not necessary in shareholding structures such as the aforementioned.

45. ECJ, C-29/04 – *Commission v. Austria* [2005], ECR I-9705.
46. E.g. the Chambers of Handicrafts or the Chambers of Industry and Commerce.
47. Same result for intermunicipal cooperation Burgi, Warum die *"kommunale Zusammenarbeit" kein vergaberechtspflichtiger Beschaffungsvorgang ist*, NZBau 2005, 208, 211 *et seq*.

4.2. The "essential part of activities" criterion

4.2.1.

The second *Teckal* criterion demands that the "in-house" entity must perform the essential part of its activities for the contracting authority.[48] This requirement must be fulfilled to justify the non-application of the public procurement rules otherwise this entity would have an unjustified advantage compared to private competitors. For a long period of time the *ECJ* did not clarify what the essential part of activities is. The *Carbotermo* decision brought clarification of paramount importance concerning the second *Tecka*l criterion.[49] Thereafter the essential part of the activities criterion was understood to mean that the activities of the entity concerned are devoted principally to the contracting authority and other activities are only of marginal significance, irrespective of who the beneficiary is, who pays the entity in question and in which territory the service is provided. The *ECJ* did not follow the idea of an analogy to Art. 23 (3) Directive 2004/17/EC for contract awards outside of procurement procedures in the water, energy, transport and telecommunications sectors. This means that the 80 % – benchmark of Art. 23 (3) Directive 2004/17/EC cannot be transferred to contract awards in the classic sector to substantiate the "essential part of activities" criterion. Subsequently, the *Asemfo* decision showed that it is sufficient if the entity provides more than 90 % of its performances to the contracting authority.[50] *German* courts mostly accept this decision although the answers to some questions remain unclear and legal uncertainty is not completely dispelled. Some *German* courts are stricter concerning the second *Teckal* criterion.[51] This case-law seems to be a kind of anticipatory obedience to *EC* law; some might say that this is typical for *Germany*.

4.2.2.

Municipal economic law may constitute a further barrier for municipal undertakings to obtain public contracts. The *Länder* have the legislative competence for municipal law. Hence there are 16 different laws regulating municipal economic activity, one for each *Land*. They have in common strict rules

48. ECJ, C-340/04 – *Carbotermo* [2006], ECR I-4137.
49. Avarkioti, The Application of EU Public Procurement Rules to "in-house" Arrangements, (2007) 16 P.P.L.R. 22.
50. ECJ, C-295/05 – Asociación Nacional des Empresas Forestales (Asemfo) v. Transformación Agraria SA (Trasga) [2007], ECR I-2999.
51. Oberlandesgericht Celle, 14.09.2006, NZBau 2007, 126 decided that 92.5 % is not enough to assume that a tendering procedure is not necessary.

for supra-local activities to guarantee acting in public interest and not only to draw profit. Although these rules are not part of German public procurement law,[52] they have an influence on public undertakings tendering in procurement procedures outside their municipality. These restrictions of municipal economic law facilitate the compliance with the second *Teckal* criterion because municipal public companies should work predominantly for the founding municipality only. Protection of municipal budgets is one important reason for this because, at the end of the day, it is always the municipality that has to pay the company's liabilities if it gets into financial trouble. Secondly, it is said, for example in § 107 (1) Local Code *North Rhine-Westphalia*, that a municipality has the right to use economic activities for executing its own affairs. These affairs are of local provenance because Art. 28 (2) BL says that the municipalities have the right (and the responsibility) to attend to all affairs of importance to the local authority. The word "affairs" in the Local Code thus means affairs of local interest. This is called the *Örtlichkeitsprinzip.*[53] It is doubtful whether a public undertaking can work in public interest in the area of another municipality because there is often no connection between this economic activity and the common good of the "home" municipality with the exception of earning money. Such an undertaking must justify its supra-local activities. It is important to note that such rules exist only for municipalities, and not for other public bodies such as universities.

For municipal companies this situation represents a dilemma because, on the one hand, they do not have the possibility to accommodate private shareholders without losing the advantage of "in-house" providing; on the other hand, they are restricted to the area of their responsible body. So there is no alternative to work more efficiently and to grow. Public companies lose customers to private competitors while at the same time struggling to acquire new customers in other areas.[54]

There are different ideas about how to abolish these barriers because municipal undertakings are at a disadvantage compared to their private competitors who can act wherever they want to. Some *Länder* allow municipal economic activity in areas of other municipalities under the precondition that the interests of these local authorities are protected.[55] A second possibility is the

52. Oberverwaltungsgericht Münster, 01.04.2008, 15 B 122/08, Eildienst Städtetag Nordrhein-Westfalen 2008, 157 *et seqq.*
53. See Burgi, *Kommunalrecht*, 2. Aufl. 2008, § 17 paras. 47 et seqq.
54. Leder, Kohärenz und Wirksamkeit des kommunalen Wirtschaftsrechts im wettbewerbsrechtlichen Umfeld, DÖV 2008, 173, 179.
55. E.g. § 107 (3) Local Code North Rhine–Westphalia.

creation of a legal possibility for municipalities to found companies that are not bound to the *Örtlichkeitsprinzip* and other restrictions. But that also means that a public authority cannot award a public contract to such an undertaking without following the tendering procedures required under *Community* legislation and national public procurement law. These kind of undertakings are called *Wettbewerbsunternehmen.* They have no advantages or disadvantages compared to private competitors and their status as a *Wettbewerbsunternehmen* is formally manifested by the municipal council.

4.3. Conclusion

To avoid legal uncertainty, it would be useful if the *European Community* would clarify the procurement directives. The only criterion should be the question whether the procuring entity beneficiary has private shareholders or not. The criteria of a control which is similar to that which the contracting authority exercises over its own departments and that the entity must carry out the essential part of its activities with the controlling public authority or authorities are not matters of public procurement law.

5. Emerging issue: Horizontal cooperation on a more contractual basis (no institutionalised relationship)

As more and more municipalities discover the benefits of mutual cooperation (on a contractual basis) and act accordingly (e.g. *Bochum* and *Dortmund* conclude a contract that allows *Bochum* to store its waste in *Dortmund's* landfill site), it did not take long until courts were asked to decide whether procurement law is applicable to these constellations or not. Both *OLG Düsseldorf*[56] and *OLG Frankfurt*[57] ruled that procurement law shall be applicable if two neighbouring cities enter into a contract in terms of which one municipality is mandated to execute certain public tasks in the other municipality while legal responsibility remains with each municipality. The *OLG Naumburg* found that procurement law is even applicable where the legal responsibility is delegated to the other city.[58] In contrast, the *OLG Düsseldorf*[59] decided on a constellation where two cities founded an entity with legal personality (*Zweckveband*) to which the legal responsibility for a certain public task (in

56. *OLG Düsseldorf*, 05.05.2004, NZBau 2004, 398.
57. *OLG Frankfurt*, 07.09.2004, NZBau 2004, 692.
58. *OLG Naumburg*, 03.11.2005, NZBau 2006, 58.
59. *OLG Düsseldorf*, 21.06.2006, NZBau, 662.

this case, waste disposal) was delegated that procurement law shall not apply. Thereby the court might have created a *sui generis* exception from procurement law for constellations where (based on statutes governing the administrative structure of cooperation) legal responsibilities are delegated from one public authority to another.

Sparked by these decisions and the *ECJ's* judgement *Commission vs. Kingdom of Spain*,[60] a controversial discussion about the future of "in-house" constellations unsurprisingly took place in *Germany*. The arguments presented varied on a broad scale. While some authors were rather sceptical about the future of "in-house" possibilities in general,[61] others took a more analytical approach.[62] Within this debate, whether so-called horizontal cooperation on an entirely contractual basis (that means without the establishment of an entity of whatever legal nature) between two or more public entities falls under the "in-house" exception as defined by *ECJ* was especially intensely discussed. However, it was often overlooked that the court only ruled that "national legislation on public contracts which excludes, *a priori*, from its scope cooperation agreements concluded between public authorities and other public undertakings, and therefore also the agreements which constitute public contracts for the purpose of those directives *constitutes an incorrect transposition* of Directives (...) 93/36 ... and 93/37 (....)."[63] Therefore, from this verdict, only vague (if any) conclusions can be drawn for the admissibility of any (and contractual horizontal in particular) "in-house" constellations. So, the judgement did not bring any more clarity and it can be considered rather fruitless for the "in-house" debate." Furthermore, it must be borne in mind that the *ECJ's* "in-house" case-law so far did not really fit to constellations where a *horizontal* cooperation is in question.

That has changed significantly since the pronouncement of the most recent *ECJ* judgement concerned with the "in-house" – subject matter. In the *Stad-*

60. ECJ C-84/03 of 13.01.2005 – Commission of the European Communities v Kingdom of Spain, OJ EU C 82, 02.04.2005, p. 2
61. See e.g. Ziekow/Siegel, Die Vergaberechtspflichtigkeit von Partnerschaften der öffentlichen Hand, Vergaberecht 2005, 152 et seqq.; Hattig/Ruhland, Kooperationen der Kommunen mit öffentlichen und privaten Partnern und ihr Verhältnis zum Vergaberecht, Vergaberecht 2005, 425 et seqq.
62. Burgi, *Warum die „kommunale Zusammenarbeit" kein vergaberechtspflichtiger Beschaffungsvorgang ist*, NZBau 2005, 208 *et seqq* and *Vergabe- und Wettbewerbsrecht als zusätzliche Maßstäbe für Verwaltungszusammenarbeit*, ZG 2006, 189 *et seqq*.
63. *ECJ* C-84/03 of 13.01.2005 – *Commission of the European Communities v Kingdom of Spain*, paras. 38, 40. Emphasis added by author.

treinigung Hamburg case[64] the court had to decide whether or not cooperation in the abovementioned horizontal constellation (i.e. purely contractual cooperation) between public authorities could also be exempted from the procurement regime. The facts of the case were rather simple[65]: Four *German* counties (Landkreise) concluded a 20-year contract with *Stadtreinigung Hamburg* (City of Hamburg Cleansing Department) for the disposal of their waste in *Hamburg's* new incineration facility. Stadtreinigung Hamburg reserved part of the incinerator's capacity for the counties, which in return paid annual fees, which where passed on to the facility's operator. The counties also made available to Stadtreinigung Hamburg their excess landfill capacity to alleviate the lack of landfill capacity of the City of Hamburg. The *ECJ* stressed that the contract at issue did not govern the relationship between Stadtreinigung Hamburg and the facility's operator, but that it was a contract between the four counties and Stadtreinigung Hamburg for the reciprocal treatment of waste. The Court analysed in detail the obligations of the parties, and concluded that the contract established a cooperation only between local authorities with the aim of performing a public-interest task. The *ECJ* reconfirmed its statement from the Coditel case that public authorities are free to perform public-interest tasks themselves or in cooperation with other public authorities regardless of any particular legal form.[66] However, the *ECJ* did not abolish all boundaries. In the view of the court, there seem to be two conditions under which such cooperation agreements are exempted from the rules on public procurement: a) the cooperation is governed solely by the pursuit of objectives in the public interest (e.g. waste disposal); and b) no private undertaking is placed in a position of advantage vis-à-vis its competitors (here: this agreement did not prejudice the award of contracts necessary for constructing or operating the waste treatment plant).

Thus, the judgement has made clear, that where *horizontal cooperation* is in question the "similar control" criterion is not applicable; the decisive factor is whether private capital is involved or not. Furthermore, the judgement constitutes a paradigm shift insofar as the Court finally paved the way for the overdue acknowledgment that horizontal cooperation between two or more public authorities does not constitute a public contract in terms of the *EU* procurement directives. As a matter of course, the judgement was welcomed

64. ECJ C-480/06 of 09.06.2009 – *Stadtreinigung Hamburg.*
65. ECJ C-480/06 of 09.06.2009 – *Stadtreinigung Hamburg*, para. 4 et seq.
66. ECJ C-480/06 of 09.06.2009 – *Stadtreinigung Hamburg*, para. 47

by the *German* organisations representing municipalities which for a long time argued towards this direction.[67]

However, within the ongoing debate in *Germany* about a reform of the financial relationship between the *Länder* and the federation, an expert report[68] presented by the *Federalism Reform Commission*[69] suggests the creation of a legislative framework on constitutional level providing for cooperation between the *Länder* especially for areas like IT and e-government where cooperation is greatly needed to improve efficiency and to reduce costs. Of course, the report is aware of the principle of the supremacy of *EU* law, but it is stated that it would send a strong signal (which hardly could be ignored) to the *EU* if the constitution of a member state considers a certain form of cooperation desirable.

This approach deserves approbation: From a procurement law perspective it does not make any difference if a member state passes legislation allowing public entities to cooperate voluntarily (on a contractual basis in order to work more efficiently) or passes legislation in terms of which the entities in question are incorporated. Otherwise the member states' organisational sovereignty would be infringed. Furthermore, states with a highly pluralistic federal system (with innumerable contracting entities on local, state and federal level) would be forced to follow the *Community* procurement rules whenever it decides to reorganise its administration (by way of amending its law governing the administrative structure); on the other hand, more centralist states (with fewer contracting entities) would be much more flexible to do so without having to obey the *EU* procurement requirements. If it remains undisputed that it is (still) up to the member states' choice to "make or buy" public tasks, the decision how to organise the "making" must remain within their discretion too as long as they do not seek to involve private capital. In any case, the contractual horizontal cooperation which is provided for in national legislation concerned with the organisational structure of the member state should be recognised as another exception from *EU* procurement law. With

67. See e.g. statement of the German association of cities and municipalities (Deutsche Städte- und Gemeindebund) of 09.06.2009, available at http://www.dstgb-vis.de (24.09.2009).
68. *Die Vereinbarkeit innerstaatlicher Kooperationsformen mit dem EG-Vergaberecht –Überlegungen zu einer grundgesetzlichen Regelung der Verwaltungszusammenarbeit aus vergaberechtlicher Sicht*, Kommissionsdrucksache 099, Berlin, 19.03.2008
69. Its official name is „*Kommission von Bundestag und Bundesrat zur Modernisierung der Bund-Länder-Finanzbeziehungen*".

its *Stadtreinigung Hamburg* decision the *ECJ* made the first step towards this direction.

6. Further problem: Service concession

For service concessions[70] the same "in-house" principles apply as for other public contracts. Nevertheless, service concessions are even more problematic due to their paramount importance especially for the completion of politically sensitive public tasks. In addition, they are covered neither by Directive 2004/18/EC[71] nor by *German* national legislation. Nonetheless, the selection of the private partner has to comply with the fundamental principles of equal treatment, transparency and mutual recognition derived from the *EC* Treaty.[72] But since the devil is often in the detail, this concept led to the challenge, for practitioners and scholars alike, to find out precisely what is required for the award of concessions in everyday procurement life to comply with this doctrine.

Some proposals have been made; inter alia, the author of this paper has suggested that a "procurement law light" should apply if the contract in question is relevant to the *European* Internal Market.[73] Such a "procurement law light" would contain a set of basic standards derived directly from the rules and principles of *Community* law. For example, the principles of equal treatment and non-discrimination on grounds of nationality imply an obligation of transparency which consists in ensuring, for the benefit of any potential tenderer, a degree of advertising sufficient to enable the services market to be

70. Defined as "(...) a contract of the same type as a public service contract except for the fact that the consideration for the provision of services consists either solely in the right to exploit the service or in this right together with payment." by Article 1 (4) of Directive 2004/18/EC.

71. See article 17.

72. See *ECJ* of 07.01.2000 C-324/98, OJ C I-10745, paras. 60 – 62 – *Teleaustria*; *European Commission*, Communication from the Commission to the European Parliament, the Council, the European Economic and Social Committee and the Committee of the Regions on Public-Private Partnerships and Community Law on Public Procurement and Concessions COM(2005) 569, 15.11.2005 and Interpretative Communication on the application of Community law on Public Procurement and Concessions to Institutionalised Public-Private Partnerships (IPPP), C(2007)6661, 05.02.2008.

73. Burgi, *Die Vergabe von Dienstleistungskonzessionen: Verfahren, Vergabekriterien, Rechtsschutz*, NZBau 2005, 610 et seqq.

opened up to competition and the impartiality of the procedures to be reviewed. A useful guideline for the potential content of a "procurement law light" can be found in the interpretative communication of the *EU* Commission on the *Community* law applicable to contract awards not or not fully subject to the provisions of the Public Procurement Directives.[74]

With the enactment of Regulation 1370/2007,[75] *Strasbourg* has now added a different piece of secondary legislation to the discussion. The regulation has brought some interesting innovations, two in particular: First, it explicitly allows the direct award of certain public service contracts to distinct legal entities over which the public authority exercises control similar to that exercised over its own departments. By defining what "similar control" implies, the regulation significantly broadens the "similar control" criterion as established by the previous *ECJ* "in-house" case-law. The relevant Article 5 (2) reads:[76]

> 2. Unless prohibited by national law, any competent local authority, whether or not it is an individual authority or a group of authorities providing integrated public passenger transport services, may decide to provide public passenger transport services *itself or to award public service contracts directly* to a legally distinct entity over which the competent local authority, or in the case of a group of authorities at least one competent local authority, exercises control similar to that exercised over its own departments. Where a competent local authority takes such a decision, the following shall apply:
>
> (a) for the purposes of determining whether the competent local authority exercises control, factors such as the degree of representation on administrative, management or supervisory bodies, specifications relating thereto in the articles of association, ownership, effective influence and control over strategic decisions and individual management decisions shall be taken into consideration. *In accordance with Community law, 100 % ownership by the competent public authority, in particular in the case of public-private partnerships, is not a mandatory requirement for establishing control within*

74. Interpretative communication of the *EU* commission on the Community law applicable to contract awards not or not fully subject to the provisions of the Public Procurement Directives, OJ EU 2006 C 179/02 of 1.8.2006.
75. Regulation (EC) No 1370/2007 of the European Parliament and of the Council of 23.10.2007 on public passenger transport services by rail and by road repealing Council Regulations (EEC) Nos 1191/69 and 1107/7, OJ L 315, 03.12.2007. For a brief assessment of the regulation see Olykke, *Regulation 1370/2007 on Public Passenger Transport*, P.P.L.R. 2008, NA 84 et seqq; Wittig, Schimanek, *Sondervergaberecht für Verkehrsdienstleistungen- Die neue EU-Verordnung über öffentliche Personenverkehrsdienste auf Schiene und Straße*, NZBau 2008, 222 *et seqq*.
76. Emphasis added by author.

the meaning of this paragraph, provided that there is a dominant public influence and that control can be established on the basis of other criteria;

(b) the condition for applying this paragraph is that the internal operator and any entity over which this operator exerts even a minimal influence perform their public passenger transport activity *within the territory of the competent local authority*, notwithstanding any outgoing lines or other ancillary elements of that activity which enter the territory of neighbouring competent local authorities, and do not take part in competitive tenders concerning the provision of public passenger transport services organised outside the territory of the competent local authority;

(c) notwithstanding point (b), an internal operator may participate in fair competitive tenders as from two years before the end of its directly awarded public service contract under the condition that a final decision has been taken to submit the public passenger transport services covered by the internal operator contract to fair competitive tender and that the internal operator has not concluded any other directly awarded public service contract;

(d) in the absence of a competent local authority, points (a), (b) and (c) shall apply to a national authority for the benefit of a geographical area which is not national, provided that the internal operator does not take part in competitive tenders concerning the provision of public passenger transport services organised outside the area for which the public service contract has been granted;

(e) if subcontracting under Article 4(7) is being considered, the internal operator shall be required to perform the major part of the public passenger transport service itself.

Second, it stipulates in Article 5 (3) which minimum standard has to be followed if a contract in terms of the regulation is awarded to an entity over which no "similar control" is exercised:

3. Any competent authority which has recourse to a third party other than an internal operator, shall award public service contracts on the basis of a *competitive tendering procedure*, except in the cases specified in paragraphs 4, 5 and 6. The procedure adopted for competitive tendering shall be *open* to all operators, shall be *fair* and shall observe the *principles of transparency and non-discrimination*. Following the submission of tenders and any preselection, the procedure may involve negotiations in accordance with these principles in order to determine how best to meet specific or complex requirements.

Moreover, an obligation is introduced for every contracting authority to publish in advance in the Official Journal of the *European Union* the public service contracts that will be tendered or directly awarded.[77]

In *Germany* Regulation 1370/2007 is often regarded as a model for how to react to the problems that have been ascertained for service concessions. However, it remains doubtful whether Regulation 1370/2007 will bring more

77. Article 7 (2).

clarity than confusion for both the "in-house" criteria and the appropriate awarding procedure for concessions.

7. Conclusion and outlook

Tackling the manifold traditional and new public tasks of regional and local authorities, in particular in times of restricted budgets, is difficult, especially for smaller authorities. Furthermore, many tasks (e.g. in the areas of energy supply, waste disposal, environmental questions, IT and public transport) are not limited to the jurisdiction of one public authority. Accordingly, in many member states public authorities at all levels are increasingly interested in (and often dependent on) cooperating with the private sector or with other public bodies in order to benefit from the synergy effects of such cooperation and to ensure public tasks are executed more efficiently and cost-effectively.

Nonetheless, public (private) cooperation is not a miracle solution for this set of problems. Instead, for each different project it is necessary to assess whether partnership really adds value to the specific service or public works in question, compared with other alternatives such as choosing a more traditional option. But the perceived lack of legal certainty and the strictness of *Community* law in relation to the involvement of private (and public) partners discourages public authorities from even considering entering into cooperation and therefore missing the (important) opportunity to explore how to execute public tasks most economically advantageously; be it in form of cooperation with other private or public entities.

In *Germany*, the disadvantageous tendency, especially on the local but also on *Länder* and federal, level can be diagnosed: cooperation often remains undone (although it might be advisable) due to the fear of establishing structures based on contracts which might subsequently turn out to be non-compliant with *EC* law and overturned by the *ECJ*.

However, even the *European* Commission (which is not likely to be suspected for being in opposition to the realisation of the *European* Internal Market) regularly confirms that Community law is neutral as regards whether public authorities choose to provide a public service themselves or to entrust it to a third party.[78]

78. E.g., European Commission, *Communication from the Commission to the European Parliament, the Council, the European Economic and Social Committee and the Committee of the Regions on Public-Private Partnerships and Community Law on Public Procurement and Concessions*, COM (2005) 569, 15.11.2005

In-House Providing in Italy: the circulation of a model

Professor Mario Comba, University of Torino, Italy

1. Introduction

This paper will address the Italian statutory and case law with reference to in-house contracts. For the notion of in-house, we will constantly refer to the paper by prof. Caranta and to the European case law described and analyzed therein. This national report is therefore a study on the way by which the European model of in-house contracts has been implemented in Italian law: it is a question of the circulation of legal models.

Given this methodological approach, it is essential to commence with a description of the Italian legislation on public procurement *prior* to the implementation of European directives on public procurements and still now applicable in default of European law. One must consider if the in-house doctrine – or something similar – was already present in Italian law before the introduction of ECJ doctrine and therefore if the latter was recognized simply as application of internal case law or if it was the introduction of a brand new legal institution.

In the following paragraphs, the questionnaire will be used as a guideline and therefore the paper will address (i) the similar control clause and how it can fit with the Italian company law; (ii) the essential part of activities clause and (iii) the four further miscellaneous issues.

2. Italian statutory and case law prior to the implementation of European directives

2.a. R.D. (Royal Decree) 18 November 1923, n. 2440 and R.D. 23 May 1924, n. 827

Italian legislation on public contracts dates back to the origins of the Italian State, established in 1861. Articles 325 and ff. of Law n. 2248 of 20 March 1865, regarding public works provide the basic rules to be followed in order to award contracts for the construction of public works. Royal Decree (R.D.) n. 2016 of 17 February 1884 coordinated the existing statutes in relation to public contracts, giving a general regulation of the sector which was modified by R.D. n. 2440 of 18 November 1923, and n. 827 of 23 May 1924, both still applicable (even if only in part).

Well before the Treaty of Rome entered into force in 1957, Italy followed the French model of the administrative State, by establishing a statutory law to regulate, in general, all contracts (including public procurement contracts) awarded by the State and by other public bodies.

R.D. 2440/23 was inspired by principles not so different from the present EC rules: art. 3, clause 2 states "*all contracts which imply an expenditure for the State have to be awarded through open or restricted tendering procedure, depending on the discretionary choice of the administration*". Art. 6 admits the possibility of negotiations without prior publicity, but only under "*special and exceptional circumstances*".

R.D. 827/24 is the regulation to execute R.D. 2440/23 in that it details the general rules provided by RD 2440/23. In particular articles 38 and 39 limit the discretion in the choice of the restricted procedure listing the cases in which the State can follow such a procedure and states that, in all other cases, only open tendering procedures can be used. Art. 41 of R.D. 827/24 lists the cases in which it is possible to use the negotiated procedure, but leaves an open door to the contracting authorities by way of clause 6, which states that the negotiated procedure can be used under "*special and exceptional circumstances*".

Case law has specified an occasion on which "*special and exceptional circumstances*" cannot be recognized – and therefore the negotiated procedure is not allowed – being an urgency caused by the contracting authority itself (*inter alios*, Consiglio di Stato, sez. V, 11.6.2001, n. 3123). In another case, art. 41 was considered applicable for the special and exceptional case of serious pollution in a river (Consiglio di Stato, sez. II, advice 13.7.1988, n. 719).

Articles 63 – 88 of R.D. 827/24 describe in detail the procedure for open negotiation; articles 89 – 92 refer to restricted negotiation (which, compared with the EC model, does not include a previous publication but only a direct invitation by the administration to participate in the procedure) and the negotiated procedure (again, admitted without a prior publication).

R.D. 2440/23 and 827/24 are still applicable in Italian public procurements, even if only in part, where compatible with EC legislation, and where EC legislation does not apply. In particular, they can still be considered as existing law for Italian public procurements of a value under the thresholds stated by European Parlament and Council directives or in other cases where EC directives do not apply (e.g. articles 12-18 of directive (EC) 2004/18[1]) but according to ECG case law, in these cases they still have to be compatible with principles stated in the EC Treaty.

It is generally considered that R.D. 2440/23 and 827/24 are only applicable to public bodies and not to bodies governed by public law, which constitutes a relevant difference from EC directives, because they only refer to public administrations as such. On the other hand, they are applicable not only to public procurements, but to all contracts which imply an expenditure for the State and therefore for all purchases of the State, including concessions for services which, on the contrary, are excluded by EC directives[2]

1. Directive (EC) 2004/18, on the coordination of procedures for the award of public works contracts, public supply contracts and public service contracts, [2004] OJ L 134/114.
2. Such seems to be the prevailing opinion of the Consiglio di Stato: see *inter alios*, Consiglio di Stato, sez. V. 7.4.2006, n. 1893. It has to be remembered however, that there is also another interpretation, now less followed but in the past almost leading, according to which R.D. 2440/23 and 827/24 are not applicable to concessions because (i) they only mention "contracts" and not "concessions" and (ii) concessions are awarded by the State on the basis of personal trust, i.e. *intuitu personae* and therefore it is not possible to choose the concessionaire by way of a public procedure. For one of the last decisions concerning this issue see Consiglio di Stato, sez. VI, 6.12.2000, n. 4688.

   The prevailing opinion of the Consiglio di Stato is consistent with EC case law and with the Commission's understanding of the EC Treaty, as described in the *Commission interpretative Communication on concessions in Community law* (C 121/2 of 29 April 2000) and in the *Commission interpretative communication on the application of Community law on Public Procurement and Concessions to institutionalised PPP (IPPP)* (C 91/4 of 12 April 2008). It is already a shared opinion in Community law that the concession of public services, even if not subject to Public procurement directives (art. 17 of Directive 2004/18) should be awarded in compliance with the Treaty principles of non discrimination, equality of treatment, transparency, mutual recognition and proportionality. Concessions of public works are, on the contrary, subject to Public procurements directives (art. 56 and ff. of Directive 2004/18).

In order to complete the picture, it should be mentioned that EC directives on public procurements were introduced in Italy with D.Lgs. (Legislative decree) n. 358/92 for public supply contracts, n. 157/95 for public service contracts and n. 158/95 for special sectors. Having enacted European Parlament and Council directives 2004/17[3] and 2004/18, D.Lgs. 164/06 presently regulates all public procurements in Italy (in addition to previous legislation which is still applicable: R.D. 2440/23 and 837/24) and in fact is known as the "Italian Public Procurements Code".[4]

2.b. Concessions of public services and "aziende municipalizzate": a case of In-House cantracts ante litteram

If R.D. 2440/23 and 827/24 are applicable to public procurements as well as to public services, this means that a contracting authority cannot award the execution of a public service – which of course implies an expenditure or a minor income – without having chosen the service provider through an open or a restricted negotiation (art. 3 RD 2440/23). In other words, prior to the implementation of EC directives, in Italian legislation the rules applicable to the award of public procurements were, in principle, the same as those for awarding public service concessions.

This general rule, however, has a significant exception: in the case of "*enti strumentali*" or "*aziende speciali*", whereby a contracting authority awards the concession of a public service to another subject (more rarely the concession of a public work). The point is all about what is considered to be "another subject": in the case of "*ente strumentale*", it is a different legal person, subject to strict control by the contracting authority; in the case of "*azienda speciale*", it is an economic subject, without autonomous legal status, subject to strict control by the contracting authority. But for the sake of this paper, the difference between these two models – i.e. the presence or lack of legal personality – is almost insignificant. It is easy to understand that this is exactly the same legal question as that for the in-house doctrine of the ECJ: the possibility for a contracting authority to award a concession to a subject which is considered to be the same legal subject as the contracting authority, even if it has a different legal status. In other words, the prevalence of the substantial

3. Directive (EC) 2004/17, coordinating the procurement procedures of entities operating in the water, energy, transport and postal services sectors, [2004] OJ L 134/1
4. For a bibliography in English about Italian public procurements see R. Caranta, *A guide to the Italian Literature on Public Procurement*, Public Procurement Law Rev. 2008, p. 156 ff.

relationship between the contracting authority and the concessionaire instead of the formal datum.

The most meaningful example is that of public services concessions supplied by Italian local governments (Municipalities and Provinces).

R.D. n. 2578 of 15.10.1925, introduced the possibility for Municipalities and Provinces to supply public services directly: it was a kind of "municipalization" of public services so far provided mostly by private companies.[5] Art. 2 of R.D. 2578/25 says that the public service undertaken by the Municipality should be managed by an "*azienda speciale*", different from the ordinary municipal administration, with a separate balance sheet and ruled by its own bylaws.

The *Azienda* is managed by a Director, to be appointed after an open competition and it is administered by an Executive Commission, appointed by the Municipal Council. Neither the Director nor the members of the Executive commission can be employees of the Municipality nor members of the municipal Council (art. 9).

It is significant to note that, according to art. 2, clause 3 of R.D. 2578/25, the *Azienda* "*can enter into any contract necessary for its activity and has standing to sue and to be sued autonomously*" and that, according to art, 2, clause 5, all profit and losses shown on the balance sheet of the *Azienda* are charged to the balance sheet of the Municipality. It was only in 1986, that the regulation for the execution of R.D. 2575/25 was approved, namely with D.P.R. n. 902 of 4.10.1986, which details the model of the *Azienda* and its relationship with the Municipality.

It has been debated for a long time whether an *Azienda* would hold autonomous legal status or if it would be an organ of the Municipality.[6] The debate was concluded when Law n. 142 of 8.6.1990 established under art. 23 that the *Azienda speciale* has an autonomous legal status, but this is more an acknowledgement of an existing situation, already recognized by case law and by the mainstream administrative lawyers, rather than an innovative amendment.

5. The reason for this political choice is to be found in the fact that, between the end of the XIX century and the beginning of the XX century, public services were supplied mainly by private companies at high costs for consumers; Municipalities wanted to provide them at reasonable costs to their citizens. See Cavallo Perin, *Comuni e Province nella gestione dei servizi pubblici*, Napoli, Jovene, 1993, p. 160 – 165
6. See R: Cavallo Perin, *Comuni e Province nella gestione dei servizi pubblici*, Napoli, Jovene, 1993, p. 166 – 178.

What is relevant however, is that notwithstanding the argument about the legal status of the *Azienda, the possibility of the Municipality to award the public service to the Azienda without any public procedure was never called into question.* With or without an autonomous legal status, the *Azienda* has always been considered as an in-house body "ante litteram" of the Municipality, which means that the question of legal status was insignificant in relation to the application of R.D. 2440/23 and 827/24. What was relevant was the financial dependence of the *Azienda* on the Municipality and the strict system of controls of the Municipal Council on the management of the *Azienda.*

The *Azienda speciale*, as created by R.D. 2578/25, no longer exists (or, at least, should not exist). Art. 17, clause 51, of Law n. 127 of 15.5.1997 encouraged Municipalities and Provinces to turn their *Aziende* into joint stock companies, authorizing a much simpler and less fiscally expensive special procedure than the ordinary one. Subsequently art. 35, clause 8 of Law n. 448 of 28.12.2001, obliged Municipalities and Provinces to turn their *Aziende* into joint stock or limited liability companies. The only *Aziende speciali* still legally existing are those of the Chambers of Commerce, pursuant to art. 2 of Law n. 580 of 29.12.1993.

The case of Italian *Aziende speciali* shows that the doctrine of in-house contracts already existed and was well rooted in the Italian legal tradition, even if not known as such with its present English label – but with the definition of "*ente strumentale*" or "*azienda speciale*" or also "*delegazione interorganica*". It is however possible to say that the core legal assumption upon which the ECJ based its in-house doctrine is almost the same as for the Italian Municipal *Aziende*: (i) a contracting authority can charge its own organs with the job of supplying services, (or works) without any specific procedure, since it is performing the activity itself and is not assigning it to third parties, (ii) the autonomous legal status is not relevant in order to qualify a subject as third party because it is only a formal datum. What is important is the famous "similar control"; therefore, (iii) if there is similar control, a contracting authority can appoint a subject to perform an activity even if this subject is – formally – a distinct and separate entity.

The problem of "similar control" was solved, for the *Aziende*, with a public law regulation (R.D. 2578/25 and D.P.R. 902/86) which defined the relation between the *Azienda* and the Municipality, established the financial dependency of the latter on the first, as well as the requirement to appoint an executive Commission composed of members of the Municipal Council and for the Municipal Council to approve the program of activities of the *Azienda.*

It seems therefore that the ECJ did not create the in-house doctrine out of the blue, but that it could rely on well rooted statutory and case law evolved in Italy in relation to the "*enti strumentali*". Furthermore: since "administration by Agencies" is a widespread phenomenon in Western Europe,[7] it is likely that similar problems were faced also in other legal contexts, and here is where comparative law is highly useful.

3. A precedent and the aftermath of Teckal: an Italian story

3.a. A precedent of Teckal: the opinion of the AG La Pergola in the BFI Holding case

Teckal[8] is unanimously considered to be the leading case concerning in-house contracts and in fact it seems to be the first case decided by the ECJ in which "*a second life independent from art. 6 of Directive 92/50/EC had begun for in-house providing*".[9] But the doctrine of in-house contracts was already set out in the opinion of Advocate General La Pergola in the case BFI Holding.[10]

The question concerned two Dutch municipalities which planned to merge the municipal waste collection services and to entrust them to a new legal entity, a public limited company called ARA. BFI Holding, a private undertaking whose business included the collection and treatment of household and industrial waste, brought a proceeding before the Dutch Courts complaining that the awarding of the waste collection service to ARA infringed Council directive 92/50.[11] The question involved several different legal issues, which were referred to by AG La Pergola in his opinion. The position of AG La

7. Gualmini, *L'amministrazione nelle democrazie contemporanee*, Roma, Laterza, 2004,
8. Case C-107/98 *Teckal* [1999] ECR I-8121
9. See Caranta, *The in-house providing: The law as it stands in the EU*, in this book, page 19.
10. Case C-360/96 *Arnhem and Reden v BFI Holding* [1998] ECR I-6821. The decision of the ECJ, of 10.11.1998, did not face the problem of in-house contracts, set out by AG La Pergola in his opinion of 19.2.1998, because it solved the question on a preliminary point. The opinion of AG La Pergola is not often cited – perhaps because it is available only in Italian – and in particular it is not cited in the *Teckal* decision, even if AG Cosmas, in his opinion for the *Teckal* case, cites it in footnote 36.
11. Council directive 92/50/EC, relating to the coordination of procedures for the award of public service contracts, [1992] OJ L 209/1.

Pergola, as set out in paragraphs 33 – 38 of the opinion, is that there is no contract between the two municipalities and ARA because ARA is not a third party in respect of the two municipalities.

In point 38 of his opinion, Advocate General La Pergola states "*there is no third party element, that is to say no essential distinction between ARA and the two municipalities, in the present case. What is involved here is a form of inter-departmental delegation that remains within the administrative ambit of the municipalities. In assigning the activities in question to ARA, the municipalities had absolutely no intention of privatising the functions they themselves had previously performed in this sector. In conclusion, it is my opinion that the relationship between the municipalities and ARA cannot be regarded as a contract within the meaning of the Directive*".

The elements by which AG La Pergola deduced that ARA was not a third party were mainly economical: the two Municipalities paid ARA a sum of money which was simply a refund of expenditures incurred by ARA and previously authorized by the Municipalities, thereby ARA had no risk in the management of its activity and therefore it was not in a third party position in respect of the two Municipalities. In addition, the same survival of ARA depended totally on the will of the two Municipalities: it had no rights towards the two Municipalities, who could decide at any moment to abolish financing ARA and organize the waste collection service by way of another method. The position of the two municipalities in respect of ARA is, using the expression of AG La Pergola, "*ius vitae ac necis*".

It is easy to perceive the analogy between the situation of ARA and the legal status of *Aziende* as described in the previous paragraph[12] and it is not unlikely that AG La Pergola, an Italian professor of public comparative law and former President of the Italian Constitutional Court, had in mind the *Aziende* model when writing his opinion on the BFI Holding case.

The richness of the AG La Pergola motivation, consisting in six paragraphs with detailed reasoning on the financial relation between ARA and the two municipalities, makes the short formula of the Teckal decision appear quite shabby; it states that there are in-house contracts: "(...) *where the local authority exercises over the person concerned a control which is similar to that which it exercises over its own departments and, at the same time, that person carries out the essential part of its activities with the controlling local authority or authorities*". Perhaps the "years of uncertainty that followed

12. One may mention here that Law 142/90 also provides for consortia between municipalities for the supply of public services, with the same characteristics of *Aziende*.

Teckal"[13] could have been shortened had the Teckal precedent and the tradition of *Aziende*, well rooted in the Italian legal system – but I am sure also in other western European systems – been known.

3.a. The aftermath of Teckal: what happened to the case before the Italian national judge?

The Teckal case was brought before the ECJ by the TAR (Tribunale Amministrativo Regionale) of Emilia-Romagna, Italy, for a preliminary ruling under Art. 177 of the EC Treaty (now Art. 234 EC) in the proceedings pending before the Court between Teckal srl and AGAC (Azienda Gas-Acqua Consorziale) of Reggio Emilia. After the ECJ decision, the TAR of Emilia-Romagna delivered its decision (decision n. 444 of 17.10.2000) which says that, since the activity performed by AGAC is not a public service, but a supply of goods, Council Directive 92/50 fully applies and therefore the award of the contract by the Municipality of Viano to AGAC without a public procedure was illegal. Had the relationship between the Municipality of Viano and AGAC been a concession of public service, the direct award would have been legitimate pursuant to art. 22 of Law 142/90. What is not clear, however, is how it can be possible that AGAC is not a third party towards the Municipality of Viano if it provides a service, while it is a third party if it supplies goods.

AGAC and the municipality of Viano appealed to the Consiglio di Stato but the appeal was later withdrawn, as stated in decision n. 334 of 8.2.2005 by the Consiglio di Stato.

At this point the story would appear to have ended happily: the TAR of Emilia-Romagna followed the decision of the ECJ and declared that the contract awarded by the Municipality of Viano to AGAC was against EC Law. In reality, the story was not ended yet.

In 1995, the TAR of Emilia Romagna decided on a case concerning exactly the same legal issue as Teckal: yet again it was Teckal against AGAC, but this time in relation to a contract awarded to Teckal by another member of the consortium: the Municipality of Reggio Emilia. In this case the TAR did not bring the case to the ECJ and admitted the claim of Teckal (decision n. 317 of 18.9.1995), with practically the same motivation used in decision n. 444 of 17.10.2000.

AGAC and the Municipality appealed before the Consiglio di Stato and the case was left pending in Rome. In the meantime the "famous" Teckal case

13. See Caranta, cited in this book, page 19.

was brought before the ECJ and the TAR of Emilia-Romagna issued its decision in October 2000. The Consiglio di Stato never decided on the merits of the "famous" Teckal case.

In 2001 the "less famous" Teckal case, which was sleeping before the Consiglio di Stato, suddenly reawakened. Decision n. 2605 of 9.5.2001 issued by the Consiglio di Stato reversed decision 317/95 of the TAR of Emilia Romagna and stated that the Municipality of Reggio Emilia had lawfully awarded the contract to AGAC. Point 4 of the motivation (which practically covers the entire motivation) explains that AGAC is not a third party in relation to the Municipality of Reggio Emilia because, being a consortium established under Law 142/90, it is like an *Azienda* for each Municipality associated to the consortium.

According to the Consiglio di Stato, the *Azienda* is "*institutionally dependent*"on its Municipality since it is – citing a precedent of the Italian constitutional Court[14] "*an element of the administrative system headed by the Municipality*": it is therefore the same administrative system, the same substantial subject, notwithstanding the formal distinction of the legal status. The awarding of the contract to AGAC is simply internal re-organization of the Municipality of Reggio Emilia and not an outsourcing of a commercial activity; it is a case of "*delegazione interorganica*".[15] The fact that AGAC has an autonomous legal status, distinct from the Municipality of Reggio Emilia, is considered irrelevant, because it is only a formal datum.

Concluding its motivation, the Consiglio di Stato faces the question of EC Law, saying that the principle of fair competition had not been violated because the ECJ decision in the Teckal case stated that the Directives on public procurement are not applicable "*where the local authority exercises over the person concerned a control which is similar to that which it exercises over its own departments and, at the same time, that person carries out the essential part of its activities with the controlling local authority or authorities*".

Thus, according to the Consiglio di Stato, the relationship between AGAC and the Municipality of Reggio Emilia fitted well within the in-house contracts model set by the ECJ in the Teckal case. This seems to be a paradox, because the ECJ decision was about exactly the same factual situation decided by the Consiglio di Stato: the relationship between the consortium AGAC and one of its members (the Municipality of Viano in the ECJ case

14. Corte costituzionale, decision n. 28 of 12.2.1996
15. The expression, which could be translated as "inter-departmental delegation" is the same used by AG La Pergola in the BFI Holding opinion

and the Municipality of Reggio Emilia, in the case decided by the Consiglio di Stato).

It appears that the Consiglio di Stato, in decision 2605/01, interpreted Teckal in the light of AG La Pergola's opinion on the BFI holding case and therefore, bypassed the Teckal formula of "similar control", recognizing that the original model of in-house contracts was that of Municipal *Aziende*.

3.c. A provisional conclusion

The aim of this lengthy and drawn out reconstruction of the precedent and the aftermaths of Teckal is to show the strict and contradictory ties between the Italian public law legal tradition of *Aziende* and the ECJ doctrine of in-house contracts.

As a provisional conclusion, one could say that the Teckal decision and in particular the often repeated holding by which Directives on Pubic procurement do not apply "*where the local authority exercises over the person concerned a control which is similar to that which it exercises over its own departments and, at the same time, that person carries out the essential part of its activities with the controlling local authority or authorities*", has wandered off course from the direction of AG La Pergola's opinion on the BFI Holding case. AG La Pergola didn't mention similar control, nor corporate governance, but the financial relationship between the Municipalities and BFI Holding, which was sufficient to say that the Municipalities had a *ius vitae ac necis*.

The Teckal formula, which can be resumed in the requisite of "similar control", is in fact almost impossible to be realized because it presumes to find in company law a kind of control that is typical of public law. If we accept that the original model for in-house contracts was that of the *Aziende*, we have to admit the control required in order to have an in-house relationship has to be a public law control. However the legal tools by which public law guarantees the control of public authorities over other subjects can be very difficult to reproduce by company law (see par. 4.b) as for example in the case of *Aziende*.

This could be the reason why, according to Prof. Caranta's paper, years of uncertainty followed Teckal and, in particular, why ASEMFO[16] can be considered a turning point. The ASEMFO decision, in fact, stresses the relevance of a public law relationship between Tragsa and its shareholders (the Spanish

16. Case 295/05, *Associacion Nacional de Impresa Forestales (Asemfo) v. Transformacion Agraria SA (Tragsa)*, [2007] ECR I-2999. I refer to Prof. Caranta's paper for comments on the case.

Kingdom and the four Local Communities) and, in particular, the point is not corporate governance, but the economic relationship, as in AG La Pergola's opinion, focusing on the power for shareholders of Tragsa to unilaterally order the supply of services. The trend opened by ASEMFO seems to be confirmed by the recent ASI decision.[17]

4. The impact of the ECJ case Law: the "similar control" and the "essential part of activities" clauses in the Italian case law

4.a. Decision n. 1/2008 of the Adunanza Plenaria of the Consiglio di Stato

With the exception of decision 2605/01 of Consiglio di Stato and a few others, the Italian case law fully upholds the Teckal formula and the subsequent ECJ case law for the definition of in-house contracts. If one looks at the decisions of the Consiglio di Stato from the year 2000 on, 46 mention the word "in-house", 34 contain the word "Teckal" and only one (decision 4711/02) cites the opinion of AG La Pergola in the BFI Holding case, which means that the in-house doctrine is almost always traced back to the Teckal case.[18]

The effort of the Italian administrative judges is to apply correctly the in-house doctrine exactly as fixed by the ECJ, without attempting to introduce original interpretations, nor to explore the possible interaction between this doctrine and the Italian tradition of *Aziende*.[19] The Italian case law on in-house contracts is therefore nothing more than an interpretation of the ECJ decisions.

17. Case 371/05, *Commission v. Republic of Italy*, [2008] OJ C 223/3.
18. The proportion changes if we look at the decisions of the TAR: 325 decisions with the word "in-house", 74 with the word "*Teckal*" and only 10 with reference to the case *BFI Holding*, but mainly to the ECJ decision and not to the AG La Pergola opinion.
19. It is also significant that in 2001 the Municipal *Aziende* were abolished: see supra, par. 2. This is another paradox: the in-house doctrine was strongly influenced by the experience of Italian Municipal *Aziende*, through the opinion of AG La Pergola in *BFI Holding*, but in 2001, when this doctrine began to be applied by the national Courts, the Italian Parliament abolished the *Aziende* and modifies art. 113 of D. Lgs. 267/00 (the Law for local government) authorizing Municipalities and Provinces to award direct public services directly only on the basis of the *Teckal* formula of "similar controll".

The Consiglio di Stato, in its Plenary Meeting (AP),[20] recently issued a decision (Consiglio di Stato, Adunanza Plenaria, decision n. 1of 3.3.2008) which provides a guideline, even if not legally binding, for all administrative judges on how to apply the in-house contracts doctrine.

The description of the Italian case law on in-house contracts will therefore be limited to the above mentioned decision of the Consiglio di Stato AP, since it is at the same time a summary of the most relevant decisions of single Divisions of the Consiglio di Stato and a kind of soft law for future decisions of administrative judges. In other words, the above mentioned decision of the Consiglio di Stato AP is a very influential description of the state of the art of Italian case law in respect of in-house contracts.

After having remembered that the EC Treaty principles apply not only to public procurements regulated by EC directives, but also to any other contract which can be of interest in the competition between companies, including concessions of public services, point 8 of decision AP 1/03 tackles the in-house contracts issue.

The first part of point 8 describes the nature of in-house contracts, remembering that the core legal point consists in the fact that the in-house subject cannot be considered a third party in relation to the contracting authority, but only an internal organ. Therefore it is not the case to follow a public procedure for the awarding of a contract, since there is no contract between two organs of the same entity.

The Consiglio di Stato then states that, in order to have an in-house relationship, two requisites have to be met: (i) similar control and (ii) a strictly instrumental relationship between the activities of the in-house undertaking and the public needs of the contracting authority. The second requisite is not the usual "essential part of activities" but seems to be something new, since it refers to the quality and not to the quantity of the activity performed by the in-house subject. Unfortunately, the decision of the Consiglio di Stato does not elaborate on this element since the motivation only talks about similar control.

20. The Consigio di Stato, when acting as Administrative Judge, is formed by three divisions (Sezione IV, V and VI). Under special circumstances, the three Divisions meet together to issue decisions of particular relevance in what is called "Adunanza Plenaria". The decisions are not legally binding, since the principle of *stare decisis* does not apply in Italy, but undoubtedly they are provided with great prestige, so that it is very rare that an administrative judge, or a single Division of the Consiglio di Stato itself, decides not to follow them.

These two requisites have to be subject to a strict scrutiny by the Courts, since in-house contracts are an exception to the general rules of EC Law.[21]

At this point, the Consiglio di Stato deals with the "similar control" requisite. Its reasoning starts by stating that in order to have similar control it is necessary to have a total public holding of the company, since the presence in the capital of a private undertaking, even if in a minority position, excludes the possibility of similar control.

Total public holding is not enough however: it is necessary for the contracting authority to have strict tools of control over the in-house subject. In particular:

a. The statute of the in-house company must rule out the possibility for a share of the capital – even a minority share – to be sold to private undertakers;
b. The board of directors of the company cannot have relevant operational powers. The contracting authority, shareholder of the in-house company, must have greater powers than those usually reserved by company law to majority shareholders;[22]
c. The company cannot expand its activity so that the contracting authority can loose its control, for example by: (i) widening the original scope of the company; (ii) increasing the capital in a short time offering it to other investors; (iii) expanding the activity to the whole Italian territory and abroad;
d. The most important decisions of the company must be subject to approval by the contracting authority;

21. This is another formula often repeated, which does not seems correct. In-house is not, in fact, an exception to EC directives (and even to EC Treaty) because these rules apply to the award of a contract by a contracting authority to a third party. If there is no third party, there is no contract and, therefore, these rules cannot be applied. One cannot say that if the municipal Council decides to build a bridge and charges the technical department of the Municipality to prepare the project, this is an exception to the EC rules on public procurement because there is no public procedure.
22. At this point the AP decision cites decision 1514/07 of Consiglio di Stato which recognizes the element of "similar control" in Zetema srl (a company owned by the Municipality of Rome), but does not say what are the specific provisions of the statute of the company which guarantees similar control. All the other decisions of the Consiglio di Stato cited in AP 1/08 refer to cases where "similar control" was found not to exist.

e. The contracting authority should be entitled to and de facto exercise the following powers:
   a. control on the approval of the budget and the balance sheet;
   b. control on the quality of the administration of the company;
   c. powers of inspection
   d. complete control on the company's policies and strategies.

The rules set out by the Consiglio di Stato are not very clear; in fact, sometimes they are contradictory and often difficult to coordinate. This is because they are the result of the collection of various decisions made by Italian national courts and by the ECJ, that the Consiglio di Stato AP has taken and strung together, without attempting to build a unitary framework. For example, it is not easy to understand the difference between the rules under points a) and c.ii) as well as under points b) and d).

What is clear is that the powers usually granted by company law to the majority shareholder (or even to the sole shareholder) are not enough: "*greater powers*" are required. What the substance and the extent of those greater powers should be is not clear, nor if they have to be granted within the company bylaws, or if it is necessary to use public law instruments. On the other hand, this is the same ambiguity which can be found in the ECJ case law and which is well described in Prof. Caranta's paper: there is a kind a negative definition of in-house but, at least until ASEMFO, it is not clear what are the positive requirements.

As already mentioned, the Consiglio di Stato does not even mention the requisite of "*essential part of activities*", but it requires that the activity performed by the in-house subject be functional to the public needs which the contracting authority has to satisfy. This is certainly another limit for a public entity that wants to create an in-house subject: the activity performed by the in-house subject cannot be any kind of economic activity, but only an activity functional to the public needs which the contracting authority is institutionally charged to satisfy. It follows that the in-house subject cannot perform any activity but only those functional to the institutional aims of the procuring entity or entities.

The interpretation introduced by the Consiglio di Stato seems to be stricter than that set out in the Teckal formula, which only requires the essential part of activity to be carried out with the controlling public authority or authorities. It is possible that this stricter interpretation is due to specific Italian legislation which forbids in-house companies to carry out any activity unless with the controlling authority or authorities (see point 5. c).

4.b. Italian company law and similar control: can the "similar control" be ensured by the instruments of national company law?

The in-house subject can have different legal statutes, since the irrelevance of its legal statutes is its peculiarity. In this paper we will examine only the case – which is the most common – in which the in-house subject is a company with liability limited by shares, leaving out the other cases, even if there are highly interesting fields of study among them, such as the case of an in-house subject incorporated as a foundation, or a trust.

Under Italian company law, there are mainly two kinds of companies with liability limited by shares: the "Società a responsabilità limitata" (Srl) and the "Società per azioni" (Spa). There is also the "Società in accomandita per azioni", but it is rarely used and almost never by public entities.

The Italian company law reform of 2003 has made a sharp distinction between the two types of company in relation to the point which interests in this paper, i.e. the possibility for the Statute of the company to grant to the contracting authority, as shareholder, a "*greater control*" over the company. In other words, the point here is to verify whether the shareholders can, through the Statute, modify the statutory rules about the distinction of competencies between the General meeting and the Board of Directors in order to decrease the powers of the latter and increase those of the former.

At the moment, the Statute of a Spa cannot increase the powers of the General Meeting, This is clearly stated in art. 2380bis of the Italian civil code, which says: "*the management of the company is exclusively up to the Directors*" and therefore the Statute cannot reserve to the General Meeting greater powers than those specifically listed in the articles of the civil code. This is a rule which has not been challenged by case law and is unanimously confirmed by literature.[23] If the General Meeting exercises a power which is not among those awarded to it by the civil code, such act is considered to be ineffective (*inefficace*) and therefore can be ignored by the Directors without the necessity of challenging it before the judge.

It is possible to conclude that in Italy the in-house subject cannot be a Spa because in this case the contracting authority as a shareholder cannot hold greater powers than those usually reserved by company law to majority shareholders, as required by the Consiglio di Stato AP. Decision 1/08 and, in particular, it cannot hold direct managing powers. However, it has to be noted that recently the Consiglio di Stato (decision 9 march 2009, n. 1365) stated

23. See F. Galgano, *Diritto commerciale – Le società* – Bologna, Zanichelli, 2003, pp. 263 and ff.

that this position is too much "company law oriented": considering the ECJ decision Coditel Brabant SA,[24] the Consiglio di Stato stated that the "similar control" can be exercised jointly by the shareholders, through a majority vote and that even if the General Assembly does not have management powers, but is only a policy settler, this is compatible with the "similar control".

As for the Srl, the situation is different. According to art. 2475, clause 1 of the Civil code, "*Unless the Statute states differently, the management of the company is up to one or more shareholders (...)*". If there are more shareholders charged with the management of the company, the Statute can decide whether they must act jointly or individually. In this case, the rule set by the Code is that majority shareholders can exercise all the powers of management of the company, with the only exception of the decisions reserved to all shareholders as such (art. 2479), and of the control powers of the minority shareholders (art. 2476).

It seems that the structure of Srl is more suitable to meet the requisites of in-house contracts, because it is possible that the contracting authority, as a majority shareholder, be entitled to the direct management of the company. One could say that this is the *normal* situation of the governance of an Srl and therefore the contracting authority, as shareholder, would not have greater powers than those usually entitled to a majority shareholder by commercial law, but the objection seems to be trivial: in fact the point is not that of greater powers, but that of similar control: if the national company law gives to the shareholder of and srl the power to exercise – in a normal way – a control which is similar to the control that the contracting authority exercices into its own department, the similar control requirement is met, even if it is not greater than the control normally awarded by company law.

When the in-house Srl is owned by more than one contracting authority, it could be difficult to meet with the similar control requisites because it is impossible for all of them to be the only managers of the Company. This problem was solved by TRAGSA with the recourse to public law tools such as the unilateral order given by a shareholder to the company on the basis of a specific statutory provision and has been recently faced by the Consiglio di Stato, with the already commented decision 1365/09.

Another possible solution, if one wants to strive to remain in the company law field, is to use the consortium (or the *società consortile*), ruled by art. 2612 and ff. of the Civil Code. Every member of the consortium, in fact, can

24. Case C-324/07 *Coditel Brabant SA v. Commune d'Uccle, Region de Bruxelles-Capitale* (ECJ 13 November 2008).

ask to the consortium to perform specific activities in its interest only (art. 2615, clause 2), which seems to be hardly admissible even in a Srl.

4.c. The assimilation of Asemfo and Coditel Brabant by the Italian statutory and case law

The Italian statutory law has not yet assimilated the ECJ case law created with Asemfo and Coditel Brabant. The Consiglio di Stato, however, has recognized the importance of Coditel Brabant in the decision 9.3.2009, n. 1365, stating that it gives the correct interpretation of Coname and Asemfo which are apparently contradictory. According to the Consiglio di Stato, it is now clear that the contracting authority can award directly contracts to an in-house company in which it is only a minority partner. The possibility to exercise a "similar control" even without the majority of shares, is in fact coherent with the pattern of in-house contracts provided that there are other public law mechanisms of control, as, for example, an Assembly of Mayors having the power to approve, prior to the General meeting, all decisions related to sales and purchases of stakes, modification of service contracts with the municipalities, appointment of corporate officers and industrial plan.

The Restatement of the decisions of Consiglio di Stato in the year 2008 (*Rassegna della giurisprudenza amministrativa e delle sezioni consultive del Consiglio di Stato – anno 2008*) states that, with the decision Commission v. Italy (C-371/05 *Commission v. Italy*, [2008] OJ C 223/3) the ECJ has overruled its precedent in Stadt Halle, admitting that, under certain circumstances, the in-house company can have private partners, if they didn't take part in the negotiations of the in-house contract (point 7.6 of Restatement 2008).

5. Further issues

5.a. Institutinal Public Private partnership

If private participation rules out the in-house character of semi-public companies,[25] it is still possible to find spaces for institutional PPP in Italy. As a general rule, the Consiglio di Stato (advice 18.4.2007, n. 456[26]) stated that a contracting authority can award a contract directly to a semi-public company, if the private shareholder was previously chosen through a public procedure. The position of the Consiglio di Stato is that, if the intention of the public

25. But, given the recent ASI case, this is doubtful.
26. The Consiglio di Stato is not only an Administrative judge, but it can also issue advice, if requested by Public administrations.

procedure was to choose a private undertaking to perform a specific activity for a limited period of time, then this activity can be awarded to a company were the private undertaking is a shareholder. It seems to be a clever solution, not so much different from what is proposed by the Commission's interpretative communication on the application of Community law on Public procurement and Concessions to institutionalized PPP (IPPP), point 2.2.[27] The Consiglio di Stato has recently confirmed its position on semi-public companies, excluding the possibility of a direct award if the activity of the company is not limited to the contract originally awarded (Consiglio di Stato, sez. VI, decision 23.9.2008, n. 4603). However, the TAR of Sicily-Catania has raised the question with the ECJ (TAR Sicilia-Catania, sez. III, 22.4.2008, n. 164).

5.b. Public interest activities

Generally speaking, the ECJ has interpreted very strictly the public interest activity of the public undertaking of art. 86 EC Treaty, while there is not such a limit for the activity of in-house subjects. But this is a question of EC law, for which this paper is not competent. It should be noted that since the Consiglio di Stato, in decision AP 1/03, stated that an in-house subject can perform only activities with a relationship strictly instrumental to the public needs of the contracting authority (see point 4), then this difference can be reduced.

5.c. Further limits to in-house companies

In Italy, D.L. (Decree law) n. 223 of 4.7.2006, art. 13, states that, in order to avoid distortion of competition, companies established by local public entities in order to perform activities instrumental to their institutional mission must operate exclusively with their shareholders' public entities and cannot supply any activity to third parties, public or private.[28] Under this perspective, the Italian statutory law for in-house is stricter than the Teckal doctrine of the ECJ, because it does not allow any activity in favour of third parties, while Teckal establishes that only the essential part of activities has to be done for shareholders of the in-house company.

Art. 13 of D.L. 223/06 has been applied extensively, not only to in-house subjects, but also to companies only partially owned by public entities and

27. 2008/C 91/02
28. Companies providing public services are excluded from the application of this article, probably because at the time a law regulating in general all the public service sector was under discussion in Parliament. Since that law was not approved, the public services remain as an exception still now.

operating without any direct award by the shareholders (Autorità per la Vigilanza sui contratti pubblici di lavori, servizi e forniture, Deliberazione n. 135 of 9.5.2007 and Parere n. 213 of 31.7.08; TAR per il Lazio, decision 5.6.2007, n. 5192). The reason being that a company whose capital is also only partially paid by a public entity, has an advantage over companies totally owned by a private subject. This seems to be an interpretation in contrast with the case law of ECJ on art. 87 EC Treaty, according to which the simple participation of a State in the capital of a company does not imply, *per se*, State aid.

The constitutional Court (decision n. 326 of 30.7.08) uphold art. 13 of D.L. 223/06, which was challenged by some Regions under various elements of unconstitutionality. The opinion of the Court (written by Justice Cassese) says that art. 13 wants to distinguish between administrative activity and economic activity, when both are performed by public entities through instruments of private law (i.e. limited liability or joint stock companies). In the first case, the company performs administrative activity which is instrumental to the public entity; in the second case the company performs economic activity in a regime of competition. Art. 13 forbids to companies of the first kind to do the activity performed by companies of the second kind. Under this perspective, it is not forbidden to companies totally or partially owned by public entities to act in a regime of competition; it is only forbidden to do so to companies which were specifically established for performing administrative activity, instrumental to the public entities. The great, unsolved question, is now to understand what is the difference between administrative activity instrumental to the public entity and economic activity.

5.d. Article 18 of the Directive

According to the in-house doctrine, it is not possible to draw up a contract between a contracting authority and a subject which is not a third party in relation to the contracting authority and thus it is not possible to apply EC Directives on Public Procurement, nor EC Treaty principles. Art. 18 of the Directive, on the other hand, highlights the case of a contract between two different legal entities which is not subject to the Directive under certain circumstances. Art. 18 is an exception to the directive; in-house contracts doctrine is a case of inapplicability of the Directive.

5.e. Italian sectorial legislation about in-house

The Italian code on public procurements (D. Lgs. 163/06), which implements EC directives 2004/17 and 2004/18, does not mention the in-house contracts doctrine. There are, however, some statutes which regulate in-house contracts in specific fields.

The most important example is art. 113 of D. Lgs. 267/00[29] (the already mentioned Code for local government) which is the heir of art. 22 of Law 241/90. Since the Municipal *Aziende* were abolished in 2001, art. 113, clause 5.c, states that a Municipality can award directly a public service contract to a company totally owned by public entities, only if the shareholder(s) entity(ies) exert(s) a control which is similar to that which it exercises over its own departments and, at the same time, the company carries out the essential part of its activities with the controlling local authority or authorities. There is also the possibility (under art. 113, clause 5.b) to award a public service contract to a semi-public company, whose private shareholder was chosen through a public procedure.[30]

The Teckal formula is copied also in Law 3.4.2006, n. 152 (the Italian code for the environment) where art. 150, clause 3 states that the public service of providing water can be awarded, under special circumstances, according to the same procedures of art. 113, clause 5 b) and c) D. Lgs. 267/00.

In the field of the Health service, D. Lgs. 30.12.1992, n. 502 regulates the National health services and says that they must be supplied by the Regions, through ASL (*Aziende sanitarie locali*) which are something similar to the old municipal *Aziende*, since they have legal status, but they completely depend on the Region for their financing.

In the field of the protection and exploitation of works of art, D. Lgs. 22.1.2004, n. 42 (the Italian code for works of art and for landscape) states, in art. 115, that public entities can establish a public consortium for the direct management of works of art (thus excluding the direct management through a company or another legal form different from a pubic consortium).

The lack of a general statutory provision introducing in-house contracts and the presence of some sectorial legislation does not mean that, in Italy, in-house contracts are admitted only where specifically stated by law. To the contrary, the case law on public procurements always implies the applicability of in-house doctrine, even if it never explicitly tackles the problem.[31] The

29. Now modified by art. 23bis of D.L. 25.6.2008, n. 112.
30. This possibility is considered contrary to EC law and thus non applicable by Consiglio di Giustizia Amministrativa della Regione Siciliana, decision n. 589 of 27.10.2006, but now see point 5.a.
31. To be precise, Consiglio di Stato, decision n. 1514 of 3 April 2007, states that in-house doctrine cannot be applied to public works because there is no specific statutory provision in Italy. The decision refers to a public works contract in the field of

Adunanza Plenaria of the Consiglio di Stato was requested, by the Sezione V, to state whether the in-house doctrine was applicable also in absence of a specific statutory provision, but it did not answer because, in the above mentioned decision 1/03, it solved the case logically on previous grounds.

However, the decision in Consiglio di Stato, AP 1/03 according to which in-house contracts consist of awarding an activity to a subject which is not a third party and therefore without a contract, induces to conclude that specific statutory authorization is not necessary.

Bibliography

Recent Italian *books* about in-house providing are: *De Nictolis* Rosanna – *Cameriero* Luigi, *Le società pubbliche in-house e miste*, Milano, Giuffré, 2008; *Guzzo* Gerardo, *Società miste e affidamenti in-house nella più recente evoluzione legislativa e giurisprudenziale*, Milano, Giuffré, 2009. Less recent, but still interesting in particular for the comparative approach is: *Casalini* Dario, *L'organismo di diritto pubblico e l'organizzazione in-house*, Napoli, Jovene, 2003.

Articles and case comments about in-house providing published on Italian Law Journals are a very numerous, impossible (and useless) to be enumerated here. The main Law Journals to be examined are: »Rivista italiana di diritto pubblico comunitario», edited by Giuffré, Milan, with particular reference to EC developments; «Rivista trimestrale degli appalti» edited by Maggioli, Rimini; «Archivio giuridico delle opere pubbliche», edited by Promedi, Roma, mainly referring to procurements of works and useful for the publication of arbitration decisions; «*I contratti dello Stato e degli altri Enti pubblici*», edited by Maggioli, Rimini; «Urbanistica e appalti», edited by IPSOA, Milan.

Since the most important recent decision of Italian Consiglio di Stato is the Adunanza plenaria n. 1/2008, cited in the paper, it may be useful to point out the comment on this decision written by Carmine Volpe, the judge who wrote the opinion for the Consiglio di Stato: Volpe Carmine, *in-house providing, Corte di giustizia, Consiglio di Stato e legislatore. Un caso di convergenze parallele?*, in «Urbanistica e appalti», 2008, p. 1401.

works of art (D. Lgs. 42/04) where a specific statutory provision allows direct award to public consortia only for the management of public goods and therefore only for services.

Case comments about in-house providing may also be found in electronic Law Journals dedicated to administrative law. The most common are: www.lexitalia.it are www.giustamm.it. Specifically on procurements is: www.appaltiecontratti.it, while www.lavoripubblici.it, devoted to public works, has a much more technical profile and publishes a high number of tenders.

Italian cases on in-house providing may be found on: www.giustizia-amministrativa.it, where all decisions of Consiglio di Stato and all Tribunali administrativi regionali (TAR) are published in full text, since the year 2000.

"In-House Providing" in Spanish Public Procurement Law

Professor Julio González García,
Complutense University of Madrid, Spain

1. General Considerations

It is a deeply rooted assumption in Spanish law that Public Administrations can rely on their own means for the execution of public works and of services. As a matter of fact, except for a brief parenthesis during the XIX Century, under the 1868 Public Works Decree, public procurement legislation has set no limits to the direct or indirect execution of services on behalf of Public Administrations. These are denominated "own" or "internal" means and technical services – *medios propios y servicios técnicos* – as exposed in the current Public Sector Contract Law.

In fact, Spanish tradition on this topic has been consistent in allowing the admissibility of these types of offerings. A conglomerate of public enterprises forming HOLSA, – Barcelona Holding Olimpico, S.A.–, executed the construction works for the XV Olympic Games that took place in Barcelona in 1992; something similar had happened during Seville's 1992 Universal Expo. Since the mid-nineties of the XX Century Public Administrations restructuring operations have resulted in the development of water infrastructure networks, irrigation, roads or railways through public companies, or the use of instrumental entities to build airports, ports and other transport infrastructure such as railways.[1] In the Autonomous Communities the development of prisons, schools, hospitals, police stations, and other projects has been undertaken with the avid participation of public companies.

The problem, from the Spanish Law perspective, is twice as complex. On the one hand, there is a general Public Sector Contract Law Decree, allowing

1. About the use of state corporations for the construction of infrastructure, please see my book *Sociedades estatales de obras públicas,* Ed. Tirant lo Blanch, Valencia (2008).

the use of the so-called "own" or "internal" means entities for the execution of works and the supply of services. On the other hand, there are changes in administrative patterns, which will be mentioned later. The question how to harmonize the Spanish legal system according to the case-law of the Court of Justice of the European Communities on *in-house*, has prompted two recent judgments in court cases related to Spanish law, namely TRAGSA[2] and CORREOS.[3] However, one must firstly consider the EU law approach to this issue.

2. Two antagonistic movements within European Union Law

The infrastructure construction process at a European level is complex. There is a growing need for such infrastructures, as stated by Community authorities, and even the citizens claim more and improved infrastructures in all areas, whether for general use or for the provision of services. Yet, we are moving towards a more restrictive economic policy, whereby the tax burden has been reduced – referring to the highest income and capital income, with the wealth redistribution problems this causes –, while maximum public expenditure limits have been set in application of the budgetary stability principle. Thus, in principle, the actual possibilities of building public works are today lower than in the past.

The principle of budgetary stability[4] has its origins in the Stability and Growth Pact that prevents Member States from reaching an excessive government deficit. Calculating the so-called funding needs by using complex accounting parameters can see this.[5] In any case, Member States cannot ex-

2. A commentary on the CJEC TRAGSA ruling is in my article "Medios propios de la administración, colaboración interadministrativa y sometimiento a la normativa comunitaria de contratación", en la Revista de Administración Pública, nº 173 (mayo-agosto 2007), pp. 217-237.
3. My detailed commentary on the CORREOS ruling about *"Prestación del servicio universal y doctrina de las prestaciones in-house"*, en la Revista Española de Derecho Europeo, nº 26 (abril-junio 2008); pp. 193-209.
4. About the principle of budget stability and public works see my book *Financiación de infraestructuras y estabilidad presupuestaria*, Ed. Tirant lo Blanch, Valencia (2007).
5. The additional step required by Eurostat comprises a formal part, – autonomy and separate accounts, – and a substantial part – a market behavior and liability towards risks of economic operations, – which requires verifying that 50% of the costs of production are borne by the 50% of sales; moreover the risks of the operation (the

ceed 3% of the GDP and the public debt should not exceed 60% of GDP (Gross Domestic Product). However, the EU authorities have been aware that a thorough control of this deficit would paralyze the authorities' possible actions and thus public interest would be impaired.

The European Commission, through its statistical office Eurostat, has adopted a number of measures to avoid the cost of construction affecting the public deficit. One is the creation of non-government entities with "market behaviour", i.e., those whose operational costs are similar to those of a private company, while being able to eventually extend their client portfolio. Provided they are liable for the financial risks associated with the construction and its operation or availability (depending on the nature of the work), these separate entities will not be included when calculating the overall public deficit. It is not a simple process, but it has become a real possibility since the decision taken by the Austrian Federal Government Corporation BIG. And this is precisely why the number of such entities has increased. The consequences of this process are easily discernible: the use of legal-financial engineering and accounting design by the public bodies in order to achieve the exclusion from the public budget deficit calculations; The process is not without risks, as it is shown by the case of the Metrosur construction by of the Autonomous Community of Madrid, through the shell company MINTRA.

At the same time, the case law of the Court of Justice has been increasingly restrictive when it comes to allowing recourse to the *in-house.* This will be discussed later. The public authorities are in a paradoxical situation: such an essential public need should not increase the debt, unless by using a differ-

construction risk and, depending on the type of infrastructure, the risks of demand or availability) must be assumed by the private company. This applies also to the manner in which the works are funded by the parent administration. Infrastructure is not paid for directly, but for the funds under the State General Administration, there are transfers of public funds dependent on the mechanism of indirect credit facilities, to the extent that Public transfers are to form the target company's own funds, which, according to the doctrine of Eurostat, eliminates the potential for consolidation. It would not, therefore, be a problem of whether the funding is budgetary or not, but how it is materialized, that is affecting the budget of origin and purpose it has. And this time, there is the displacement of the payment to the contractor for the execution of the work, which is made by the corporation. This also has to be complemented with the corporation, at least formally, taking the risks of the contract with the contractor carrying out the works, the construction is that it pays the costs from its own funds or other collect-and-operating in its dual, as the Administration does not pay more.

ent budget allocation, thus requiring the establishment of separate entities. In this same line, the ECJ has chosen requirements for the characterisation of *in-house* entities, which are untenable from the perspective of budgetary stability. And in the meantime, public needs are not fulfilled, unless through a privatization process, which is clearly not the most suitable means for a number of political, legal, social and economic reasons.

3. EU case law relating to In-House services: a distorted vision of Antitrust Law

The ECJ case law on in-house contracts is mainly based on the *Teckal* ruling and is centred on the following point: we are not looking at a contract within the meaning of the Directive which is absent "in the case where the local authority exercises over the person concerned a control which is similar to that which it exercises over its own departments and, at the same time, that person carries out the essential part of its activities with the controlling local authority or authorities."

In my opinion, with this ruling the Court holds what can be considered a distorted view of competition law, which forces the State towards privatisation. The phenomenon of the instrumental use of *in-house* entities for the provision of infrastructure has always been considered normal, insofar as it merely represent a possible administrative organisational option, allowing the effectiveness and efficiency gains of separating a certain service from the main Administration.

In fact, when the system of relations between the parent Administration and its instrumental organisation is carefully examined, such relations will prove to be very similar to those existing within the administrative system. An element of some inconsistency is to be noted in the requirement excluding the *in-house* character of entities providing a sizeable part of their services for entities other than those controlling them, as seen in the *CORREOS* case. This also means putting limits to the possible choices of the Administration, in that it forces it to have recourse to the market, and consequently diminishing the public powers of control over economic activities. It causes a financial loss for the public administration due to funds being transferred outside the public sector, despite the administration itself having enough means to provide the service. Finally, as was shown in the *TRASGA* case, it makes co-operation between different public authorities more complicated. Which is by itself questionable considering that in many sectors different authorities share competence and anyway the different territorial allocation of competencies may not lead to obliterate the fact that what is at issues are in any case public powers and functions.

Moreover, the public benefit involved is not clear. Becoming competitive is a factor to be considered along with other factors that may be more or less important when analyzing how things should to be done. Moreover, the Court is imposing these obligations on the public sector, while such requirements do not apply to the private sector, this being unreasonably discriminatory towards the public sector, as pointed out in Spain by Sosa and Fuertes.[6] As observed by REBOLLO, one may reasonably reach a conclusion based on "common sense" that "the Administration is not obliged to hire what can be done by its own means, even although such means are personified".[7] In the end it should be up to the public authorities to decide what to keep and what to leave to the competitive market

A totally different matter refers to certain anti-competition practices agreed between the government and its controlled undertaking, which is GOCs, something that can and should be penalised in order to protect the market. But this is a different problem; let's just say that according the EC case law, there is always here an anti-competitive behaviour, which is not true.

4. Authorized companies undertaking Public Works (Sociedades de obras públicas con habilitación legal).

The current system for the construction of public works by State owned companies is based on the provisions of article 158 of Act 13/1996 of 30 December, on fiscal, administrative and social order, which introduces a new procedure specifically called direct management of the construction and / or exploitation of certain public works. This procedure has enabled the creation of one or more companies for the management of road and water infrastructure works. Two years later, a similar provision was added in connection with irrigation infrastructures in article 99 of Act 50/1998 of December 30, on Fiscal, Administrative and Social Order measures, and in 2004 for the railway system. In this way, the State Company for road construction and maintenance set up after the Government's approval of the State Plan of the Land Transport Infrastructure could expand its action in the railway sector.

6. Sosa Wagner, F. y Fuertes, M.; "¿Pueden los contratos quedar en casa? (European issues arising over in-house considerations) in the Law Journal LA LEY

7. Rebollo Puig, M., *"Los entes..."*, *op. cit.*, p. 379.

Under the current model of state-controlled companies, the General State Administration holds 18 of these companies, either alone or, in two cases, in collaboration with regional governments. These 18 companies are currently managing over 50% of public investment in infrastructure in the relevant sectors.

4.1. Company incorporation. In particular the role of statutes in the company incorporation and the contents of the Council of Ministers' authorisation.

One of the features of State owned companies worth remarking is that despite their being incorporated under private law, their model does not respond precisely to the typical corporate prototype because their corporate purpose is linked to the exercise of public administrative functions, such as those linked to public works. This means that there are certain particular features involved in the company incorporation by the government bodies, contrary to the simplicity of normal incorporation, even those involving public capital. So the next step in the development of the public undertakings system consists in determining its process of incorporation and the main elements of its legal regime, in which one must harmonize public law on the one hand and company law on the other.

The process of the creation of public undertakings for the construction and operation of public works will be realized through a procedure with two separate stages: the first one, of a public law nature, in turn comprising two parts: one in which legislation is going to define the entity structure-type, enabling the identification of the next phases of the process – in particular, specifying the type of business to be developed and its main elements, and a second part concerning the specific authorisation to incorporate the company (for most companies, this will fall within the jurisdiction of the Council of Ministers), in order to set up the company under a specific corporate regime by virtue of a statutory authorisation.

Once the part of the procedure subject to the administrative law requirements has been concluded, the next phase begins, which has a private law character and therefore the public nature of the founder will not provide sufficient elements for an adequate differentiation from other similar company incorporation acts. In any case, it is part of the process in which the actual company incorporation will take place. At this point, we reach a different issue, which is to determine, once that it is set up, what kind of relationship the company will have with the parent administration with reference to the infrastructure construction, and how it is defined and what powers are retained by the company founder.

Precisely because of this, the law plays a key role. The system for creating organs and structures within the government is subject to legislative regulation, as set forth in article 103.2 of the Constitution: "the organs of state administration are created, coordinated and governed *in accordance with* the law," – the italics are mine. The constitutional approach has a double purpose: on the one hand, to enforce a series of legal requirements (a definition should be provided by the legislature), that design the model of government organisation to serve the public interest and, on the other, to enable the public Administration, within this legal framework, to organize itself according to needs that have arisen, subject to the provisions previously enacted by the legislature. Thus, within the framework laid down in art. 103.2, the lawmaker plays a key role in the process of company incorporation and in the design of all other forms of public organisation, Obviously, here the legislature is subject to certain limits, according to other constitutional provisions affecting government organisation.

Therefore, in order to provide the administration with authority to alter the system of work performance, the Council of Ministers needs to be legally empowered to be able to create such companies. And this is so to such an extent that, as the doctrine has pointed out, "it is not a mere authorization, yet a compulsory requirement of our legal system." Obviously, doing so without undergoing the initial parliament screening would imply an alteration of the public contracts law system and, in particular, a waiver of the administrative powers that are contained in the Contract Act. In the absence of parliamentary authorisation, the new company will be acting under the private law only, albeit in co-operation with the parent public authority, even if it will exercise mostly public powers in relation to its contractual activities. Under these circumstances, however, the new company activities will not be relevant when assessing the overall public budget deficit under EU/EC rules. This explains why a specific scheme has to be established for the exercise of the public powers recognised to the parent administration. Under Art. 158.2 Act 16/1996, a requisite content to be included in the agreement between the government body and the dependant public undertaking is precisely to determine "the powers of the State General Administration regarding the management, control, supervision and acceptance of the work, powers it formally holds in any case."

Once the government has been authorized to incorporate the companies, these go, as it was already said, through a dual process: one under public law and another under private law, something that is logical given that the creator of the company is a government entity and has to meet the requirements concerning its own decision making processes in order to guarantee that the entity is properly established. It is a guarantee for the general interest, and serves also as a mechanism that controls the administrative activity. This dual-stage is due, on the one hand, to the fact that permission for the establishment of the company is required, to be granted by the responsible authority of the founding entity, this usually being the Council of Ministers. Secondly, to the extent that the process intends to set up in a corporation, the authorisation must be consistent with the relevant procedure appropriate for the entity being created. Therefore, the procedure will have to comply with the general requirements established by the Corporations Act and, by extension, the Law on Limited Liability Companies, with the added complication that in most cases the company incorporated will have a sole shareholder or a sole participation unit holder according the case.

On the basis of the role for the development of corporate activities, the agreement authorising the establishment of the state company will be structured according to the following points: i) identification of the corporate purpose upon implementation of the statutory authorisation; ii) specifying whether or not the public undertaking may acquire participation in other entities; iii) adaptation and development of the legal clauses that determine the rules for the transfer of shares, either by free sale, by restricting the sale to certain buyers, or by completely prohibiting the operation; iv) definition of the company's economic-financial policy; v) definition of the geographical areas in which it is to operate, either in all or in part of the national territory, the company not having to power to alter its pre-defined sphere of influence. This issue is one over which the legal rules are less definite and therefore the Council of Ministers enjoys a very wide discretion by virtue of its authority to organize. An example of the great flexibility in this regard is the distribution of functions among the four state companies for agricultural infrastructures; vi) a essential aspect for the development of the company business is that under article 166.2 LPAP the supervision of the companies is conferred to the ministry more closely connected with the company's activities vii) the period for which the company is created, which must be connected to the audit of the conditions for its establishment, to the extent that this mechanism of indirect control should determine whether it should have a limited life-limited to a specific need- or, rather, extended indefinitely in time.

Furthermore, in the particular case under Art. 62.1 f) LOFAGE, – company incorporation by public bodies, – the creation of a corporation is justified by the fact that it is "essential to the achievement of the objectives assigned," which involves giving the reasons why a more traditionally structured administrative body is not suitable.

One of the most notable issues in connection with the evolution of public undertaking public works is the widening of their possible corporate purpose, which has gone from being limited to the performance of public works to an early involvement from the initial stages in the work project all the way to the last stage of participating in the operation and exploitation of the public works. This change, as we shall see in due course, is a result of the maximisation of the benefits from the company's creation sought by the government, which has changed from being a mere way of circumventing the regulations established for government contracts to become the dissociation of the cost of infrastructure construction from the public budget. This means that the State and the other procuring entities have had to adapt the corporate purposes and operating requirements of the public undertakings being created, by bringing them in line with Eurostat's guidelines. This translates in the need to implement the requirements of the ESA 95, which, as we will see, exclude from the public sector only those companies being market-oriented. But, of course, this need has to be translated into the clauses of the instruments of incorporation, which define the purposes of the new company, allowing the development of its activities in a manner appropriate to the achievement of the same purposes.

4.2. Rules applicable to contracts passed by public undertakings

As a rule, public undertakings are only charged with the management of public works procurement procedures. It is highly unusual that they themselves carry out the works. In fact, they normally lack the technical capacity for executing the works themselves, to undertake the work directly. We will now examine the procurement procedures they should follow

The question of what procedural format for the award of contracts should followed by companies whose capital is held by procuring entities has ceased to be of great theoretical interest. This is due to the progress made in implementing Community Law, which must be uniformly applied across the Community, which encourages transparency and equal treatment. Exactly how administrative practice has developed is a different matter, also taking into account the number of companies of this type created in recent years. Since the formation of these entities for the purposes of bypassing public procurement procedures has ceased to be of great interest (having been replaced by the interest in avoiding the constraints of budget stability) we have seen an improvement in compliance with public procurement rules.

Indeed, the precedents set by the Court of Justice regarding the implementation of the directives give a wide and functional, interpretation of the three criteria used for deciding which bodies are procuring entities under Community law, namely (a) established for the specific purpose of meeting needs in the general interest, not having an industrial or commercial character; (b) having legal personality; and (c) financed, for the most part, by the State, regional or local authorities, or other bodies governed by public law; or subject to management supervision by those bodies; or having an administrative, managerial or supervisory board, more than half of whose members are appointed by the State, regional or local authorities, or by other bodies governed by public law. The case law reasonably enough considers that entities in principle ruled by private are to be considered procuring entities anyway when the requirements of the directive are fulfilled.

4.3. Financial rules applicable to public undertakings responsible for public works

The *public undertakings responsible for public works* are primarily funded from public contributions or through the payment of services they provide to other entities, public or private which, as we have seen, they are permitted to do upon incorporation. Public financing will come from the funds to which they have access, as well as from contributions by the entities on which they rely,. The latter will usually take the form of additions in the capital of the company, although this is not the only manner. Finally, these public undertakings will be able to have recourse to the financial market for credit along the normal rules, debt having increased in the past years with the diversification of its possible sources.

Financing as a result of undertaking activities for third parties – whether those third parties be other public entities or future users of the infrastructure – means that most of the construction costs are determined in a conventional manner rather than applying the mandatory mechanisms required under the law; this was the case with the legislation, governing water works which was originally established in the Water Works Act of 1911. In any case, and notwithstanding understandable criticism, in general, the percentage of works subsidised by individuals should be 50%. This mechanism ensures that these public undertakings acquire a market-like status meeting the requirements of the current legal environment

One of the basic elements in order to examine the functioning of the system of state companies undertaking public works is its financial aspect, which is structured on its operating budget and capital budget. Under Art. LGP 64.1. both types of budgets must be approved; they "must indicate the annual budgets and resources to cover costs" Notwithstanding its approximate nature, to which I will revert in the next chapter, its fundamental importance stems from fact that it has to guide the actions of the company, as it is provided for by art. 67.1 LGP "public undertakings and public entities manage their business operations to achieve the objectives arising from the approach reflected in their operating budgets."

The operating budget and capital budget have similar contents. In accordance with the provisions of Art. 64.2 LGP, "they shall consist of expected income and financing table for the financial year. As an annex to that budget an estimate of the entity's balance sheet will be attached", along with any further documentation to be decided by the Ministry of Economy and Finance. Companies implementing public policy must also submit a description of the policies that will be pursued during the financial exercise showing the objectives to be achieved. Moreover, they must submit an annex listing to their investment projects classified by province, indicating whether it is a new investment or if it had already started in previous budget years.

Public funding to cover work to be performed is based on four types of budgetary items: operational subsidies, capital subsidies, capital and asset investment, and loans. Of these, the most important are the first and the third, the last one being almost irrelevant within the total sum contributed by the State General Administration. In public undertakings responsible for public works, the most important source for funding is the capital investment.

When analyzing the relationship between the parent administration's annual budget and those of public undertakings, two realities must be accounted for: first, the budget of the latter must be merged into the budget of the Authority and, on the other hand, this implies the combination of two different types of budgets corresponding to two different types of entities; this will account for some amount of distortion in the merging process and even the approval of the public undertaking's budgets.

The merging of the two budgets takes place by incorporating the company's budget in the State Budget, as provided for in Art. 33.1.b. LGP, which requires the inclusion, insofar as being part of their content, of "the budgets of current operations and capital and financial operations of public sector business entities and public sector foundational entities." It is an approach that is clearly logical in view of the relationship between the parent Administration and the corporation, also considering that public undertakings are part of the public sector, as required by Art. 2.c) of the General Budget Law, and therefore, the results of the company should be somehow projected on their parent administrations.

4.4. Financing public undertakings

The performance of the works, the development of pluri-annual programs of action and implementation of operating budget and capital depends on there being sufficient funding to address corporate projects. These funds may come from various sources, such as equity – mostly transfers from the parent administration – other types of transfers from the parent administration, funds from the European Union or those acquired through capital transactions in financial markets.

In principle, these funding mechanisms are the result of the company structure, which acts as a limit. It is true that the developments in recent years have meant an expansion of the activity, with a corresponding increase of funding opportunities and, simultaneously, of the risks undertaken by the public undertakings. In any event, even today, by the very nature of its business, the company's capacity of generating income may be limited – beyond any income generated through works carried out in the interest of third parties or, where appropriate, due to certain payments made by the users of the service, either directly or by the Administration in its own name – and in any case, depending on the decision of the parent Administration regarding the infrastructure built in its name. Hence the need of resorting to forms of indirect financing of public funds, and at the same time, forms of external financing, which are often linked and operating at different times.

The modalities of budgetary financing that can be applied to the public undertakings would be classified among those that are considered indirect financing to the extent that despite the budgetary nature of the money at issue the disbursement is not directly processed by the parent Administration but through the public undertaking. Among these mechanisms there are three ways in which the Administration can make the payments: capital transfers – to be recorded as public expenditure at the time that the obligation to pay arises corporate capital contributions, and, thirdly, through participatory credits. We can also find cases of deferred financing, that is payments made by the parent Administration as for instance shadow toll payments, – depending on the use of infrastructure – or availability payments – payments based on the availability of the infrastructure with a certain quality standard – and payments for infrastructure management services – which will be used for the improvement of previously built infrastructures through reform or by adding complementary services. In any case, as we shall see in the next chapter, if one intends to dissociate the infrastructure cost from the parent Administration, there are restrictions both on the budget from which the transfers originate – because they cannot affect the government funding needs, and on the amount, as it must have a market behaviour, under conditions set by Eurostat.

In any case, this public funding, both indirect and delayed, will be based on those transfers of public funds through the mechanisms foreseen in the General Budget Act and will compensate the fulfilment of the commitments undertaken with the parent Administration through the relevant agreements, as we noted in the previous chapter. Among them, an important role is played by the monetary contribution to the capital of public companies, which has no effect on the public deficit, as will be seen in the following chapter, to the extent that, under certain conditions, it does not affect the government's funding requirements, which is causing continuous capital increases to cover the cost of infrastructure, as shown by virtually all infrastructure management agreements and, especially by the "Direct Management Agreement on the management and/or operation of hydraulic works in the Jucar Basin", signed in October 2006 between the Ministry of Environment and the Water State corporation of the Júcar.

4.5. Financial means derived from users and from relations with public administrations different from the parent one. The specific case of water companies.

Besides the means by which the money is acquired, which is defined in the Convention, the main problem that arises with reference to water companies is "the disappearance (referred to the undertakings performed) of the tax system of waterworks funding now regulated in art. 114 of the revised Water Law (with reference to fees and taxes on water use). The forced disappearance of the tax regime is more than anecdotal, and has a profound meaning when one considers that in the future the weight of investment in this field will fall on those companies, which could convert the legal tax system regulated in the Water Law, to a mere appearance without substance, or, and in any case in a system of residual application to the works built before the creation and operation of the State undertakings."

However, the problem is not merely the determination of the amounts, but how the public undertakings are to recover the construction costs considering that, under normal conditions, they are supposed to shoulder part of the same costs. Logically, all these issues are dealt with in the Direct Management Agreement entered into between the parent administration and the parent undertaking.

As for the economic and financial system of the works performed by public works state companies with the users, there is the possibility that the company may wholly or partly perform and/or operate the waterworks by agreeing tariffs with the relevant users. The scheme differs from the general system of financing the works that is provided for in art. 114 of the water law, and a regime is thus agreed that will have to comply with the following two rules: i) Up to 50% of the investment will be funded from the company's own funds. ii) The remaining amount, by setting prices charged to the users and/or by selling products or services resulting from the exploitation of the work. “These sums, though defined as taxes in the agreements, are in fact private prices”.

Resorting to the state-run public works companies may have an impact on the financial arrangements to be applied to the construction of those works subsidised by users. As noted earlier, in water issues, for example, we find that both the State company and water users share costs for the completion of works, so the administration pays a flat rate of 50% of the cost of construction. The individual, all being the result of an agreement signed between the two, will pay the remainder. From here two issues arise: how can this be harmonized with the principle of cost recovery foreseen in the EU directives and which is the real effect on the regime imposed by the law.

The principle of cost recovery, which has a strong commutative nature, has been included in Community law, specifically in the Directive 2000/60/EC of the European Parliament and the Council of 23 October 2000, which establishes an EC performance framework in the field of water policy, and has been reflected in art. 111 of the Water Act. The principle of cost recovery is based on two key points: a) the cost principle, which requires each user to compensate the cost of their usage; b) the principle of utility, requiring all who benefit from the a public work or service to contribute to its financing to the extent of such benefit or advantage, which leads to the need to distinguish between users and beneficiaries of the hydraulic project, as they are in a similar but not in the same situation. The problem is how to harmonize a conventional system that involves a payment by the government of half of the work, as we have seen previously in connection with the waterworks, with the principle of cost recovery.

It is true that the latter is not an absolute principle, – even the directive states that it is a principle that national authorities will “take into account” – and the directive itself establishes tempering mechanisms in view of other legally relevant factors, such as “social, environmental and economic effects of the recovery and the geographic and climatic conditions in the region or regions involved” (art. 9). This leads to a problem concerning the exemption foreseen in art. 42.1 f) TRLA. The problem arises because State companies are automatically applying the rule of 50% in all agreements reached with the users of water, something that certainly does not seem to fit in with the system. There are no “legal reasons that should encourage such a uniform generalization of the public subsidy in any circumstance (regardless of the type of works, geographical location, user capacity or specific conditions of the territory), which in the future will inevitably result in compatibility issues with the EU Framework Directive concerning the principle of cost recovery.”

4.6. Control methods and direction from the main Administration

One of the most important elements of the structural organization of a State corporation, as was already noted in some parts of this study, is the appointment of a "Supervising Ministry." The choice is made by the measure authorising the establishment of the company, which is foreseen in art. 176.1 LPAP "upon authorising the creation of a corporation of the type foreseen in article 166.2 of the Act, the Council of Ministers may appoint a ministry, whose powers are relevant to the specific object of the company, as a supervisory authority".

The most prominent issue in the daily management of the company and especially for the accomplishment of the objectives of general interest that motivated its creation is the definition of the management powers held by that Ministry with regard to the company's operations. This is certainly a point in which the relations arising from a meta-legal perspective are as important as those expressly set out in the legislation. Moreover, the presence of senior officials from the supervising Ministries in the Management of all public works companies has removed much drama from the issue of the limits placed on the ministerial power to get involved into the management of the public undertakings. These officials allow a more fluid transmission of the ministerial concerns to the companies involved. What happens is that at the same time the very independent existence of State corporations is questioned and we are really faced with an institutional unit, as defined by Eurostat, in line with what has been seen in the previous chapter.

The third component of the power of supervision is the responsibility of the parent Administration, through the ministry, for the performance by the State corporations of public works. Although being a company under private law, its public component cannot be forgotten and the Minister is required to give reason of the performances before the Parliament. This recording and reporting of the corporation's business activities is to be performed by the Ministry, as required by art. 177.1 LPAP: the supervising Ministry will be responsible for reporting to the Spanish Parliament "in the sense that the political control of the companies' results, through various mechanisms that are listed in the Parliament regulations, will be the responsibility of the Ministry exercising guardianship".

5. General regime of the "In-House technical services" in the Administration

In parallel with this special system, the Law on Public Sector contracts, as did all the previous regulation, sets forth the rules of the so-called *in-house* technical services of the public administration (in Spanish "Medios propios y servicios técnicos"). In principle, the aim of any the classification of an entity as "Medios propios y servicios técnicos", is to remove any possibility to consider that entity as legally distinct from the administration having set it up, with the consequence that the activities it performs are directly imputed to the administration.

Under Art. 24.6 of the Law on Public Sector contracts, the *in-house* nature of the service has to be spelt out in the articles of association. According to this provision, "The internal or technical nature of the service of entities that meet the criteria listed in this paragraph should be recognized explicitly by the regulations whereby it was created or by its articles of association, defining the institutions for which this condition applies, the tasks that may be performed for them, or the conditions under which they may be awarded contracts, at the same time laying down a prohibition for these entities to participate in public procurement procedures called by the authorities from which they depend; in any case, when there are no bidders, they can undertake the rendering of the service in question". After the TRAGSA ruling, on June 6, 2008 the Council of Ministers proposed the amendment to the legal regime of all companies providing services to the Administration, so as to make sure they comply with the requirements for *in-house* providing, being paid a fee for the tasks performed; this will include the power of the administration to give the necessary instructions for the performance of the work. This is a formalistic response, in keeping with the EC case law, which also displays excessive formalism.

As noted by DE LA QUADRA in connection with former art. 152 of the Law on Public Service Contracts, now 26.1 of the Law on Public Sector contracts, quite independently from the existence or not of a separate legal entity, the recourse to *in-house* providing is allowed when four different types of conditions are present. Two of them refer to the specific capacities of the *in-house* entity (hypothesis a) and b) detailed later); four more refer to operating considerations (c), d) f) and I); however c) can also be considered to concern the expediency of the *in-house* provision; finally, an exceptional ground concerns the performance of building services on the basis of background design only (h). More into the details, these grounds are: a) the Administration's factories, arsenals, armories or technical or industrial support facilities should be suitable to carry out the provision, in which case the implementation system should usually be used, b) the Administration should have recourse to its employees when this would lead to an economy of more than 5 percent of the amount of the contract or a more rapid execution, in both cases being evident the benefits of the *in-house* option. c) A previous tender. d) In the case of an emergency event, as stipulated in Article 97. e) If the nature of the work renders impossible the pre-determination of a certain price or a budget based on units of work. f) It is necessary to exempt the contractor from doing certain work units due to failure to agree on contradictory price quotations. g) Works of mere preservation and maintenance, as defined in Article 106.5. h) Exceptionally, the performance of building services on the basis of background design only provided Art. 134.3.a) does not apply. i) Cases foreseen in paragraph d) of Art. 206.

Every case is conditioned on its availability to address it through its own means, except for exceptional cases of cooperation with private individuals as legally stipulated. We therefore need to consider when corporations satisfy this requirement, because otherwise the procurement should be subject to the general public sector contracting rules and awarded in accordance with the procedures statutorily outlined, thus being open to the participation of private contractors who could theoretically be awarded the contract.

An essential factor in this respect is that the procuring entity must exercise over the *in-house* structure a control similar to that it exercises over its own services. Following *Tragsa* this is the case if the procuring entity may pass orders that the *in-house* entity is bound to fulfil in accordance with instructions given to it, including as to the remuneration which is determined by reference to rates approved by the parent public entity. This is precisely why it is understood that the nature of the legal relationship in such cases is not contractual but mandatory; consequently, the obligations of the party need not to be written down in a formal contractual document. Simple instructions from the parent Administration in the form of an administrative act would be sufficient. As noted by REBOLLO it can and should be done through an administrative act and, even when appearing in the form of agreement, this does not change the true nature. Indeed, the *in-house* bodies – simple instruments belonging to the Parent Administration – should carry out the assignments with no refusal being possible; their judgement is not relevant and consent is not necessary.[8]

8. REBOLLO PUIG, «Los entes institucionales de la Junta de Andalucía y su utilización como medio propio», in Number 161 of this LAW JOURNAL (May-August 2003), page. 377.

However, it is standard procedure to sign an agreement, as shown in art. 4.1.n), a case exempted from the application of the Law on Public Sector contracts: "Those legal acts whereby an *in-house* entity is charged, according to Article 24.6, with the performance of a particular task. However, contracts to be passed by the *in-house* entities for the performance of the services committed to them, shall be subject to this law, in terms that are derived according to the nature of the entity who is party to the contract and the type and amount thereof, and in any case, in the case of contracts for works, supplies or services which exceed the threshold amounts set forth in Section 2. Chapter II of the preliminary section, the Private law entities must follow in its preparation and allocation rules set out in articles 121.1 and 174."

The third requirement is that the *in-house* entity should be one entirely owned by public administration. This point is apparent from the LCSP, leading to the conclusion that "where companies are concerned, in addition, their entire capital must be publicly owned" – either by a public entity or by several public administrations jointly creating such an entity based of efficiency motives.[9] Its capital should be entirely public and this is the only thing that ensures that the only element that characterises the company is to achieve an objective of general interest. Private partners always aim to achieve other interests, which are private, and in addition, "participation, albeit small, of a private company in the capital of a company which is also involved in the procuring entity in question excludes in any case the chance of it exercising authority over the said company similar to that the control exercised over their own services."[10]

Obviously, in the event of a joint venture of two or more government administrations, an agreement between them must be passed. In the words of Malaret, "because it is a State corporation, the performance of assignments from other public administrations requires a formal agreement between the two governments involved, the parent Administration and the other administration performing the task (art. 15 LRJPAC). This requirement is substan-

9. This possibility, which mitigates the problem that will be after the corporations that are considered "means" another government, it is expressly permitted in STJCE of May 11, 2006, and Consorzio Carbotermo Alisei. Here what is required is that "where several local authorities control a company, the requirement relating to the essence of this activity can be considered fulfilled if the company makes most of its activity, not necessarily *one or the other These local authorities, but such local* taken together." STJCE of May 11, 2006, and Consorzio Carbotermo Alisei, Ace 340/04.

10. Among others, see rulings from ECJ January 5th, 2005, *Stadt Halle*, As. C-26/03 and November 10th 2005, *Commission v. Austria*, As. C-29/04.

tive, not a mere formality, since its existence or not entails important practical implications."[11]

6. Final Notes

The above-mentioned elements are critical of the European Union case law but serve as an explanation of a reality not altogether presenting a promising scenario. The promotion of public undertakings must be understood as a privatisation of infrastructure development, something that is happening in all countries and offers different perspectives. In all economic areas there are two distinct situations: first, those cases of privatization to enable a greater participation by private individuals; other cases have meant wider a privatisation of the legal system. And there is one last change, particularly noticeable in our country, which is the wider acceptance of the cost compensation model which due to Community pressure to reduce budget imbalances, pushes in the direction of cost recovery from users. This process, beyond any ideological criticism that would not be suitable at this time, has fewer positive than negative aspects.

In my view, there is no advantage either for the effectiveness or efficiency of the service, and it certainly causes problems in administrative transparency and democratic control. The control of activities is inferior to that of public entities and accounting control is also problematic. The main issue, however, is how this public activity is taking place now. The principle of budgetary stability, the reduction of the tax burden, added to what is in my opinion the excessive reliance on competition law, all these are leading to inevitable difficulties in the exercise of public function. It must not be forgotten, in this sense that the Administration is objectively serving the public interest.

11. Malaret García, E. *Sociedades...*, *op. cit.* p. 124.

“In-House” Providing in Polish Public Procurement Law

Professor Marcin Spyra,
Jagellonian University of Cracow, Poland

1. Introduction

Polish legislation has not avoided an ambiguity concerning the possibility of not applying public procurement rules by awarding contracts to a separate entity which functionally operates as an “in-house” structure of a contracting authority. The purpose of this paper it to analyse the development of the “in-house” providing concept in Poland in the context of European law.

The borderline between having recourse to internal sources and externalisation of public operations has not been set precisely in Polish Law. The Public Procurement Act of 1994 (hereafter: PPA) did not contain any specific provision relating to the subsidiaries of contracting authorities. It required instead the application of awarding procedures to some cases of the internal arrangements between the authority and its departments. The Public Procurement Law of 2004 (thereafter: PPL), which replaced the Act of 1994, limits its scope of application to the contractual relations of procuring entities. It does not contain any provision on the special status of entities controlled by procuring authorities, either. There are some other statutes, which have been referred to during the academic debates and several litigations on the notion of “in-house” providing. Article 2 of the Municipal Management Act of 1996 (hereafter: MMA) provides, that a local government unit may carry out its statutory tasks engaging its departments or companies incorporated by this unit. According to Article 3 of MMA a local government unit may entrust its statutory tasks to natural persons or other entities on a contractual basis, in compliance with the provisions on public finances or respectively on public procurement or public utility entities.[1]

2. Traditional restrictive approach

Until 2005 the question of avoiding the procurement rules in the case of awarding a contract to an entity controlled by contracting authority had not been subject to lively debate in Polish literature and practice. Surprisingly so far the debate has been limited to the activity of local government units. It was commonly accepted, that public authorities had to apply procurement rules in all cases of externalisation of their operations which included relations with their subsidiaries. Contracting authorities were bound to apply procurement rules also in certain cases which evidently belonged to the category of "in-house" providing. The criterion applied by PPA was not a contract for pecuniary interest but the expense of public financial means.[2] Therefore arrangements between a public authority and its financially independent departments did not automatically fall outside the scope of PPA, although these departments did not enjoy the status of a separate entity. Article 6 sec. 1 (3a) of PPA exempted from public procurement regulation only agreements between awarding authorities and its departments which were reached in the course of ordinary operations of the authority. All other cases fell within the scope of PPA. There were no doubts, that contractual relations with companies and other separate entities owned by a public authority required a prior public tendering procedure, or other procedures regulated by PPA.[3] It was stressed that even if having recourse to a public authority's own departments

1. Local government unit may subsidise the entity, to which it has entrusted the performance of public tasks, using public law instruments regulated in the Public Finances Act or provide financing to this entity on a contractual basis, which requires applying public procurement procedures. There are also special tendering procedures in the field of public health protection, protection of national and ethnic minorities, and public utility organisations. N. Kowal, *Tworzenie i rejestracja organizacji pożytku publicznego.* (Warszawa 2005) 76.
2. The expense of public financial means was understood as a budget category, therefore it covered also a transfer of an amount from the account of a public authority to the account of its financially independent department.
3. J Pieróg, W. Łysakowski, *Ustawa o zamówieniach publicznych. Komentarz* (Warszawa 1999) 78

had not fallen within the scope of PPA it could violate antitrust law.[4] The legality of an award of a public contract to the entity controlled by a public authority was analysed mainly from the perspective of the subsidiarity principle, which had been raised to the status of a constitutional value by the preamble of the Constitution of 1997. It was assumed that not only an award of a contract, but also the existence of a company incorporated by a public authority are justified only if the company performed assigned tasks better and cheaper than other entities.[5] This shows, that there is no space for administrative discretion to decide, whether to have recourse to internal sources, to incorporate a subsidiary or to outsource needed works, goods or services from private entities. The choice depends on economical efficiency. To compare the efficiency of different possible arrangements it is necessary to apply tendering procedures, which verify the value of the market alternative to the own operations of the public authority. It was accepted that a subsidiary of a public authority which had failed to submit the most advantageous tender in several procedures should be wound up.[6] The requirement of applying the procurement regulation in the case of an award made to a subsidiary of a contracting authority was backed by the principle of business entities equality.

Most of these views and opinions remain relevant after PPL came into force in 2004. The most significant change is the adoption of a contract criterion instead of an expense criterion, thus purely administrative arrangements between public authorities and their financially independent departments have definitively fallen outside the scope of Polish procurement law. The prevailing attitude towards the status of separate entities controlled by public authorities has not been changed.[7]

4. C. Balasiński w: C. Balasiński, M. Kulesza, *Ustawa o gospodarce komunalnej. Komentarz.* (Warszawa 2002)
5. A Szewc, Artykuł 9, A. Szewc, G. Czyż, Z. Pławecki, *Ustawa o samorządzie gminnym- Komentarz.* (Warszawa 2005) 79.
6. M. Ciepiela, *Formy komunalnej działalności gospodarczej.* PUG 2001/6, 22.
7. G. Wicik, P, Wiśniewski, *Prawo zamówień publicznych.* (Warszawa 2007) 16-17, K. Żuk, *Powierzanie zadań publicznych w ramach gospodarki komunalnej.* A, Miszczuk, M. Miszu, K. Zuk, *Gospodarka samorządu terytorialnego.* (Warszawa 2007) 147

3. There and back again; judicial decisions of 2005

3.1. The Municipality of Luboń case.

"T." sp. z o.o. is a limited company incorporated in 1991 by the Municipality of Luboń, which holds 100% of its share capital. "T" has been created to perform statutory municipal tasks related to public transport (Article 7 [4] of the Municipal Local Government Act). The Municipality of Luboń provided the company with assets of its transport department acquired by "T" as a contribution in kind. The Municipality exercises control over "T" not only as the only shareholder but also on the basis of certain powers vested in the local government by law. According to Article 8 sec. 1 of the Prices Act of 2001 a municipal council may introduce official prices for public transport services on the territory of the municipality. A municipal council may also lay down the categories of persons entitled to free-of-charge and special price services. A company active in the field of public transport is obliged to render free-of-charge and partly paid services, if a municipality finances the deficit resulting from these services. This refinancing is provided on a contractual basis. The Municipality of Luboń entered into such a contract with "T". The duty not to exceed official prices and the right of refinancing the costs of price reductions and exemptions pertain to both public and private entities.[8]

The contract between Municipality of Luboń and "T" concerning the performance of public transport services was signed in 1991.[9] In 2002 the parties were to amend the contract. The Municipality intended to assume a contractual duty to refinance business activities of "T".[10] The Mayor of Luboń applied to the President of the Public Procurement Office (thereafter: PPO) for the approval of the amendment without a call for tender. The basis for the petition was inter alia the Article 71 sec. 1(1) of the PPA of 1994, which allows a direct award, if for technical reasons of an objective character the supplies, services or works may be provided by only one economic operator . Neither the applicant nor the PPO President considered the question of in-house providing. The President of PPO questioned the technical necessity of awarding the contract to "T" and refused the approval.

8. Finance Ministry Statement ST1-4834-417/2007/807 of 29 May 2007 at [6]
9. The contract between Luboń and "T" was executed before PPA came into force, and therefore at that stage the legality of direct award was not disputed.
10. Previously the costs of public transport services were refinanced on a public law basis, what according to the Regional Audit Chamber (Regionalna Izba Obrachunkowa) infringed public finances regulation.

Against this decision of the Municipality of Luboń brought proceedings before the Regional Administrative Court (Wojewódzki Sąd Administracyjny) in Warsaw. One of the grounds for the claim for the reversal of the disputed decision was the incompleteness of the decision relating to the consideration of the scope of public procurement regulation. The claimant expressed the view that the Public Procurement Act does not apply to the relations between a local government unit and a company controlled by this unit. In the claimant's opinion municipal management regulation differentiated between companies owned by a local government unit and other entities. It was pointed out that contrary to Article 3 of MMA, which pertains to the local government tasks carried out by private entities, Article 2, which allows the performance of public tasks by a company owned by local government unit, does not require the application of public procurement procedure. According to the claimant a company owned by local government unit is in fact not a business organization and therefore it is obvious that it can perform public tasks better and cheaper than a private entity, which has primarily business objectives.

The Regional Administrative Court rejected the claim stating that the only exemptions from public procurement regulation result from Article 6 of PPA.[11] The Court took the view that MMA does not regulate public procurement procedure and any reference in this field has no normative value.

The Municipality of Luboń brought an appeal against that judgment before the Supreme Administrative Court (Naczelny Sąd Administracyjny), which set aside the disputed judgment and remitted the case to a lower instance.[12] The starting point of the Supreme Administrative Court's deliberations was the observation that normally the contract was an instrument applied only in the relations between the local government unit and private entities. The Court found, that in the case of a company controlled by a municipality, the relation normally was structured by corporate governance instruments. The Company's duty to carry out public tasks may result not from contractual obligation but from the articles of incorporation determining a company's objectives and from decisions taken by a municipality as a shareholder. In the Court's opinion this situation is not covered by the scope of PPL, which regulates only contractual relations. According to this doctrine the public procurement regulation may apply to the relations between a local government unit and its subsidiary, if a contract between these parties per-

11. Decision of 13 Oct. 2004, Case II SA 1921/03, Lex no. 159886.
12. Decision of 11 Aug. 2005, Case II GSK 105/05, Lex no. 180740 = ONSAiWSA 2006/2/62

tains to a task, which has not been given to the company in the articles of incorporation.

In the second judgment the Regional Administrative Court in Warsaw bound by the opinion of the Supreme Administrative Court set aside the disputed decision of the PPO President.[13] The Court took the position, that due to the 100% holding in "T" the Municipality and the company, though represented by different natural persons, could be treated as one entity. The Court held, that the Municipality, as a shareholder, had an effective power to order the company's directors to render certain services, which made any contractual relation unnecessary. This reasoning was also backed by the reference to the ECJ decision in the case *Stadt Halle*. It was assumed a contrario that the exclusive holding in the share capital indicates decisively that a municipality exercises over a company control similar to that which it exercises over its own departments. Therefore the Court reached the conclusion that public procurement regulation did not apply to the relations between a local government unit and companies where this unit was a single shareholder.

3.2. The Municipality of Buczkowice case

In the same year the Regional Administrative Court in Warsaw heard the case of the Municipality of Buczkowice. The facts resembled the *Arnhem* case decided by ECJ.[14] In 1996 municipalities Buczkowice and Wilkowice incorporated a limited company "E" sp. z o.o. to carry out their own statutory tasks relating to waste management and maintaining refuse dumps. Each of the municipalities held 50% of the company's share capital. To finance the share capital of "E" the Municipality of Buczkowice transferred, as a contribution in kind, equipment and installations necessary for the operation of the company. "E" provided services relating to waste disposal to the inhabitants of municipalities Buczkowice and Wilkowice. Its activity covered also ecological education and administration of the refuse dump common for both municipalities. "E" operated only on the territory of its shareholders.

In order to promote the recycling of wasted materials and to stimulate dump segregation Buczkowice and W. Municipal Councils decided to finance the costs of the segregation and disposal of recyclable materials. These services were free of charge for the inhabitants. All the fees charged by "E" were paid directly by the municipalities. According to the Article 6 sec. 2 of the Cleanness and Tidiness Act the Municipal Councils of Buczkowice and

13. Decision of 14 Dec. 2005, Case III SA/Wa 2815/05, Lex no. 200785.
14. Case C- 360/96 *Arnhem*, [1998] ECR I-06821

Wilkowice decided on the level of tariffs applied by "E" in case of waste disposal services.[15] The tariffs reflected a socially acceptable level of prices, thus the company's revenues were significantly smaller than the costs. To cover this difference Buczkowice and Wilkowice entered into a contract with "E" assuming a permanent duty to provide the company with financial means necessary to guarantee its solvability and to maintain its business operations.

In the 2005 the Municipality of Buczkowice applied to the President of PPO for the approval of a procedure without a prior call for tender. The Municipality of Buczkowice intended to award to "E" a three-year contract relating to waste management services and the administration of a municipal refuse dump. According to the Municipality, "E" was for technical reasons of objective character the only economic operator which could provide the requested services (Article 67 sec. 1.1[a] PPL). The President of PPO refused the approval finding no grounds for the conclusion that there were objective circumstances of a technical nature excluding the possibility of a call for tender. He pointed out that the municipal refuse dump had been only administered by "E" while it was owned commonly by the municipalities. As an co-owner Buczkowice had all technical possibilities to award the contract also to other entities. The PPO President expressed the view, that the PPL did not differentiate between companies owned by private and public entities.

The Municipality of Buczkowice challenged this decision before the Regional Administrative Court in Warsaw. The question of the "in-house" providing was not raised by Buczkowice, nevertheless the cognition of an administrative court is not limited to the statements of an applicant. The Regional Administrative Court set aside the disputed decision due to the incompleteness of the inquiry, as the President of PPO failed to consider whether the application of the Municipality actually related to the case covered by the scope of PPL.[16] The Court repeated reasoning developed by the Supreme Administrative Court in the case Luboń and stated that this doctrine applies also to the companies whose share capital is held by several local government units without any private participation. It held that to decide on the case, it was necessary to clarify the objectives of "E" determined by its articles of incorporation and the content of its contractual relations with the Municipality. The Court made no reference to the fact that neither of the municipalities owned the holding which guaranteed independent control over the company.

15. According to this provision of Cleanness and Tidiness Act the municipal council fixes official maximal prices for the waste disposal services rendered to owners of real estates on the territory of the municipality.
16. Judgment as of 10.11.2005, Case III SA/Wa 2445/05, Lex no. 191902.

There was also no reference to the possible conflict of interests between the municipalities.

3.3. Comments on Luboń and Buczkowice

The decisions in cases of Luboń and of Buczkowice have been decisive for the development of an "in-house" providing practice in Poland. PPO has released an interpretative opinion on the relations between local government units and companies controlled by these units.[17] The opinion follows the approach of the Supreme Administrative Court without any further explanations.

The first comments on the decisions in the cases of Luboń and of Buczkowice were rather critical. It was pointed out that in view of the ECJ decision in the *Parking Brixen* case, the judgment of the Supreme Administrative Court had not been conforming to European law.[18] It was, however, a minority opinion. The majority rejected the critics and assumed there was no significant parallel between those cases due to the private participation in Stadtwerke Brixen AG, while "T" sp. z o.o. remained wholly owned a by public authority.[19]

The idea that the relations between a local government authority and a limited company structured by the act of an incorporation, bylaws, contributions, shareholder resolutions and other corporate acts are not subject to public procurement regulation was widely accepted.[20] There are nevertheless at least two points of the Supreme Administrative Court's reasoning that remain unclear. It was emphasised that the public services or a services concession contract between a local government unit and the company controlled by this unit is unnecessary. The Court however did not refer expressively to the situation, when a controlling authority concludes a public services contract or a service concession with the controlled company. Both the Supreme Administrative Court and the Regional Administrative Court in Warsaw mentioned that the public procurement regulation is applicable in the case of a contract

17. Interpretative Release on Awarding Public Tasks to the Subsidiaries of the Local Government Units (in Polish) available on www.uzp.gov.pl.
18. A. Stawicki, *Trybunał kwestionuje bezpośrednie zlecenie*, Rzeczpospolita of 7 Nov. 2005, C3
19. Z. Czarnik, *Glosa do wyroku NSA z dnia 11 sierpnia 2005 r.*, II GSK 105/05. ST 2006/5 76, A. Kisielewicz, *Nasze orzecznictwo nie jest sprzeczne z europejskim*, Rzeczpospolita of 12 Dec. 2005, C3.
20. Z. Czarnik, 73, R. Szostak, *Glosa do wyroku NSA z dnia 11 sierpnia 2005 r.*, II GSK 105/05. ST 2006/1-2, 141, M. Szydło: *Umowne powierzanie zadań z zakresu gospodarki komunalnej przez jednostki samorządu terytorialnego.* FK 2007/7, 17.

executed between a public authority and a company controlled by this authority, if it does not pertain to the objectives of the company set out in the articles of incorporation. Nothing was said about the contracts that were covered by the scope of these objectives. This is quite an important lack in the courts' opinions as in both analysed cases claimants' statements prove that the relations between the municipalities and their companies were not limited to the corporate investor relations. The Municipality of Luboń concluded a contract with "T" to regulate the performance of public transport activities and to refinance the deficit suffered by the company due to compulsory application of reduced price tickets and transport services rendered free of charge for certain categories of clients. The Municipality of Buczkowice paid for the services of segregated waste disposal and partly reimbursed the costs of other activities of "E". It appears that the courts did not ignore those facts but assumed that they were irrelevant from the point of view of duties arising from a public procurement regulation and EC Treaty provisions.

Some authors have tried to explain this assessment claiming that the contract to refinance partly the costs of special-price-tickets and free-of-charge services cannot be deemed to be neither a public service contract nor a part of a service concession. It has been suggested that in the case of such a contract the payment is executed not in consideration for services rendered by a company but that it is rather a kind of a donation.[21] Other authors characterised a company controlled by a municipality as a contracting authority which can be directly awarded a public service contract on the basis of an exclusive right which it enjoys pursuant to an administrative provision.[22] Companies which perform tasks of the local government and in which the majority of the share capital is held by local government units belong to the category of contracting authorities due to Article 3 sec. 1 (3) PPL. The resolution of a municipal council that gives certain public tasks to a company owned by the municipality was treated by those authors as an administrative provision constituting an exclusive right.

It is difficult to accept that the contract to refinance partly the costs of public transport services is a kind of a donation. A public transport company performs the statutory duty of a municipality. The financial means provided to the company on contractual bases are closely related to this performance. The payment depends on the performance of transport services. The amount depends on the quantity and quality of the services rendered for a reduced price

21. R. Szostak, 142.
22. Z. Czarnik, 78.

or free of charge. These circumstances confirm the conclusion that a contract between a municipality and a pubic transport company is a commitment to refinance the specified cots of the transport activity in exchange for the transport services rendered to the public.

The idea that a resolution of a municipal council to incorporate a limited company and to entrust it with the performance of statutory duties of the municipality may constitute a legitimate administrative provision referred to in the Article 18 of the Directive 2004/18/EC should also be rejected. A company wholly owned by the local government units fulfils the requirement concerning the status of a contracting authority. An administrative provision awarding an exclusive right to provide waste management or public transport services to the entity directly chosen by municipal council limits the freedom to provide services. It is also contrary to the principles of transparency and non-discrimination. It is difficult to point out any adequate and proportional reason which could justify such a restriction in the field of public transport and waste disposal. Creating of a local services monopoly by municipal council resolution is also inconsistent with national legislation on the freedom of the enterprise, which does not grant such a power to the municipality.

Both of the referred opinions seem to have gone beyond the reasoning of the Courts in the analysed cases. Neither the Supreme Administrative Court nor the Regional Administrative Court in Warsaw analysed the cases in view of the exclusive right exception. It is also doubtful that they considered the financing agreement as a kind of a donation. The Courts seem rather to have acknowledged that if the company's duty to perform municipal tasks results from a non- contractual source, it is not important what specific instruments the parties use to manage their relations. They can be of a corporate, contractual or administrative nature. These instruments establish additional conditions and play a only technical and supplementary role in the relation which, as a whole, has not been established by a public service contract. The reference to the *Stadt Halle* justifies the supposition that at least the Regional Administrative Court in Warsaw considered the contracts concluded by the municipalities as cases of "in-house" providing. This is, of course, only an attempt to interpret partly inarticulate motives of both decisions.

In light of the *Teckal* doctrine, as it has been developed by subsequent ECJ judgments, the commented decisions seem erroneous. The Courts assumed that the position of a shareholder guaranteed the powers that enabled public authorities to control and to manage the companies effectively. They did not consider the level of an independence provided to company directors by Polish law. Nothing indicates that the bylaws of the companies provided the municipalities with special voting, control or decision powers other than the standard statutory shareholder rights. In the Municipality of Buczkowice case it was not considered that the holding of 50% of shares did not allow the municipality to influence the activity of the company independently. In fact neither of the municipalities could enjoy over "E" the level of control which would be comparable to the control they enjoyed over their departments. No decision of the shareholders' meeting could be made without the consent of the other shareholder. Regarding the fact that the municipalities did not have any other instruments of influence upon the company than shareholder rights it is clear that the first *Teckal* condition was not fulfilled in this case.[23]

The fact that municipalities fix tariffs for waste disposal and public transport is also not decisive for characterising the relation between a public authority and a company as an "in-house" relation. In *Correos* ECJ stated that "the mere fact that that company has no choice ... as to the tariff for its services cannot automatically entail that no contract was concluded between the two entities."[24] The official prices set by a municipal council bind all entities rendering relevant services in the territory of the municipality. According to the Article 9 of Prices Act (2001) the official prices are the maximal prices, unless a proper public authority decides otherwise. In both analysed cases it was possible to apply lower prices. It was up to the management of the company to decide on the business strategy including prices and other conditions of contracts executed by the company. The companies negotiated contracts with the municipalities. There was no legal duty to either accept the conditions offered by the municipalities or to enter into the refinancing contract. The companies had also a right to terminate contracts with municipalities for a valid reason. Therefore it is impossible to acknowledge that in actual fact in the referred cases, municipalities could structure the relation with their subsidiaries by a unilateral administrative measure creating obligations solely for the subsidiaries and departing significantly from the normal conditions of a commercial offer made by them.[25]

23. ECJ acknowledged that majority holding is not always necessary to meet the first *Teckal* requirement. Asemfo case- par. [60]-[61]. There is an important difference between the position of municipality B in "E" sp. z o.o. and the position of the Autonomous Communities in Tragsa. Spanish law requires Tragsa to carry out the orders given it by the Autonomous Communities notwithstanding their minority holding in the share capital of the company. Polish municipalities do not have any special statutory powers to give orders and instructions to directors of companies, whose shares are owned by these municipalities.
24. At [53].
25. Case 220/06, *Correos* at [54] and [85].

3.4. The Municipality of Kraśnik case

The decision of the Supreme Administrative Court in the Luboń case has not put an end to the controversies relating to the duty of a public tender in the case of awarding public contracts and concessions to subsidiaries of local government units. In the same year the Circuit Court in Lublin and the Appellate Court in Lublin delivered decisions in the case of the Municipality of Kraśnik, which may be considered opposite to the decision of the Supreme Administrative Court in the Luboń case. In 2004 the Municipality of Kraśnik awarded directly to Kraśnickie Przedsiębiorstwo Mieszkaniowe sp. z o.o. (hereafter: KPM) a contract to manage municipal housing resources. KPM is a single member limited company wholly owned by the Municipality of Kraśnik. The President of PPO brought before the Regional Court in Lublin proceedings against the Municipality of Kraśnik and KPM to declare that the direct award of the contract concluded between the defendants had been an infringement of public procurement law and that the contract was void. The plaintiff expressed the opinion that a company, which was a separate entity from the municipality, could be awarded a public service contract only in a procedure provided by PPL. The defendants contested the claim stating that a wholly owned subsidiary of a municipality could not be regarded as a separate entity from the point of view of public procurement regulation, as its only task was to perform statutory tasks of the municipality entrusted to it on a contractual basis. They also declared that the disputed contract had been exempted from the public tender requirement due to the Article 189 of Real Estate Management Act of 1997, which stated that central or local government might entrust managing and administration of housing and real estate resources to entities created by the state or local government units, provided the resources were administered by employees, which were licensed real estate managers. The Regional Court in Lublin rejected this reasoning and declared the contract illegal and void.[26]

The defendants filed an appeal against this decision to the Appellate Court in Lublin. They repeated most of the arguments of the plea. They also quoted the decision of the Supreme Administrative Court in the case Luboń to confirm the opinion that contractual relations between a municipality and its subsidiary incorporated to perform statutory tasks of the municipality were exempted from the requirement of a public tendering procedure. The Appelate Court did not share this view and rejected the appeal, having entirely ap-

26. Decision of 21 Jul. 2005, I C 421/05- unpublished.

proved the motives of the Circuit Court decision.[27] It distinguished the case from the Luboń case stating that the decision of the Supreme Administrative Court related only to situations, when statutory municipal tasks were given to the subsidiary by virtue of an act of and incorporation or a shareholders resolution.[28] Nevertheless it was emphasised, that in case of contractual relations the public procurement regulation is applicable no matter what the company's objectives are. The Court stressed that an incorporation of a company owned by a municipality, and a direct award of a public contract to this company would be a breech of the subsidiarity principle, if there are private entities capable of performing the tasks given to the municipality's subsidiary. The only way to verify the subsidiarity criterion is to follow procedures regulated by public procurement law. According to the court a direct award of the contract to the company owned by the municipality would be also contrary to the equality principle and could be detrimental for the competition on a local market. With regard to the Article 189 of the Real Estate Management Act of 1997 the Appellate Court observed that this provision pertains only the possibility of an award of a management services contract to an entity created by the state or local government unit but not to the awarding procedure, which is regulated in PPL.

4. Draft Public Procurement Law Amendment of 2008

In April 2008 the Polish Government submitted to the Parliament a draft amendment of PPL. Its main goal was to simplify the contract awarding procedures and adjust some inconsistencies of PPL with European law. The draft included also provision on "in-house" providing. The prospective Article 4 sec. 1 (11) of PPL was to clarify that "The Act does not apply to contracts awarded by a local government unit or a union of local government units to the company referred to in the provisions on municipal management, if the following conditions are jointly fulfilled:

a) the activity of the corporation pertains to the performance of the own tasks of the local government unit, local government units or a the association of local government units and it is carried out only on the territory where

27. Decision of 14 Nov. 2005, I A Ca 791/05- unpublished.
28. The Court admitted, that the Supreme Administrative Court's opinion in the Luboń case had not been transmitted either to it or to PPO, and that it had relied only on the summary of the case presented by PPO.

the local government unit performs public tasks given to it by the agreement regulated in the provisions on a municipal, county or regional government,

b) a local government unit or units or a union of local government units control the company in the way similar to that which they exercise over their departments without legal personality, which particularly means an influence on the strategic and individual decisions pertaining to the administration of the company's affairs,
c) all the shares of the company are owned by a local government unit, local government units or a association of local government units."

From the perspective of Polish law this provision could be important, as it was aimed to solve finally the dispute on the permissibility to award directly public tasks to local government units subsidiaries not only on corporate but also contractual basis. The provision was the fruit of an effort to comply with European law, nevertheless the usage of the quotations from the motives of several ECJ decisions was not the optimal legislative technique. The independent expertise ordered by the Parliamentary Bureau of Analyses warned that the governmental proposition might not reach its goals, and that it was likely to cause uncertainty, and controversies similar to those relating to the *Teckal* line of judgements. It also pointed out that there was no reason for limiting the scope of an "in-house" providing exception to the contracts awarded by local government units.[29] The Parliamentary Commission of Economy unanimously recommended the Parliament to adopt the governmental draft amendment of PPL without the provision on in-house providing. It was mainly the worry of an extensive interpretation of the provision and of its negative impact on the competition, which motivated the recommendation. Thus the attempt to regulate the problem of in-house providing by statutory instrument was put to an end.

5. Direct application of the *Teckal* doctrine

The members of the Parliamentary Commission of Economy took the view that without specific statutory provision the direct award of public contracts and concessions to companies controlled by local government units is impos-

29. A. Sołtysińska, Opinia prawna do rządowego projektu ustawy o zmianie ustawy – Prawo zamówień publicznych oraz niektórych innych ustaw (druk sejmowy nr 471). Analysis no. 1388I, 6-8.

sible. The Appellate Court in Lublin took a similar position. The principles of subsidiaryty and equality of business entities adopted in national law may justify this conclusion. Although the European law acknowledges the possibility of the direct award of the contract to the "in-house" entities, it does not preclude stricter requirements of national law.

The prevailing opinion represented in the most recent academic commentaries is quite different. The majority of authors accept the possibility of direct application of the *Teckal* doctrine in Polish public procurement law.[30] Even these authors differ over the consequences of its application in the Polish legal environment. It is disputed, whether the satisfaction of requirements defined by ECJ is possible in Polish law. The disagreement concerns mainly the first *Teckal* criterion.

6. The control criterion

6.1. Corporate law as an instrument of control

Is it possible to achieve the level of the level of control required by ECJ by the means of corporate law? There has been no ECJ decision, in which the Court has found that the influence of the procuring authority exercised by means of corporate governance satisfies the first *Teckal* requirement. Nevertheless it has not excluded such a possibility. The Court took the position that the fact that a contracting authority holds, alone or together with other public authorities, all of the share capital in a successful tenderer tends to indicate that that contracting authority exercises over that company a control similar to that which it exercises over its own departments.[31] The exclusively public ownership of the corporation is, in the Court's view, not a decisive factor to determine the fulfilment of the first *Teckal* criterion. The independent position of a company's management and the fact, that the contracting authority enjoys the rights and powers of every ordinary shareholder attenuate the status of the contracting authority to the effect that the company cannot be characterised as an "in-house" entity.[32] This, however, should not prompt the conclusion that the instruments of corporate governance can in no case guarantee a level of control similar to that exercised over departments of a contracting authority. The internal structure of corporations, duties, powers and liabilities of corporate bodies have not been harmonised in Community

30. M. Stachowiak, Article 2 at [33], M. Szydło (Warszawa 2008) Article 3 at [10].
31. Case C 340/04, *Carbotermo* at [37], Case C 295/05 *Asemfo* at [57].
32. Case C 458/03 *Parking Brixen* at [69], Case C 340/04, *Carbotermo* at [38].

law.[33] It is therefore impossible to asses the question of corporate governance as an instrument of control of an "in-house" entity without the reference to the particular national legislation. It cannot be excluded that a corporate law of a member state enables the controlling shareholder to influence a company in the way that in actual fact his decisions are a unilateral administrative measure creating obligations solely for the company and departing significantly from the normal conditions of a commercial offer made by this company. It appears that the decisive factor for the satisfaction of the first *Teckal* requirement is the level of control, exercised by contracting authority, and not the kind of instruments, which serve this purpose.

Two questions should be asked in order to analyse the national corporate law in the context of "in-house" providing: 1) Do the standard rights of a majority shareholder allow to exercise over the company the control similar to that which a public authority exercises over its departments? 2) Is it possible to constitute in the company's act of incorporation special rights and privileges which can guarantee this level of control?

1) With respect to Polish corporate law the answer to the first question appears obvious. Neither standard shareholder rights in a joint stock company (*spółka akcyjna*) nor in a private limited company (*spółka z ograniczoną odpowiedzialnością*) guarantee the level of control over the company, which could be compared to the control, which a public authority exercises over its departments. The managing board of a joint stock company is generally independent from shareholders. It is not appointed by shareholders' resolution but by a decision of supervisory board (Article 368 § 4 of Commercial Companies Code thereafter: CCC).[34] It enjoys all competences in the field of the company's management except for the powers and competences expressly reserved for the supervisory board or the shareholders' meeting. The management of the company is not bound by any orders and directions given by the shareholders meeting or the supervisory board (Article 375^1 CCC). The powers of the shareholders meetings are restricted to strategic decisions. The shareholders meeting may dismiss the managing board members at any time for any reason (Article 368 § 4 and Article 370 § 1 CCC). Shareholders have limited access to information on the company. Apart from generally accessible sources of information on company's affairs they can only claim informa-

33. The harmonisation in the field of shareholders' rights in the publicly listed companies or regulation of specific entities of European law (e.g. Societas Europea) is still rather an exception than a rule.
34. All CCC quotations come from the translation of K. Michałowska, *Polish Commercial Companies Code*. (Warszawa 2004).

tion relevant to the agenda of the shareholders' meeting (Article 428 CCC). Limited influence on companies' everyday operations and restricted information rights preclude the possibility, that even a single shareholder in the Polish joint stock company could achieve in the company the level of control, which could satisfy the first of *Teckal* criteria. Shareholders of a private limited company enjoy a stronger position. They may at any time inspect the books and documents of the company, draw up a balance sheet or request explanations from the managing board (Article 212 § 1 CCC). They appoint and dismiss managing board members. Nevertheless, their power to influence the decisions of the management is limited to the authorisation of several strategic decisions enumerated in the Code (e.g. Articles 228-230 CCC). The competence to give positive orders and instructions is excluded.[35] In view of the *Carbotermo* and *Asemfo* decisions such a narrow influence on company's affairs precludes the characterisation of standard shareholder rights in a private limited company as an instrument of control similar to that exercised over a contracting authoritys' own departments.

2) It appears also impossible to alter the standard model of shareholders' rights in a Polish joint stock company in order to fulfil the first *Tecal* requirement. Article 375^1, which determines nonbinding character of shareholders directions and instructions given to the management of company is a mandatory provision.[36] There is also general consent to the opinion, that a joint stock company's bylaws cannot grant individual control rights to a shareholder.[37] It is possible only to broaden the list of cases, when the decision of the managing board requires shareholders' authorisation.[38] The opinion has been expressed, that to fulfil the first *Teckal* condition it is enough to introduce the requirement of authorisation regarding all of the management's

35. A. Rachwał, „*Spółka z ograniczoną odpowiedzialnością*", *Prawo spółek handlowych*. S. Włodyka ed. vol. 2nd A (Warszawa 2007) 971-972, I. Weiss, „*Spółka z ograniczoną odpowiedzialnością*", W. Pyzioł, I. Weiss, A. Szumański, Prawo spółek. (Bydgoszcz 2005) 254.
36. A. Kidyba, „Zarząd w spółce akcyjnej", *Prawo spółek handlowych*. S. Włodyka ed. vol. 2nd B (Warszawa 2007) 317-318.
37. M. Bielecki, *Uprawnienia informacyjno-kontrolne akcjonariuszy w spółce akcyjnej*. Pr.Sp. 2004/1 10, M. Michaldo, *Prawo do informacji akcjonariusza w spółce akcyjnej*. PPW 2001/6, s. 15, A. Szumański „*Spółka akcyjna*", W. Pyzioł, I. Weiss, A. Szumański, 671.
38. It should be stressed, that according to the Article 17 CCC the lack of authorization required by articles of incorporation, contrary to cases, when shareholders' authorization is required by a statute, has no effect with regard to third parties.

decisions, which pertain to assets or liabilities beyond a specified value.[39] This opinion appears disputable. It is doubtful whether a contracting authority, which has only a right to reject authorisation of managing board decisions, enjoys over the company the level of control required by the *Teckal* doctrine. In such a situation shareholders can only prevent the managing board from taking certain decisions. It is however impossible to impose on the managing board a legally binding obligation to take a demanded action. It is therefore impossible to compare the power to reject authorisation to the unilateral administrative measure referred to in the ECJ *Asemfo* and *Correos* decisions.[40]

The autonomy of the shareholders in a private limited company is much broader. According to the prevailing opinion the act of incorporation may require the managing board of a private limited company to follow instructions, orders and directions given by the shareholders' meeting.[41] This pertains not only to strategic decisions but also to ordinary business of the company. In this situation it is possible not only to prevent the managing board from taking certain decisions, but also to impose on it a duty to take an action demanded by the shareholders.[42] This approximates the position of a majority shareholder to the level of control exercised by a public authority over its departments. There are, however, several important differences. A majority shareholder, who holds capital of the company with other shareholder(s), to exercise the power to give the instructions needs to fulfil procedural requirements necessary for the convocation of the shareholders meeting.[43] It makes

39. M. Szydło, (Warszawa 2008) 120.
40. M. Stachowiak, 86.
41. A. Opalski, A.W. *Wiśniewski, W sprawie autonomii zarządu spółki z o.o.* PPH 2005/1 52, A. Rachwał, 990-991, M. Rodzynkiewicz, *Kodeks spółek handlowych. Komentarz* (Warszawa 2007) 349, R.T. Stroiński, *Dopuszczalność wydawania zarządowi wiążących poleceń przez organ właścicielski spółki kapitałowej*. PPH 2005/3 29. Some authors find the binding character of shareholders' instructions inconsistent with the nature of corporation. A. Szumański, *Normy instruktażowe w Kodeksie spółek handlowych.* PPH 2002/10 28, J. Szwaja, R.L. Kwaśnicki, *W sprawie wykładni nowego art. 3751 a także art. 375, 207 oraz art. 219 § 2 k.s.h.* PPH 2004/8 33. The majority of commentaries stresses, however, the autonomy of shareholders in the field of structuring private company's bylaws.
42. The obligation to follow shareholders' instructions may be imposed on a managing board and not on a company. As the performance of the duty is legally enforceable, it is the company, which is directed by shareholders' instructions.
43. According to the Article 235 § 3 CCC the articles of incorporation may grant a right to call a shareholders meeting also to a shareholder. M. Wyrwiński, *Spółka z ograniczoną odpowiedzialnością*. (Warszawa 2003) 89.

it impossible to take any decision without consent of other shareholders earlier than two weeks after the last notice of convocation has been sent. The resolution taken by the meeting may be challenged before the court due to unfair prejudice of the company's interest or minority shareholders' rights (Article 249 § 1 CCC). The fact that a contracting authority which is a majority shareholder cannot pursue only its own objectives but is limited by the legitimate interests and expectations of the minority shareholders in the light of *Stadt Halle* decision excludes characterisation of a private limited company as an "in-house" entity.[44] Also the procedural requirements, and possible suspending effect of a suit by the minority shareholders' differ the influence of the majority shareholder on a private limited company from the influence, that a contracting authority may exercise on its own departments.

The assessment of the position of a contracting authority as a single shareholder in a private limited company, whose articles empower the shareholder to give binding instructions to the managing board, is less evident. There are no minority shareholders, whose legitimate interests may affect the company's activities, and there are no procedural obstacles, that would hamper an immediate action of the shareholder. There are, however, other factors, which limit the freedom to pursue public objectives of a contracting authority and to impose on the company obligations departing significantly from the normal market conditions. The management of the company owes fiduciary duties not to the shareholders but to the company, which operates as a separate entity.[45] It should take into consideration not only the interests of the single shareholder but also of other company stakeholders (e.g. creditors and employees). The fact, that a company is a separate entity with limited assets and resources, exposes company stakeholders to significant risks. The management is obliged to reject any institutions, that would be detrimental to the company's financial good standing and to creditors' interests. It does not mean that it is impossible to impose on a management the duty to act in the way, which differs from the normal business behaviour. It means, that even in the case of a wholly-owned subsidiary of a contracting authority stakeholders' (mainly financial) interests limit the possibility of pursuing public tasks.[46] It is, however, at this level of generalisation, not a significant differ-

44. Case C 26/03 *Stadt Halle*, at [50].
45. A. Malinowski: *Członek zarządu- funkcjonariusz spółki, czy powiernik interesu dominującego akcjonariusza.* Pr.Sp. 2001/10 2.
46. This principle does not only preclude management from taking actions, which evidently cause insolvency but also from exposing creditors to extensive risk not adequate to company's available bargains.

ence from the situation of a public authority, whose duty to satisfy creditors' claims may put limits to the obligation of carrying out tasks in the public interest. In this context the characterisation of a private limited company which is a wholly-owned subsidiary of contracting entity as an "in-house" entity cannot be excluded.

Shareholders instructions may bind the management of a private limited company only in the internal relations. Members of managing board represent the company in all court proceedings and out of court dealings of the company. The right to represent the company may not be restricted with legal effect vis-à-vis third parties (Article 204 CCC). The actions taken by the management in breach of shareholders' instruction bind the company. This attenuates the control exercised by the shareholders. As this provision is similar to Article 129 of Spanish Ley de Sociedades Anonimas, it appears that in view of the *Asemfo* judgment the unrestricted freedom of management to represent the company does not prompt the conclusion that this company cannot be characterised as an "in-house" structure.

6.2. Structure of holdings in the "In-House" entity's capital

ECJ in several decisions referred to capital structure of holdings in share capital as a relevant factor for the characterisation of a company as an "in-house" entity. In *Stadt Halle* the Court took the view, that exclusively public ownership of an entity is an indispensable condition for the fulfilment of the first *Teckal* criterion.[47] In *Coname* the Court pointed out, that the 0.97% holding is so small as to preclude an effective control over the entity.[48] In *Asemfo* even less significant holdings of the Autonomous Communities did not preclude the "in-house" relation between the Communities and Tragsa.[49]

In Polish academic commentaries the position taken by ECJ in *Stadt Halle* has been commonly accepted.[50] It has been already mentioned that Polish corporate law requires considering legitimate minority shareholders' interests. The opinion that any private participation in a company changes considerably principles of its operations is valid also for Polish corporate law. Neither Polish courts nor ECJ recognised the participation of several contracting authorities as a problem in se. In *Coname* ECJ analysed this situation from the perspective of the influence which may be exercised by one of several contracting authorities which hold shares in an alleged "in-house" company.

47. Case C 26/03 *Stadt Halle,* at [50].
48. Case C 231/03 *Coname* at [24].
49. Case C 295/05 *Asemfo* at [58]- [60].
50. M. Szydło (Warszawa 2008) 124, M. Stachowiak, 86.

The Regional Administrative Court in Warsaw in the Buczkowice case did not take into consideration the control criterion, so the necessity of unanimous action of two municipalities to exercise any influence on the controlled company was not perceived as a relevant circumstance for the decision. The fact of the possible conflict of interests between public authorities which entrust their tasks to the same entity should be taken into consideration as a factor which attenuates the control exercised over an entity. If the control over a company is based solely on shareholder's rights and privileges, it is likely that also minority participation of other public authorities precludes the characterisation of the company as an "in-hose" entity of the majority shareholder.

It should be also acknowledged, that there is no inconsistence between ECJ opinion in *Coname* and its reasoning in the *Asemfo* decision. The minority holding in *Coname* precluded any significant influence of the contracting authority, as it enjoyed but a standard shareholder rights in the company, which had been directly awarded a service concession. The Autonomous Communities exercised over Tragsa control, which satisfied the first *Teckal* criterion, not due to the holding in the share capital of the company but due to the statutory right to oblige the company by a unilateral administrative act. It appears, that in the Court's opinion the decisive factor is not the size of the holding but the effectiveness of control.

6.3. Public law instruments of control

Polish law generally does not grant to the local government units any special instruments of control over their subsidiaries. The influence is generally based on corporate governance regulation. The main administrative instrument of control is the right of a unit's council to introduce tariffs on public utility services rendered by the company.

More instruments to influence the activity of an undertaking have been granted to the national government. According to the Article 5a of the Act on Exercising Rights of the State Treasury a state legal person[51] in order to alienate, pledge or lease the fixed assets, whose market value exceeds 50,000 €, requires consent of the Minister of the State Treasury. The contract concluded without consent is void. The decision of the Minister is subject to the

51. The notion of a state legal person covers the State Treasury, state enterprises, state universities, Polish Academy of Sciences, state research institutes and companies wholly owned by the State Treasury. The Supreme Court decision of 19 May 1992, III CZP 49/92, OSN 1992/11/200.

judicial review.[52] In case of the companies wholly owned by the central government the central government enjoys also powers to impose on certain entities duties to perform public tasks. The government has the competence to apply these measures mainly to satisfy the needs of the national defence and the state security or to mitigate the effects of natural disasters or to fulfil international obligations. The duty to perform specified tasks may be imposed on a state enterprise by a ministry which supervises this enterprise (Article 60 of the State Enterprises Act of 1983) or on a transport company by the Minister of Transport (Article 9 sec. 1 of the Transport Act of 1984).[53] The Minister of Transport has been granted more competences in "Porty Lotnicze" (hereafter: PPL), a state enterprise created to manage and administer state airports. Besides powers similar to that, exercised in other state enterprises the Minister may assign to PPL tasks relating to the management of airports, control of the air traffic and "important social and economic needs" (Articles 4 and 52 of The Act on "Porty Lotnicze" of 1987).

In all these cases unilateral administrative measures applied by governmental agencies do not exclude contractual relations between government and an entity which performs public duty. The duty is imposed by an administrative decision, which specifies the content of the imposed obligation and the government department responsible for refinancing the costs resulting from the performance of the obligation. Then the obliged entity enters into the contract which entitles it to claim remuneration for works, supplies and services performed in order to carry out the assigned task.

Most of the entities subject to these regulations do not satisfy the *Teckal* criteria. The duty to perform transport services may be imposed both on public and private entities. State enterprises operate as business entities and most of them do not fulfil the second criterion. The "in-house" characterisation may be considered in the case of PPL and its subsidiaries.

52. The rejection of the consent is reviewed by the civil division of the regional court. There are several exceptions to the requirement of the consent pertaining mainly to alienation publicly traded securities and situations, when authorisation by virtue of articles of incorporation is granted by the Minister acting as shareholders' meeting. The power to authorise the decisions of management is characterised as a measure of private law.
53. In the case of a natural disaster the duty may be imposed also by a local government unit.

7. The essential part of "In-House" entity activities criterion

Due to the lack of national judicial explanations relating to the second Teckal criterion the academic reflections on that matter are much more cautious. They generally follow the understanding of this criterion expressed by ECJ in *Carbotermo*. It is accepted that the rationale of the second criterion is preventing distortions of competition.[54] The fact that an "in-house" entity carries out the essential part of its activities with the controlling authority should ensure that when the procuring entity operates in the market in competition with other providers it is not treated differently from private undertakings because of its public nature.[55] According to the prevailing opinion the main factor to decide, whether the entity carries out the essential part of its activities with the controlling public authority should be the value of the turnover gained by the entity from the controlling authority. The qualitative assessment of activities relates to their importance on the local market for works, supplies or services performed be the entity.[56] Before *Carbotermo* some authors tended to follow the idea that the threshold of 80%, should be accepted as the criterion of essential part of an entity's activities.[57] All these opinions are of purely academic nature, as there has been so far no national judicial or administrative decision, which would refer to the second *Teckal* requirement.

From the perspective of the *Carbotermo* judgment it is only the core business of the entity, which is relevant for the verification of the second *Teckal* criterion. The rationale of the criterion relates to works, supplies and services provided by the entity. The ancillary activities as for example issuing bonds and other debentures, receiving loans and subcontracting remain irrelevant. Nevertheless these activities may attenuate the influence of the controlling authority, if it is based on the corporate governance instruments. Banks and bondholders may be granted contractual rights which empower them to influence strategic decisions on a company's business and limit the influence of shareholders.

54. Case C 340/04 *Carbotermo* at [59].
55. A.G. Leger in opinion on case C 94/99 *ARGE* at [72], F. Avriakoti, 31.
56. M. Szydło (Warszawa 2008), Article 3 at [9].
57. *Ibidem*.

8. Public procurement and Institutionalised Private Public Partnership

The public private partnership in Poland has been regulated in the Act on Private Public Partnership of 2005 (hereafter: PPPA). The private partner is selected in public tendering procedure regulated in PPL (Article 14 PPPA). The Article 15 of PPPA excludes application of several provisions of the public procurement law. The negotiated procedure with prior publication of a contract notice may not be applied for the selection of the private partner. The tender evaluation criteria may pertain to the characteristics of the economic operator, and in particular to its economic, technical or financial credibility. The contracting authority has no right to terminate the contract due to the material change of circumstances, which makes the performance of the contract unfavorable to the contracting authority. It is, however, possible to renegotiate the contract and to change its content, even if the amendment pertains to criteria of the tender which were the basis for the choice of the private partner.

The contract between the public authority and the selected private partner defines the project, necessary contributions of the private partner, the procedures of public supervision over performance of the project and the remuneration for the private partner's activities. In order to perform the common project the parties may agree to incorporate a company (Article 19 PPPA). In this case the contract defines rights and duties of the prospective company (Article 18 (13) PPPA). It appears that to enter into the contract with the company the public authority is not required to apply any tendering procedures. The content of the contract and the duty to conclude it with the specified company result from the earlier contract with the private partner. The contracting authority is bound to enter into the contract with the company incorporated to perform the tasks given to the private partner. There is therefore no space for tendering procedure.[58] As no public private partnership project has been completed so far in Poland[59] this opinion has not been verified by any judicial or administrative decision.

58. M. Bitner, A. Kozłowska, M. Kulesza, *Ustawa o partnerstwie publiczno-prawnym. Komentarz*. (Warszawa 2006), M. Szydło (Warszawa 2008) Article 3 at [10].
59. M. Zieniewski, D. Sześciło, *Nadchodzi koniunktura na PPP*? Rzeczpospolita of 29 Aug. 2008 B10.

9. Procedures relating to UEFA EURO 2012 Championships

New questions relating to the scope of application of the public procurement regulation and the "in-house" providing concept in Poland result from the adoption of the regulatory framework for the investment programme before the UEFA 2012 Championships. In 2007 the Parliament adopted the Act on the Preparations for the UEFA EURO 2012 Final Tournament. According to the Act the State Treasury and the municipalities which host EURO 2012 events may incorporate private limited companies which will serve as Special Purpose Vehicles (hereafter: SPV) for the investment projects. The Minister of Physical Culture and Sport, other agencies of the State Treasury, local government units and business entities active in the field of public transport may directly award to SPVs contracts relating to the performance of the public tasks enumerated in the governmental regulation on the Euro 2012 Championships investment projects. The question of compatibility of the direct award with European law of public procurement was not discussed during parliamentary debates. The SPVs do not enjoy an exclusive right to render services referred to in the Article 18 of the 2004/18/EC Directive. The awarding authorities may decide whether to enter into the contract with SPV or to select a private partner according to the provisions of PPPA. It appears that SPVs are treated as "in-house" entities of awarding authorities.

SPVs are wholly owned by the State Treasury or municipalities. The shares may not be alienated or pledged before all public tasks assigned to an SPV have been performed. SPVs' activity is limited only to the performance of tasks given to them in relation to the EURO 2012 investment programme. They may not create other entities or acquire shares of other companies. The Minister of Physical Culture and Sport may wind up an SPV after all tasks assigned to it have been fulfilled or in the case of breach of contractual duties to awarding authorities. The Minister of Physical Culture and Sport in relation to SPVs owned by the State Treasury and a mayor of the city in relation to SPVs owned by a municipality exercises the right to authorise contracts referred to in Article 5a of the Act on Exercising Rights of the State Treasury.

The scope of activity of SPV companies fulfils the second *Teckal* requirement. The Act on Preparations for the UEFA EURO 2012 Final Tournament precludes any other activity than performance of public tasks listed in the governmental regulation and given to the companies by public authorities. More ambiguous remains the question of the control criterion. According to Article 17 of the Act the public tasks are assigned to SPVs on a contractual basis. There is no provision that enables public authorities to oblige an SPV by unilateral measures to perform public tasks related to the EURO 2012 investment programme. Public authorities to exercise control over SPVs may use mainly instruments of corporate governance and contractual arrangements. In practice the management does not have a choice to enter or not to enter into a contract with the authority which holds shares of the company. The articles of incorporation limit the objectives of the company and its scope of activity to the performance of certain investment projects. The controlling authority may dismiss the managing board members at any time. The content of the awarded contract is however a result of negotiations between the company and an awarding authority. Article 17 sec. 5 of the Act provides that the management of an SPV drafts the contract with the awarding authority. These circumstances make characterisation of SPVs as "in-house" entities uncertain. Nevertheless it appears that in the case of the wholly owned subsidiaries of a public authority which are incorporated only to perform a specified task, the corporate governance provides measures which may satisfy the first *Teckal* criterion.

In-House Providing in Denmark

Professor Steen Treumer,
University of Copenhagen, Denmark

1. Introduction

The fundamental distinction between in-house and ex-house providing is well-known in both theory and practice.[1] Its importance cannot be underestimated, as the consequence of the categorization as in-house is that the arrangement falls outside the scope of the EC public procurement rules. This is the consequence with regard to arrangements that otherwise would have been covered by the public procurement directives but also the consequence with regard to an arrangement that would solely have been covered by the Treaty and the general principles of EC law.[2] However, it can be extremely difficult to determine whether the arrangement is in-house or not, and the interpretation of the concept differs from Member State to Member State. In spite of its importance, the issue has not been the subject of many public procurement cases in Denmark and the treatment in the legal literature has until recently been rather limited and is still highly focused on the Teckal case law, which concerns in-house arrangements with a separate legal entity, cf. *C-107/98, Teckal.*[3]

1. This article is an updated and slightly extended version of the my article "*Den danske tilgangsvinkel til in-house arrangementer i EU-retlig belysning*" in Festskrift til Det Danske Selskab for Byggeret (2009) pp. 311-327. Another and related very recent publication on in-house is the article of H.P. Rosenmeier "*in-house-spørgsmålet i udbudsretten*" in the same publication pp. 265-276.
2. The European Court of Justice established in *C-231/03, Coname* that the in-house exception previously established in the Teckal case also applied to a services concession where the relevant public procurement directive (the Services Directive) clearly was not applicable.
3. Ruth Nielsen, *Udbud af offentlige kontrakter*, 3rd ed. 2005 pp. 193-202; Jesper Fabricius and René Offersen, *EU's udbudsregler i praksis*, 2nd. ed. 2006, especially pp. 95-103; Simon Evers Hjelmborg, Peter Stig Jakobsen and Sune Troels Poulsen, *Public Procurement Law-the EU directive on public contracts*, 2006 pp. 80-106; Michael

The Danish implementation of the EU public procurement directives is atypical. The Danish legislator has chosen to maintain the exact text of the public procurement directives when implementing the directives and has thereby in practice refrained from making any substantial changes in the directives. There is therefore no definition of in-house providing in the Danish legislation implementing the public procurement directives. This means that the questions of interpretation facing Danish practitioners and enforcement bodies are as closely linked to the EC public procurement directives and the case law from the European Court of Justice as they can possibly be. Practitioners and enforcement bodies thereby enjoy the privilege of interpreting the procurement rules without the usual interference and qualifications to the interpretations made by a national legislator.

The Complaints Board for Public Procurement (hereafter the Complaints Board) has the primary responsibility for the enforcement of the EC public procurement rules in Denmark and has the power to grant interim measures, the power to establish that the rules have been violated, the power to issue set aside orders and can award damages. The public procurement disputes concerning in-house providing have typically been dealt with by the Complaints Board and the Competition Authority. The Competition authority can deal with complaints concerning alleged infringements. However, the Authority cannot issue a binding order in the field of public procurement. It can instead bring a case before the Complaints Board if a contracting authority does not comply with the recommendations of the Competition Authority.[4] The ordinary courts have only played a marginal role in this respect. The rulings from the Board can be appealed to the ordinary courts, but this happens only in about 1 out of 10 cases.[5]

As the primary purpose of this article is to cast light on the Danish approach to in-house providing emphasis will be put on particularities of the

Steinicke and Lise Groesmeyer, *EU's Udbudsdirektiver med kommentarer*, 2nd ed 2008 pp. 165-188; H.P.Rosenmeier, "*in-house-spørgsmålet i udbudsretten*" in Festskrift til Det Danske Selskab for Byggeret (2009) pp. 265-276; Michael Steinicke, "*Den udbudsretlige in-house-regel – en kritik af udviklingen i EF-domstolens praksis* in Juridiske emner ved Syddansk Universitet (ed. Hans Viggo Godsk Pedersen) 2009, pp. 260-273.

4. The Competition Authority has only used this access in a very limited number of cases.
5. Compare with H.P. Rosenmeier, "*Det danske klagesystem*" in Jens Fejø & Steen Treumer (eds.) in EU's udbudsregler – implementering og håndhævelse i Norden, 2006 that assessed that about 15 % of the rulings of the Complaints Board had been appealed.

Danish state of law and on issues that have been disputed in Denmark, be it in theory or public procurement case law. The concept of in-house providing is analyzed in section 2 with focus on the in-house arrangements between a contracting authority and a separate legal entity. The treatment of in-house tenderes in procedures covered by the EC public procurement rules (in Denmark so-called control bids) is considered in section 3, and section 4 is the conclusion.

2. The concept of In-House Providing

As mentioned above there is no definition of in-house providing in the Danish legislation implementing the public procurement directives. The Danish interpretation in practice and literature therefore adopts the classical starting point that only a contract between separate legal entities should be tendered out and that activities provided by the contracting authority's own resources are not covered by the duty to tender out. The written guide to the EC public procurement directives from the Danish Competition Authority[6] expresses the traditional official Danish interpretation of in-house with regard to the State. This interpretation is worth noticing, as it deviates from the interpretation in many other Member States i.e. from the interpretation in Germany.[7] The State is not considered to a be a single unit which implies that the providing of a service from one ministry to another would be considered as ex-house providing and therefore covered by the public procurement rules.[8] However, a ministry and its affiliated agencies and authorities are considered as a single unit, as they are under the command of the minister in question. The official Danish interpretation might be in a process of change, as the

6. The guide can be found on the homepage of the Competition Authority (www.ks.dk) and is updated on a regular basis. The above-mentioned is based on the version from October 2009 and its section 3.2 about "in-house production (selvudførte ydelser)" in the *pdf.-version* of the guide. In the other version of the guide that can be found on the homepage the remarks about the State and the in-house concept have been deleted. It appears that the latter version is the most recently updated. The background for the deviation between the two guides is not clarified.
7. See the article of Martin Burgi in this publication.
8. See Jesper Fabricius and René Offersen, *EU's udbudsregler i praksis*, 2nd. ed. 2006 p. 99. These authors emphasize that the question is disputed and that it appears to be common in several Member States considering deliveries between different branches of the State as falling outside the scope of the public procurement rules. See also Ruth Nielsen, *Udbud af offentlige kontrakter*, 3rd ed. 2005 p. 194.

most recent update of the guide from the Competition Authority contains no remarks on the issue, cf. footnote 3 in this article. It is also questionable whether the traditional interpretation of the question is correct, as the State is normally considered as one legal entity in Danish law and the ruling of the European Court of Justice in *C-295/05, Asemfo* seems to imply a different interpretation. In the latter case the State owned 99% of the company Asemfo and the State was considered as a single unit.

In 1999 the European Court of Justice widened the concept of in-house in an obiter dictum in the ruling *C-107/98, Teckal*, which is one of the leading cases in the field of public procurement law. The Court clarified in this case that an arrangement with a *separate* legal entity in specific circumstances also can be an in-house arrangement. This exception is sometimes also referred to as the extended in-house rule and this expression will also be applied in this article. It is interesting that the Danish Complaints Board *prior* to this ruling had reached a similar result in a *ruling of 11 October 1996, Luis Madsen and others against Odense Kommune*.[9] This case concerned contracts with a couple of recently established limited companies that were fully owned by a municipality. The Complaints Board held that the arrangement could take place without a tender as the transactions were perceived as a split up of the total activities of the municipality that is to say an internal reorganization. The municipality owned all of the shares in the limited companies and was therefore perceived as having the determining influence of the company. This fact was emphasized by the Complaints Board in its ruling.

From this it appears at first glance that the first Teckal criterion – which was not established at the time of the ruling – was met. However, subsequent case law from the European Court of Justice has clarified that full ownership of a company does not necessarily implly that the Teckal control criterion is meet, cf. *C-458/03, Parking Brixen.*[10] In this case a municipality was the only shareholder in the public limited company, but the Court nevertheless held that the control criterion was not met based on a concrete assessment of all

9. Compare with Ruth Nielsen, *Udbud af offentlige kontrakter*, 3rd ed. 2005 p. 202 which questions the result in the concrete ruling and her starting point is that there most likely was a duty to tender in the concrete case, cf. the rulings in C-*107/98, Teckal* and *C-26/03, Stadt Halle* but with no further elaboration on this point.

10. The Advocate General Kokott was more flexible in her approach. See in particular consideration 68 in her proposal of 1 March 2005. Kokott argues against a requirement according to which the public shareholder should have the same possibilities in law in relation to the contractor as it has in relation to its own departments which would make it almost impossible for the first Teckal criterion to be fulfilled in respect of capital companies incorporated under private law.

the legislative provisions and relevant circumstances. The European Court of Justice emphasized a number of elements in this connection including 1) the conversion from a special undertaking of the Gemeinde Brixen into a company limited by shares and the nature of that type of company; 2) the broadening of its objects as the company had started to work in significant new fields; 3) the obligatory opening of the company, in the short term, to other capital; 4) the expansion of the geographical area of the company's activities, to the whole of Italy and; 5) the considerable powers conferred on its Administrative Board with in practice no management control by the municipality, cf. paragraph 67 of the judgment. In paragraph 68 the European Court further stressed that the statutes of the company limited by shares gave the board very broad powers to manage the company, since it had the power to carry out all acts which it considered necessary for the attainment of the company's objective. Furthermore, the Board had the power to provide guarantees up to € 5 million or to effect other transactions without the prior authority of the shareholders' meeting showing that the company had broad independence with regard to its shareholders.

The case that was brought before the Danish Complaints Board against the municipality of Odense had some of the same features. The municipality established a couple of public limited companies, broadened the object of the companies as they were expected partly to sell their services on market terms and expanded the geographical scope of the activities to the Danish and international market. However, it appears that contrary to the facts in Parking Brixen there was no obligatory opening of the companies to other capital, and it seems that the powers conferred on the Administrative Boards of the companies were limited to those assigned to such a board under Danish company law. Furthermore, the municipality still owned the installations and regulated the prices of the services of the companies. On the basis of this the control criterion was presumably in the case.

It is of interest to assess whether the second Teckal criterion was also fulfilled. According to this criterion the supplying entity must carry out "the essential part of its activities with the controlling local authority or authorities". The purpose of the company was to take over the activities of the municipality regarding water supply and renovation. However, the statutes of the company allowed the company to sell services in this area both in Denmark and abroad. It follows from the explanations in the procedure before the Complaints Board that the sale of these services to external customers only was about 1-3 percent of the turnover in the two companies. It was therefore evident that the limited companies carried out the essential part of their activities with the controlling municipality and that the second Teckal criterion was also meet in the concrete case even though the criterion was not addressed in the ruling of the Complaints Board.

It is of particular interest to establish how the Danish Competition Authority, the Complaints Board and the ordinary Danish courts have taken into account the Teckal ruling and related subsequent case law from the European Court of Justice and to consider whether these entities have clarified questions still not answered by the European Court of Justice. Unlike the situation at central European level, there are only few cases where the extended in-house rule established by the Teckal ruling has been considered in Danish public procurement disputes.

One of these cases is a ruling from the Complaints Board of *10 March 2006, Fælles Fagligt Forbund and Landsorganisationen i Danmark against Viborg Amts Fælleskommunale Trafikselskab and others.* This case concerned a cooperation between a group of contracting authorities which was governed by a cooperation agreement. The cooperation was established in order to run a computer system and an office that could receive orders outside of normal opening hours. The complainant claimed that the activities in the cooperation was covered by Annex I A in the Services Directive and therefore covered by the duty to tender according to the directive. From the cooperation agreement followed that each contracting member had a member in a steering group and all decisions in the steering group required unanimity. Furthermore, the cooperation could not commit the participants outside the budget without separate agreement.

The Complaints Board made an explicit reference to the Teckal ruling and several of the subsequent rulings from the European Court of Justice on the in-house issue. After listing the two conditions for the application of the extended in-house rule, it considered whether these conditions were fulfilled in the concrete case. The Board held that both conditions were met in the concrete case. Each member of the cooperation had full control over the activities of the cooperation as decisions in the steering group required unanimity and all the activities of the cooperation were delivered to the contracting authorities participating in the cooperation. The case represents a straightforward application of the conditions established in the case law of the European Court of Justice. The case is of interest because the Complaints Board held that the control criterion was met due to contractual regulation and not due to legislation and ownership. The necessary degree of control will typically arise from ownership but can be established on another basis i.e. the law or contractual regulation.[11]

The Complaints Board stated in an obiter dictum[12] – with reference to *C-107/98, Teckal* and *C-26/03, Stadt Halle* – that the control criterion implies that "the contacting authority owns and controls the company in question 100%" in its ruling of from *7 September 2005, Dansk Byggeri against Vejle Kommune*. This is a misunderstanding of the case law from the European Court of Justice.[13] However, it was not of importance in the concrete case, as the issue was not whether the in-house rule applied but whether the contracting authority had violated the Services Directive on various points, which the Board ruled was the case.

Another case dealt with by the Danish Competition Authority in 2003 related to the consequences of shared ownership as it is relevant to ask whether shared ownership implies that the control criterion is not met. In his opinion the Advocate General in the Teckal ruling expressed the view that it was unlikely that one out of 45 municipalities that had set up a consortium could exercise over that kind of consortium the kind of control which an entity exercises over an internal body, cf. consideration 61 in the opinion.[14] The Danish Competition Authority took the same approach in a case from 2003 where a company was owned by 12 municipalities.[15] This line of reasoning is easy to follow as, it is evident that the higher degree of shared ownership the lower the influence of the respective owners will normally be.

However, the European Court of Justice has in its most recent case law after Teckal interpreted the law in a way that appears to reduce the importance of shared ownership in the assessment of whether the control criterion is met. In *C-340/04, Carbotermo* the Court held that the fact that the contracting authority holds, alone or together with other public authorities, all of the share capital in a successful tenderer tends to indicate, generally, that that contract-

11. See Michael Steinicke and Lise Groesmeyer, EU's *Udbudsdirektiver med kommentarer*, 2nd ed. 2008 on p. 176.
12. The Board wanted to remedy a statement from a chief legal adviser employed by the contracting authority, as he had stated to the Board that an EC public procurement procedure had not been necessary based on the in-house exception.
13. As pointed out by Jesper Fabricius and René Offersen, *EU's udbudsregler i praksis*, 2nd ed. 2006.
14. The Court of Justice did not consider the question in the case. Compare with the key paragraph of the judgment paragraph 50.
15. Statement from the Competition Authority of 4 March 2003 (Jysk Miljølaboratorium). A summary in Danish can be found on the homepage of the Competition Authority (www.ks.dk).

ing authority exercises over that company a control similar to that which it exercises over its own departments, cf. paragraph 37 in the judgment.

This line of reasoning was taken much further in *C-295/05, Asemfo,* by attributing shared ownership little weight in the assessment of whether the control criterion was met. In the concrete case 99 percent of the capital of the company in question (Asemfo) was held by the Spanish State itself (and through a holding company and a guarantee fund) and four Autonomous Communities, each with one share, holding 1 percent of the capital.[16] The Court did not accept the argument that the control criterion was met only for contracts performed by the Spanish State, excluding those which were the subject of a demand from the four Autonomous Communities that jointly held only 1 percent of the share capital, cf. paragraph 59 of the judgment. The Court emphasized in this context that Asemfo according to Spanish law was required to carry out the orders given it by the public authorities, including the Autonomous Communities, that Asemfo was not free to fix the tariff for its actions and that its relationship with them were not contractual, cf. paragraph 60 in the judgment. This ruling clarifies that the control criterion can be met even though the degree of ownership of the respective owners is extremely limited. However, the facts of the Asemfo case were quite unusual and shared ownership must still be of importance for the assessment of whether the control criterion is met in accordance with the rationale of the Advocate General in Teckal and of the Danish Competition Authority in 2003.

The European Court of Justice also attributed little weight to shared ownership in the latest judgment concerning the issue, cf. C-324/07, *Coditel Brabrant*. This ruling could also be used in support of an interpretation to the effect that shared ownership in general is of insignificant importance for the assessment of whether the control criterion is met. The case did not concern the question of the duties following from the public procurement directives but instead the question of whether the transparency obligation which follows from the fundamental provisions and principles of the EC Treaty[17] was not relevant due to the extended in-house rule, cf. the Teckal ruling.

Subject to verification of the facts by the referring national court, the European Court of Justice established that the control criterion was met

16. The Danish version of the judgment has been translated incorrectly on this point. Paragraph 58 of the Danish version states that 99 percent of the capital was owned by the state and that the rest by "four Autonomous Communities which each owns 1 percent of this capital".
17. Cf. *C-324/98, Telaustria* and subsequent case law.

which was remarkable, considering the facts of the case.[18] The supplying entity was an inter-municipal cooperative society whose members are municipalities and an inter-municipal association whose members in turn are solely municipalities. The entity was not open to private members and carried out the essential part of its activities with its members. However, its governing council, which consisted of representatives of the municipalities, enjoyed "the widest powers" including the power to establish the tariffs for the services of the entity. Nevertheless, the European Court of Justice emphasized that the entity was an inter-municipal corporative governed by the Law on inter-municipal coorporatives and that these according to this law are not to have a commercial character. The Court therefore established that the control criterion was met in spite of the fact that the governing council enjoyed the widest powers.

As submitted by H.P. Rosenmeier and Roberto Caranta,[19] the judgment could be interpreted as a fundamental deviation from prior case law on the issue, and it is possible that the ruling is the forerunner of a new formulation of the conditions for the use of the extended in-house rule. As pointed out by Rosenmeier the formulation of the control criterion is now misleading due to the developments in the case law from the European Court of Justice. However, the case is from a Chamber, and it was without further ado established that the second condition for the application of the extended in-house rule was fulfilled. The latter follows from paragraph 27 where the Court remarks that it is stated in the order for the reference for a preliminary ruling that the entity carries out the essential part of its activities. It is therefore submitted that there is *not* sufficient ground for assuming that the European Court of Justice has merged the two criteria for the application of the extended in-house rule to one criterion.[20]

The increased flexibility as regards the requirements of "similar control" is closely linked to another extremely interesting and fundamental development in recent case law, cf. *C-480/06, Commission v Germany*[21] regarding public

18. For a more extensive account of the facts in Danish please, see H.P.Rosenmeier, "*in-house-spørgsmålet i udbudsretten*" in Festskrift til Det Danske Selskab for Byggeret (2009), pp. 265-276.
19. H.P. Rosenmeier, *op.cit. and Roberto Caranta in section 4 of the article,* "The in-house Providing: The Law as It Stands in the EU" in this publication.
20. Compare with H.P.Rosenmeier, *op.cit.* and especially with the very end of section 2 of his article.
21. See Roberto Caranta's article, "*The in-house Providing: The Law as It Stands in the EU*" in the current publication and François Lichère, Semaine juridique – Administration et collectivités territoriales, 26 October 2009, no. 2248.

partnership. In this case the European Court of Justice essentially interpreted the scope of the EC public procurement rules in a very innovative and surprising manner. The Court thereby overruled both the Advocate General and the European Commission that had addressed the disputed behavior based on the traditional interpretation and approach to the scope of the rules.

As the facts of the case has been presented earlier in this publication[22] there will only be given a brief summary of the facts of the case here. The case concerned a directly concluded contract between four administrative districts (Landkreise) and the refuse collection of the City of Hamburg concerning waste disposal without there having been a call for tenders. The Commission essentially argued that the contract should have been concluded in accordance with the open or restricted procedures in accordance with the Services Directive which it had obviously not been. Germany invoked various arguments in its defense including the argument that the contract should be considered as an in-house arrangement. The Advocate General was to the point and assessed that nothing indicated that the administrative districts exercised similar control and that the first condition (similar control) for the application of the extended in-house rule was therefore not met, cf. consideration 47 of the opinion. Furthermore, the Advocate General stated that "I can find nothing which indicates that the contract in dispute does not constitute a public service contract for the purpose of Directive 92/50. That means that it could only lawfully have been awarded in accordance with that directive".

In the light of these statements which were clearly based on a logic and coherent interpretation of the relevant public procurement directive and previous case law of the European Court of Justice it was to be expected that Germany lost the case. However, the European Court of Justice adopted a different approach. In the start of its findings the Court made clear that the four administrative districts did not exercise any control which could be described as similar, cf. para 36 of the judgment. From this is apparent that the court considered that the contract was not covered by the exception originally established by *C-107/98, Teckal*. Nevertheless, the European Court of Justice did not establish that the contract should have been tendered out according to the public procurement rules but instead dismissed the Commission's action. With this acceptance of the conclusion of the contract the European Court of Justice in reality created a new exception to the scope of the public procure-

22. See Roberto Caranta's article, "*The in-house Providing: The Law as It Stands in the EU*" in the current publication.

ment directives.[23] It is difficult to assess the field of application of this new exception as it is conditioned and the circumstances of the concrete case were rather special.

The European Court of Justice emphasized several points. Firstly, that the contract at issue established a cooperation between local authorities (contracting authorities) with the aim of ensuring that a public task that they all had to perform, namely waste disposal was carried out. Actually this was also a community task as it related to secondary EU regulation. Secondly, the contract was atypical in the sense that the contractor of the four administrative districts (the refuse collection of the City of Hamburg) only received a payment corresponding to the charges the contractor had to pay to a the operator of the facility, cf. para 43 of the judgment. So in other words the contractor did not gain any profit from the arrangement with the four administrative districts but was simply reimbursed for the payments to the operator. Thirdly, the contract was the basis and the legal framework for a cooperation between public authorities, without the participation of any private party, and it appears that it could just as well have taken place by means of the creation of a body governed by public law to which the various local authorities concerned entrusted the performance of the task in the public interest. Fourthly, the European Court of Justice stressed that there was nothing in the case that indicated that the authorities at issue had contemplated to circumvent the rules on public procurement.[24]

As François Lichère has pointed out the French courts including the Conseil d'Etat had ruled along the same lines in recent case law prior to the judgment of the European Court of Justice in *C-480/06, Commission v Germany* and the Rapporteur on the case within the European Court of Justice was the French judge Bonichot. The case thereby appears to be a very interesting example of a national interpretation of procurement law as an inspira-

23. For the same point of view see François Lichère, Semaine juridique – Administration et collectivités territoriales, 26 October 2009, no. 2248 with an interesting analysis of the case and its interpretation.

24. The intention of a contracting authority has also been considered by the Danish Complaints Board for Public Procurement in other contexts for instance regarding technical dialogue prior to submission of bids which may or must lead to exclusion from the subsequent tender procedure. Compare with François Lichère, Semaine juridique – Administration et collectivités territoriales, 26 October 2009, no. 2248 that adds that this adds a new element to EC public procurement law.

tion for the European Court of Justice for an important development in EC public procurement law.[25]

It will be very interesting to see the follow-up to this recent development in both the case law of the European Court of Justice and the Member States.

There is no Danish case law where it is considered whether "similar control" can be ensured by the instruments of national company law. As mentioned previously, case law from the European Court of Justice has clarified that full ownership of a company does not necessarily imply that the Teckal control criterion is met, cf. *C-458/03, Parking Brixen*. From this follows that what is normally considered as control over a company in a company law context is not necessarily sufficient to meet the control criterion.[26] The complexity of the issue is underlined by the fact that a contracting company can be perceived as having control in the in-house context in a situation where it is evident that it does not have control in a company law context, cf. *C-295/05, Asemfo*, which has just been commented above.

The starting point appears to be that the "similar control" criterion is not meet, even though the contracting authority owns more than 50 percent of the shares in the company. It follows from the case law of the European Court of Justice that the in-house concept is to be interpreted very narrowly and the Court has stressed that company law as a starting point "places considerable limits on its power to influence the decisions of those [connected] companies", cf. *C-340/04, Carbotermo* paragraph 38. According to Danish company law the board of directors and the management manage the company, and the day-to-day management is handled by a managing director. A shareholder which controls the company will therefore as a starting point have to influence the management of the company through the general meeting decisions and cannot give orders to the managers and board of directors like in a public entity. Furthermore, the management and board of directors only have to comply with the general meeting decisions if they are lawful and in accordance with the best interests of the company.

The development in the field of EC public procurement law has had a very interesting spillover effect on the Danish legislation on public procurement which applies to certain contracts that are *not* covered by the EC public pro-

25. See the conclusion of the article of François Lichère, Semaine juridique – Administration et collectivités territoriales, 26 October 2009, no. 2248.
26. See H.P. Rosenmeier, *op.cit.* on p. 270 of his article, where he states "It appears almost as if the European Court of Justice had overlooked or did not want to consider that a majority shareholder – regardless of the statutes of the company – normally has decisive influence in reality" [translated by the undersigned].

curement directives. This law – which in the following is referred to as the Danish Public Procurement Act[27] – was in 2001 supplemented with a Ministerial Order. The Ministerial Order in the version of 2001 contained a provision in §6 according to which connected companies were considered as one company. In §6 it was further specified that companies were to be considered as connected when one company owns more than 20 percent of the other company. However, the Danish public procurement Act from 2005 has not repeated the provision in §6.[28] It follows from the Competition Authority's guide to the Danish public procurement law[29] that a contract cannot be considered as internal just because of 20 percent ownership. Furthermore, the guide specifies that the question of whether a contract is internal (in-house) or not is to be decided in accordance with the practice regarding the public sector directive, EC Directive 2004/18.[30]

3. Treatment of In-House tenders in procedures covered by the EC public procurement rules (control bids)

It is seen in practice in Denmark and other Member States[31] that a tender procedure involves both external tenders and an internal tender. The latter is called a control bid in Denmark. The decision on whether to contract out is based on the outcome of the competition between the external tenderers and the internal tenderer. Procedures with control bids have given cause to various questions and public procurement disputes in Denmark.

In 1996 a Danish Member of the European Parliament Karin Riis-Jørgensen posed several questions to the European Commission on treatment

27. Tilbudsloven (lov om indhentning af tilbud på visse offentlige og offentligt støttede kontrakter), Law no. 338 of 18 May 2005 as amended by Law no. 572 of 6 June 2007.
28. The Danish public procurement law from 2005 repealed the Ministerial Order from 2001, cf. §17(2) in the Law.
29. See the guide from 18 August 2005 on page 8 (Konkurrencestyrelsens vejledning til tilbudsloven 2005 (lov om indhentning af tilbud i bygge- og anlægssektoren)). The guide can be found on the website of the Competition Authority (www.ks.dk).
30. A similar point of view is submitted by H.P. Rosenmeier on p. 274 of his article "*in-house-spørgsmålet i udbudsretten*", Festskrift til Det Danske Selskab for Byggeret, 2009.
31. See the article of Martin Trybus in this publication regarding United Kingdom and Sue Arrowsmith, *The Law of Public and Utilities Procurement*, 2nd ed. 2005, pp. 394-396.

of in-house tenderers in procedures covered by the EC public procurement rules.[32] The questions related to the Danish Finance Ministry's circular on tendering and out-sourcing of state operational tasks and works,[33] which makes it possible for a government authority calling for tenders to take part in an EC tendering procedure itself by drawing up what is known as a 'control bid', i.e. its own tender. A rule in the aforementioned circular also allowed the government authority to increase private-sector tenderers' bids by automatically adding to them an amount corresponding to the costs it would incur, e.g. in retraining staff and paying wages to civil servants with no work to do, if it lost the function put out to tender which it used to perform. The essential question was whether this practice by automatically increasing private-sector bids constitutes discrimination in favor of the public sector.

The Commission answered that the circular simply provided a methodology allowing contracting authorities to decide on an objective basis when to cancel an award procedure rather than a series of provisions applicable to the comparison of tenders. In this perspective, the circular should be seen as dealing with a subject matter which is not regulated by the directives and therefore legitimate unless contrary to the general provisions and principles of the Treaty. The Commission did not find the circular contrary to any general provisions of the Treaty. As regards in particular the principle of equal treatment, the system introduced by the circular does not seem to lead to any inequality of treatment of any of the (external) tenderers and is therefore not contrary to that principle. However, the Commission was of the view that the award procedure is subject to the directives from the very beginning, and this remains so even if it does not result in a contract being concluded with an external bidder. This means that the publication of a tender notice and the application of all the provisions of the directive are obligatory as soon as the normal conditions (value above the relevant threshold, directives applicable both ratione materiae and ratione personae) are met.[34] As the circular was assessed as in conformity with Community law, no further action was taken in the matter.

32. Written question No. 2699/96 of 15 October 1996. See the O.J. 1997 C60/112 of 26 February 1997, which contains the question and the supplementary answer given by Mr Monti on behalf of the European Commission.
33. No. 42 of 1 March 1994. Now No. 159 of 17 December 2002. The Circular is currently under revision.
34. Compare with the similar remarks made by Potts J. in *R v Secretary of State for the Environment Ex p. Bury* [1997] EWHC Admin 213, CA. On this point see Sue Arrowsmith, *The Law of Public and Utilities Procurement*, 2nd ed. 2005, p. 395.

Shortly after the above-mentioned answer from the Commission a complainant contested the legality of a municipality's use of a control bid in a procedure where the municipality also had reserved the right to terminate the tender procedure without an award if the control bid was the economically most advantageous. Even though the municipality was not covered by the Finance Ministry's circular on tendering and out-sourcing of state operational tasks and works, it had followed the rules established in this circular.[35] The Complainant supported its view on the point of view of the Ministry of Housing and Building, which was based on the principle of equal treatment of tenderers. This Ministry had – in a letter sent to the complainant before the complaints case – stated that a contracting authority was not likely to be allowed to submit and assess a control bid, as this was contrary to the principle of equal treatment of tenderers. The Ministry repeated and elaborated on this point of view in a letter from the end of August 1998.

The Complaints Board rejected the complaint in its ruling of 18 September 1998, *Foreningen af Rådgivende Ingeniører against Frederiksberg Kommune*, and established that a control bid is not to be perceived as a "bid" in the sense of the EC public procurement rules but as a methodology allowing contracting authorities to decide on an objective basis when it is relevant to contract out. The Board also pointed out that the access to terminate the tender procedure without an award if a control bid is better than the external offers is a consequence of a general right to terminate the tender procedure if the contracting authority does not find any of the tenderers satisfactory. The Board concluded that a procedure with a control bid was not a violation of the EC public procurement rules and referred also to the fact that the European Commission shared this point of view, cf. the statement from the European Commission in response to the question of Karin Riis-Jørgensen mentioned above.

This case is of particular interest for various reasons. Firstly, a ministry disagreed with the European Commission and the disagreement was maintained in a case brought before a national review body. Secondly, the Complaints Board ruled in accordance with the point of view of the European Commission, thereby rejecting the point of view of the ministry. Thirdly, it is interesting to observe that similar questions were considered about the same time in a public procurement dispute in another Member State (United King-

35. The control bids from municipalities and regions were recently regulated by law in Denmark. See Act No. 224 of 8 April 2008 and Ministerial Order No. 607 of 24 June 2008.

dom) with a similar outcome[36] and that the parties involved appeared not to be aware of each other's actions. Nor did the Court of Appeal in the Portsmouth case seem to be aware of the question posed to the European Commission by the Danish member of the European Parliament mentioned above. Nevertheless, an important difference was that in the Portsmouth case the British Court of Appeal argued that the contracting authority could terminate the procedure even though the internal tender was *not* the best tender. The Danish Complaints Board ruled on the assumption that the internal tender was the best tender.

However, it is very possible that the European Court of Justice would impose some obligations to the respective treatment of in-house and external bidders once a public procurement procedure has begun based on the principle of equal treatment of tenderers.[37] The Complaints Board has had similar considerations in its ruling of *27 April 2001, Dansk Transport og Logistik against Nykøbing Falster Kommune*. The Board stated in this ruling that it is possible that an in-house tender could be favoured during a tender procedure and in the award phase in a manner which would violate the principle of equal treatment in the EC public procurement rules. However, the Complaints Board added that the question was open to doubt and did not establish a breach in the concrete case.

Such a violation could for instance relate to the bid evaluation where at least some national rules obligate the contracting authority to treat the in-house tender just like external bids for the evaluation process.[38] The Danish Finance Ministry's circular on tendering and outsourcing of state operational tasks and works also contains a provision in §10 (6) according to which em-

36. The common outcome being that the EC public procurement rules do not regulate the treatment of in-house tenderers as against external tenderers. See *R Portsmouth City Council Ex p. Coles and Ex p. George Austin* (Builders) Ltd (1997) 95 L.G.R. 494 (CA) and the case note of Peter Kunzlik, Public Procurement Law Review 1997 CS 73; Sue Arrowsmith, *The Law of Public and Utilities Procurement*, 2nd ed. 2005 p. 394 and the article of Martin Trybus in this publication.
37. For a similar reasoning see also Sue Arrowsmith's note on *R. v. Portsmouth City Council, ex p. Bonaco Builders*, Public Procurement Law Review 1996 CS 90 on p. CS 96. However, she appears not to have repeated that point of view in later publications.
38. The UK regulation is an example of this. See further on this Sue Arrowsmith, *The Law of Public and Utilities Procurement*, 2nd ed. 2005, pp. 395 and 396. The Court of Appeal held in Portsmouth that these provisions go further than the EC public procurement directives in this respect.

ployees that have elaborated the control bid cannot participate in the subsequent evaluation of the submitted bids.[39]

The ban on negotiations based on the principle of equal treatment of tenderers is also likely to have implications for the treatment of an internal tenderer. However, some authors[40] argue that a contracting authority must be allowed to enter into discussions with its own specialists that so far has solved the task in-house and must be entitled to discuss possible improvements that would make it irrelevant to contract with an external party. These authors also state that only the most rabid public procurement theorists could image that a contracting authority should decide on the issue blindfolded.

The issue was considered in the ruling from the Complaints Board of *27 April 2001, Dansk Transport og Logistik against Nykøbing Falster Kommune.* One of the arguments of the complainant was that a municipality had violated the principle of equal treatment in the EC public procurement rules by negotiating after the submission of bids with the in-house department that had submitted the internal offer. The Complaints Board held that a subsequent meeting between the evaluators and the in-house department after the submission of bids might have been a violation of the ban on negotiation if it had concerned an external tenderer. However, the complaint was rejected on this point. Firstly, because it was considered doubtful that the principle of equal treatment and thereby the ban on negotiations is relevant in the relationship between a contracting authority and an in-house department. Secondly, because the Board assessed that the internal department had not been favoured in the assessment of the bids and that the reality was that the tender procedure was annulled because the contracting authority could solve the task at a lower price than the external tenderers. The second part of the reasoning is worth noticing. It is very possible that the Board had established a breach of the principle of equal treatment on this point if the Board had assessed that the reality was that the internal department had been favoured. As this was not the case the Board could avoid ruling on an unclear point of law.

39. Jesper Fabricius and René Offersen, *EU's udbudsregler i praksis*, 2nd ed. 2006, presume on p. 97 that this provision does not apply to tender procedures covered by the EC public procurement rules, cf. §7 (4) in the circular. It is submitted that this interpretation is incorrect and that the rules in the circular simply supplement the EC public procurement rules. §7 (4) in the circular merely states that a contract award covered by the EC public procurement rules must be tendered out according to the EC public procurement regime.

40. See Jesper Fabricius and René Offersen, *EU's udbudsregler i praksis*, 2nd ed. 2006 p. 97.

It has been a common perception in Denmark that a contracting authority should announce in the tender notice or tender conditions that it expects a control bid (an internal offer). This also follows from §10 (1) in the Danish Finance Ministry's circular on tendering and outsourcing of state operational tasks and works. However, it is unclear whether such a requirement follows from EC public procurement law.[41] The issue was raised in the ruling from the Complaints Board of *27 April 2001, Dansk Transport og Logistik against Nykøbing Falster Kommune*, where the complainant also argued that the EC public procurement rules had been violated because it was not announced that there would be a control bid.[42] The Complaints Board rejected the complaint on this point and added that the EC public procurement rules do not require that the Danish rules on control bids should be followed and that violations of the latter rules fall outside of the competence of the Complaints Board. It is submitted that the Complaints Board ruling was correct on this point, but one could very well argue that such an obligation follows from the principle of transparency as the information could significantly influence the potential tenderers' decision on whether to participate in the tender procedure or not.[43]

Finally it is relevant to comment on a case, *ISS Facility Services A/S and Danish Industri against Silkeborg Kommune,*[44] which was recently considered by the Danish Court of Appeal (Vestre Landsret) which is the continuation of a complaint to the Competition Authority[45] and a ruling from the Danish Complaints Board for Public Procurement. The Competition Authority chose to submit a complaint to the Complaints Board for Public Procurement in continuation of the complaint it had received. This has only happened in very few cases, and the Competition Authority based this decision on the

41. Jesper Fabricius and René Offersen, *EU's udbudsregler i praksis*, 2nd ed. 2006 p. 98 find this doubtful, whereas Michael Steinicke and Lise Groesmeyer, *EU's Udbudsdirektiver med kommentarer*, 2nd ed 2008 p. 493 are more inclined to deduce such an obligation from the principle of transparency.
42. The Complainant also claimed that the contracting authority should have explicitly reserved the right to terminate the tender procedures without an award if the control bid proved to be the economically most advantageous. This claim was also rejected by the Complaints Board.
43. See also Michael Steinicke and Lise Groesmeyer, *EU's Udbudsdirektiver med kommentarer*, 2nd ed. 2008, p. 493.
44. Judgment of 15 May 2009 (V.L. B-0257-08).
45. Complaint of 5 April 2006 concerning the municipality of Silkeborg's termination of a tender procedure without an award. See the webpage of the Competition Authority under the date 22 November 2006 (the date of the completion of the initial treatment of the case within the Competition Authority).

fundamental questions raised in the case. The Complaints Board held in its ruling of *24 April 2007, Konkurrencestyrelsen mod Silkeborg Kommune,* that the contracting authority had violated the principles of equal treatment of tenderers and transparency by termination of the tender procedure without an award.

The contracting authority was a municipality, and the tender related to the cleaning of a public school. The municipality terminated the tender procedures, as it assessed that the tender which was the economically most advantageous and fulfilled the stipulated contract terms concerning working environment, cleaning standard and quality could not satisfy the working conditions that were wished for the relevant group of employees. It was decided to opt for a new modernized type of in-house solution. It is worth stressing that the municipality had submitted an internal offer in this case and that this offer had been evaluated as the second least advantageous tender out of a total of six submitted tenders. Furthermore, the Head of school, a committee on education in the municipality and apparently also the financial committee of the municipality had instead suggested the acceptance of the economically most advantageous tender. The case is an excellent example of the fundamental challenges regarding equal treatment and transparency that may occur when a tender procedure involves both an internal offer and external offers.

According to the judgment of 15 May 2009 the Danish Court of Appeal the municipality (Silkeborg Kommune) had not violated the EU principles of equal treatment of tenderers and the principle of transparency when it terminated the tender procedures as outlined above. The reasoning of the Court of Appeal has various weaknesses and is on some points at least highly questionable. Furthermore, the implications of this ruling are far-reaching as it allows contracting authorities an extremely wide discretion when it comes to termination of the tender procedures without an award. Not surprisingly the case will be appealed to the Danish Supreme Court.

4. Conclusion

The issue of in-house providings has not been the subject of many public procurement cases in Denmark, and the treatment in literature is relatively limited. The public procurement disputes have focused on the so-called extended in-house rule as dealt with in C-107/98, Teckal and several subsequent cases by the European Court of Justice. However, also the treatment of in-house tenderers in procedures covered by the EC public procurement rules has been the subject of debate and dispute and is likely to be at least as interesting for readers outside of Denmark.

The Danish authorities – including the Complaints Board for Public Procurement, which has the primary responsibility for the enforcement of the EC public procurement rules in Denmark – have in general been well aware of the complex developments in the case law of the European Court of Justice on in-house providing. The authorities have also generally adopted interpretations in compliance with EC public procurement law, although some exceptions to the rule can be detected in practice.[46]

Examples of the latter are the Complaints Board's ruling of *7 September 2005, Dansk Byggeri against Vejle Kommune* covered in section 2 of this article and the Ministry of Housing and Building's interpretation in 1998 related to the Complaints Board's ruling of *18 September 1998, Foreningen af Rådgivende Ingeniører against Frederiksberg Kommune* analysed in section 3 of this article. However, in the latter case the Complaints Board overruled the point of view of the above-mentioned ministry and ruled in accordance with the interpretation of the European Commission. The ruling has subsequently been generally accepted in Danish public procurement law literature.

As pointed out in section 2 of this article, the Danish legislation on public procurement, which applies to contracts that are not covered by the EC public procurement directives, was originally also not in strict compliance with EC public procurement law. The law contained a far too generous definition of connected companies and consequently a too broad interpretation of the in-house exception. However, the misleading provision entered into force as early as 2001 and was repealed in 2005 at which time the European Court of Justice had clarified that the extended in-house rule established by C-107/98, *Teckal* also applies to arrangements falling outside of the public procurement directives.[47]

It is also very interesting that the Complaints Board prior to the ruling of the European Court of Justice in *C-107/98, Teckal* had reached a similar result in a ruling of *11 October 1996, Luis Madsen and others against Odense Kommune*, cf. section 2 of this article.

46. Compare with H.P. Rosenmeier in section 5 of his article "*in-house-spørgsmålet i udbudsretten*", Festskrift til Det Danske Selskab for Byggeret, 2009, p.276. Rosenmeier briefly mentions a couple of the rulings from the Complaints Board and remarks that these rulings appear to be in conformity with the case law of the European Court of Justice.

47. Cf. *C-231/03, Coname.* See footnote 1.

Finally, it is noteworthy that the Complaints Board appears to be open-minded when it comes to imposing some obligations with regard to the respective treatment of in-house tenderers and external tenderers. This follows from the considerations of the Board in its ruling of *27 April 2001, Dansk Transport og Logistik against Nykøbing Falster Kommune,* cf. section 3 of this article. The Board stated in this ruling that it is possible that an in-house tender could be favoured during a tender procedure and in the award phase in a manner which would violate the principle of equal treatment in the EC public procurement rules. As mentioned above in section 3 it is very possible that the European Court of Justice will impose some obligations with regard to the respective treatment of in-house and external tenderers based on the principles of equal treatment and transparency. This issue has not been considered by the European Court of Justice in spite of its obvious importance in practice.

From the indivisible Crown to Teckal: the In-House provision of works and services in the United Kingdom

Professor Martin Trybus,
University of Birmingham, United Kingdom

1. Introduction*

Especially since the 1980s public authorities in the United Kingdom of Great Britain and Northern Ireland have reorganised by introducing separate units with varying degrees of independence. These units provide various types of public services, including construction. Frequently they operate as private companies, fully or partly owned by the public authority that created them. Moreover, the respective public authority is often represented in the management of these units or companies and even supervises their activities. Due to such arrangements of ownership and control, these reorganised units frequently qualify as in-house providers of services. This reorganisation occurred particularly in the context of local government but can also be found in the regional government structures of Scotland, Wales and Northern Ireland, as well as in the central government of the United Kingdom as a whole.

This chapter will discuss the treatment of in-house providers of works and services in the law of the United Kingdom. First, the analysis will provide a historical perspective. This will look at how United Kingdom law dealt with in-house providers during the period of the 1980s and 1990s, before this area became largely determined by European Community public procurement law. An understanding of the legislative initiatives and political context of these decades is essential for the understanding of the treatment of in-house

* The author wishes to thank Mr Paul Mora, Research Assistant of the Birmingham Law School, for research support on this chapter and Roberto Caranta, University of Turin, for his useful comments. All mistakes, however, remain the responsibility of the author.

providers in the current statutory and case law framework. Second, the chapter will consider the treatment of in-house providers in the statutory instruments implementing the Public Sector Directive 2004/18/EC in the United Kingdom, namely the Public Contracts Regulations 2006 applicable in England, Wales, and Northern Ireland. In Scotland separate Public Contract (Scotland) Regulations 2006 were implemented and the chapter will generally focus on England, Wales, and Northern Ireland with only limited applicability to Scotland with its increasingly devolved government. Third, two leading cases from the highest courts of the United Kingdom dealing with the in-house provision of services will be discussed, namely the rulings in *Portsmouth* and *Risk Management*. The chapter is aimed at providing an overview of the current legal situation of in-house providers in the laws of the United Kingdom. It will be shown that today the question of in-house provision of services in the United Kingdom is largely based on and meeting the requirements of the relevant Community law.

2. The 1980s and 1990s: Compulsory Competitive Tendering (CCT)

The reorganisation of the public sector outlined above posed the fundamental question of the relationship of especially local governments with these new units with respect to the procurement of services. The United Kingdom central government followed a market testing policy whereby departments, agencies, and local governments were to test whether services currently carried out by these units could be provided more efficiently and cost effectively by the private sector. The possible result of such an exercise was of course the downsizing or even closure of the in-house unit which would be with considerably less or completely without work. With respect to central government departments and agencies and the National Health Service (NHS), a policy of market testing was implemented on an administrative basis rather than on the basis of legally binding rules.[1] Similarly, with respect to local government the initial approach was based on encouraging market testing on a voluntary basis.[2] However, while there was an increase in central government services being carried out by the private sector based on this 'soft law' approach, there was significant resistance to the policy in many local authori-

1. Arrowsmith, "*Developments in Compulsory Competitive Tendering*" (1994) 3 Public Procurement Law Review CS153-172.
2. Ibid.

ties. Therefore, under the Local Government (Planning and Land) Act 1980 and the Local Government Act 1988, introduced by the Conservative governments of the 1980s, local authorities were forced to open up services provided by their own units to private competition. This requirement was called 'Compulsory Competitive Tendering (hereinafter CCT)'. The policy was related to other policies, namely, the externalisation of central government functions, compulsory market testing in the health service, and the privatisation of utilities and nationalised industries.[3] While the economic rationale for CCT might have been the dominant factor, it also needs to be taken into account that the Conservative governments in London saw many local governments and their workforce as a power base of the opposition Labour Party and the trade unions. CCT was designed to achieve value for money and efficiency but also to cut the workforce of the local authorities, which were mostly controlled by the then opposition. Another aspect to emphasise is that CCT was introduced before the major reform of European Community public procurement law which culminated in the new Directives of the early 1990s: 92/50/EEC, 93/36/EC, 93/37/EC and 93/38/EC.

Services identified for CCT were only allowed to be carried out by the in-house organisation if it won the tender for the contract to provide those services in an open competition against private sector companies. Local authority in-house organisations were known as 'direct service', or 'direct labour', organisations. The Local Government Acts of the 1980s prescribed CCT for 'blue collar' services. Services subject to CCT through the Local Government (Planning and Land) Act 1980 were: new construction; building maintenance; and some highways work. Activities defined for CCT through the Local Government Act 1988 were: refuse collection; building cleaning; street cleaning; schools and welfare catering; other catering; grounds maintenance; repair and maintenance of vehicles; and management of sports and leisure facilities. Through powers granted by the Local Government Act 1992 to the Secretary of State, CCT was also to be extended to a number of 'white collar' services, namely part or all of fleet management; security; architectural; engineering; property management; finance; personnel; legal; computing; corporate and administrative; housing management; home-to-school transport; libraries and theatres.[4] In putting work out to CCT, local authorities had to abide by a set

3. Badcoe, "*The national procurement strategy for local government*" (2004) 12 Public Procurement Law Review NA181-192, at 182.
4. This list was compiled by Frederick in "*Why Compulsory Competitive Tendering for Local Government Services is not as Good as Privatisation*", Economic Notes

of regulations, designed principally to avoid anti-competitive behaviour. The Local Government (Direct Service Organisation) Competition Regulations 1993 were adopted under the 1988 and 1992 Local Government Acts to regulate the details of the CCT procedures.[5] The standing orders issued by the local authorities themselves had to comply with these requirements.

CCT had certain benefits. Badcoe points out that it "improved management of services, via explicit specification of requirements, analysis of tasks, methodology and costs, and the introduction of monitoring arrangements."[6] CCT is also considered to have brought benefits in the form of cost savings and improvements in service quality. While there have been cases where the in-house provider was replaced by a more cost efficient private company, it appears that putting the relevant services out to tender resulted in most contracts being awarded to the in-house providers.[7] These had slimmed down, became more cost-conscious and responsive and improved their productivity and quality.[8]

CCT was increasingly criticised during the 1990s. The main criticism was that it created a separation between client and provider even when the latter comprised of directly employed in-house staff, the so-called 'client/contractor split'. While many local councils made it as difficult as possible for a private provider to win the contract, if a private sector provider had actually won the contract, an adversarial relationship developed between the two sides of the split: many local governments saw the private sector as the enemy.[9] This approach was often continued in the contract management phase, making it hard for the providers to deliver efficiently and according to the specifications. However, as a result of the adversarial, penalty and dispute focused style of management, the split also applied when the in-house provider had won the contract.[10] As many private providers lost interest in bidding for such a contract, the market for local government services shrunk considerably.

No. 52, Libertarian Alliance, London, 1994, at http://www.libertarian.co.uk/-lapubs/econn/econn052.pdf.

5. For an analysis of these Regulations see Arrowsmith, "*Developments*" *supra* note 1, at CS 161-169.
6. Badcoe, *supra* note 3, at NA 182.
7. Frederick, supra note 4, at 1.
8. *Ibid.*
9. Badcoe, *supra* note 3, at NA 182.
10. *Ibid.*

In a 1998 consultation paper of the Department of Environment, Transport and Regions[11] the rationale for the later abolition of CCT was summarised as follows:

"Under Compulsory Competitive Tendering service quality has often been neglected and efficiency gains have been uneven and uncertain, and it has proved inflexible in practice. There have been significant costs for employees, often leading to high staff turnover and the demoralisation of those expected to provide quality services. Compulsion has also bred antagonism, so that neither local authorities nor private sector suppliers have been able to realise the benefits that flow from a healthy partnership. All too often the process of competition has become an end in itself, distracting attention from the services that are actually provided to local people. CCT will therefore be abolished."

After the 1999 elections, which brought the Labour Party to power, CCT was largely replaced by 'Best Value'.[12] Under the 1999 Local Government Act,[13] which entered into force in April 2000, local councils, police and fire authorities have a legal obligation to deliver a continuous improvement in the standard and efficiency of their services, bringing in outside contractors where appropriate. 'Best value' replaces CCT, which, it is thought, placed too much emphasis on cost-cutting at the expense of quality of service. Local councils are required to draw up an annual Best Value Performance Plan (BVPP) and their progress is measured against Best Value Performance Indicators (BVPI), which is monitored by the Audit Commission.[14]

While the years of CCT are long gone and 'Best Value' has replaced it and changed practices to a large degree, the effects of the 1980s and 1990s can still be felt today. Many local authorities have acquired a negative reputation as a procurement client which makes it difficult for them to attract good quality competition for their contracts from the private sector.[15] Moreover, in-house providers suffered as a result of the uncertainty created by the policy by loosing managers and staff. These effects also feature prominently in the case law discussed below.

11. Department of the Environment, Transport and the Regions (1998) *Improving local services through best value*: Consultation Paper London, DETR, at s. 1.5.
12. For a more detailed account see: Bullivant, "*Replacing compulsory competitive tendering with a duty of best value: a review of the Government's proposals*" (1997) 6 Public Procurement Law Review CS238-241.
13. http://www.opsi.gov.uk/acts/acts1999/ukpga_19990027_en_1.
14. Independent body that monitors the performance and efficiency of local authorities, health authorities, police and fire authorities.
15. Badcoe, *supra* note 3, at NA 182.

3. Statutory law

The *United Kingdom* Regulation SI 2006/6 implemented Directive 2004/17/EC and Regulation SI 2006/5 implemented Directive 2004/17/EC. Both entered into force on 31st January 2006.[16] These Regulations apply in England, Wales, and Northern Ireland. Scotland has implemented separately and the new Scottish Regulations also entered into force on 31st January 2006. With the further progress of devolution, separate instruments for the devolved assemblies in Wales and Northern Ireland are possible. The Regulations apply only to public and utilities contracts within the field of application of the Directives, most importantly to contracts above the value thresholds of these instruments.

Article 18 Public Sector Directive 2004/18/EC was implemented with Regulation 6 (2) (l) Public Contracts Regulations 2006. It reads:

> "These Regulations do not apply to the seeking of offers in relation to a proposed public contract, framework agreement or dynamic purchasing system [...] under which *services are to be provided by a contracting authority*, or by a person which is a contracting authority in another relevant state for the purposes of the [Public Sector Directive] because that contracting authority or person has an exclusive rights, or ...
>
> (i) to provide the services, or
> (ii) which is necessary for the provision of the services;
>
> in accordance with any published law, regulation, or administrative provision, which is compatible with the EC Treaty, [...]"

This implementation is compliant with Article 18 Directive 2004/18/EC.[17] This follows the general approach of United Kingdom legal instruments im-

16. See: www.opsi.gov.uk/si/si200600.htm. The OGC web site (www.ogc.gov.uk) also contains associated guidance, including guidance on central purchasing bodies: (2006) 15 Public Procurement Law Review NA82-90. For detailed commentary on implementation for England, Wales, and Northern Ireland see S. Arrowsmith, "*Implementation of the New EC Procurement Directives and the Alcatel Ruling in England and Wales and Northern Ireland: a Review of the New Legislation and Guidance*" (2006) 15 Public Procurement Law Review 86.
17. Article 18 Directive 2004/18/EC reads:
"This Directive shall not apply to public service contracts awarded by a contracting authority to another contracting authority or to an association of contracting authorities on the basis of an exclusive right which they enjoy pursuant to a published law, regulation or administrative provision which is compatible with the Treaty."

plementing public procurement directives whereby most of the directives are implemented verbatim with only minor adjustments. The Scottish Public Contracts (Scotland) Regulations (SSI 2006/01) contain a similar provision. However, this situation is different from that under the Public Contracts Regulation in place before the implementation of 2006.[18] The latter applied to the entire United Kingdom; there was no separate Scottish instrument.

4. The Crown is indivisible

As a starting point it needs to be pointed out that even without Article 6 of the Public Contracts Regulations 2006 and the Public Contracts (Scotland) Regulations 2006 the rules do not apply to arrangements between organisations which are part of the same legal person. At United Kingdom central government level, legal powers, in general, derive from the Crown. In United Kingdom law, the Crown is indivisible, the Crown is a single legal entity and each Crown body discharges functions on behalf of the Crown. The Crown is one legal person, and as such services provided from one Crown body to another are considered 'in-house' service provision.

5. The In-House exception in case law

In addition to the indivisibility of the Crown, the rules do not apply to arrangements between organisations which, although legally separate, are so closely connected that it would be inappropriate to make their dealings subject to the rules, and are, for procurement purposes, considered to be indistinguishable. This is the 'in-house' exception which was first established by the European Court of Justice in the case of *Teckal*[19] and, as outlined above, is now part of the statutory implementation in both the United Kingdom Public Contracts Regulations 2006 and the Public Contracts (Scotland) Regulations 2006. The details and precise application in the United Kingdom, however, are best illustrated by case law, namely the rulings in *Portsmouth* and *Risk Management.*

18. See s. Arrowsmith, *The Law of Public and Utilities Procurement* (Sweet & Maxwell: London, 2nd ed. 2005), at 394-396.
19. Case C-107/98, *Teckal SrL* v *Commune di Viano* [1999] ECR I-8121. See the discussion in chapter 00 by Caranta, at 000-000.

a. The *Portsmouth* Case 1995-1997

The leading case of *R. v Portsmouth City Council ex parte Peter Coles and Colwick Builders Limited and e parte George Austin Limited*[20] (hereinafter '*Portsmouth*') was first the subject of a High Court judgment in *R. v Portsmouth City Council, ex p. Bonaco Builders* (see below) before it was decided by the Court of Appeal.

i. The facts

The case concerned three contracts for the local authority housing estates of Portsmouth City Council. More specifically there was a maintenance contract over a three year period, an improvement contract (for example replacing kitchen and bathroom fittings), and a BISF contract (external renovation of a specific group of houses). Parts of this work had previously been carried out by the Council's in-house Portsmouth Contract Services (PCS). Contract notices for the maintenance contract and possibly the BISF were placed in the Official Journal. The notice stipulated on award criteria that "Tenders will be accepted on the basis of best value for money. The Council do not bind themselves to accept the lowest or any tender." The improvement and the BISF contract were later advertised in the local press. A report to the Council's Policy and Resources Committee noted that PCS had previously carried out maintenance work worth about £1.6 million and said regarding the improvement and BSIF contracts that "[t]he cumulative effect of a reduction in the work awarded to PCS under both contracts would involve very substantial redundancy payments." The Committee then considered all three contracts at the same time, taking account of another report which stated that on the basis of value for money PCS would get £135,000 per annum under the maintenance contract and nothing under the other two contracts. This would have meant that money could be saved on the housing revenue account at the expense of the general fund of the Council. The Council then decided to award 40% of the works contract, 60% under the improvement contract, and all the work of the BISF contract to PCS. It is important to emphasise that what emanates from the facts is that the tenderers did not know about redundancy costs being an award criterion since the Council itself had not decided on this issue at the time it called for tender.[21] The applicants had been the lowest ten-

20. *R. v Portsmouth City Council Ex p. Coles and Ex. p. George Austin (Builders) Ltd.* [1997] 95 LGR 494 (Court of Appeal).
21. Craig, "*Public works procurement: the Portsmouth case*" (1999) 15 Construction Law Journal 88-110, at 107.

derers under the maintenance contract and the improvement contract respectively and applied for judicial review.

ii. The High Court judgment

In the Queen's Bench division of the High Court Keen J. held that the Public Works Regulations 1991 applied to the improvement contract but not to the maintenance and BSIF contracts.[22] Regulation 20 stipulated that

> "[w]here a contracting authority intends to award a public works contract on the basis of the offer which is the most economically advantageous it shall state the criteria on which it intends to base its decision, [...] in the contract notice or in the contract documents."

The judge held that:

> "[...] if the Council was proposing to adopt the approach which it did, it should have stated in a contract notice or in the contract documents that it intended to take account of the effects of any award on its overall financial position, including the financial consequences for itself as the employer of a direct labour force"

There was no obligation to award the contract to the lowest tender but the Council had violated Regulation 20 by failing to state the criteria in one of the ways required there. With regard to the maintenance contract to which the Regulations did not apply, Article 29 of the Works Directive 93/37/EC was considered to have direct effect, since at the relevant time the deadline for the implementation of the Directive had passed without the United Kingdom having had implemented it. Keene J. repeated the same view he had expressed with respect to the Regulation containing the same rule and held that insofar as they had suffered a loss as a result of a breach of Article 29 (2) of the Works Directive the applicants would have a claim for damages.

Generally, two important aspects of the award of contracts to in-house bidders where considered in this judgment. First: can a contracting authority take the redundancy costs which it would cause by not awarding the work to the in-house provider into account as a factor in favour of that in-house service? Keene J. rejected the argument that redundancy costs can be regarded as an aspect of lowest price since many of the factors expressly listed as an illustration in the Directives and Regulations for the economically most advantageous offer criterion rather than the lowest price criterion relate to costs.

22. Judgment of 6th June 1995, see annotations by Arrowsmith, "*Interpretation of the Procurement Directives and Regulations: a note on R. v. Portsmouth City Council, ex p. Bonaco Builders*" (1996) 5 Public Procurement Law Review CS90-96.

The judge then ruled that redundancy costs can be considered in the context of assessing the economically most advantageous offer. Arrowsmith agreed as this was an objective criterion which relates to the economic advantages of the bid concerned.[23]

Second, can an authority terminate an award procedure to retain the contract in-house? The United Kingdom Regulations did already provide that a bid by another part of the same purchaser is required to be treated as an offer just like any other (external bid) for the purpose of the rules on the evaluation of bids.[24] While it is clear that the award can only be made in accordance with the Directives and Regulations, an award made on the basis of an economic criterion which was not listed in the contract notice as was the case here, is unlawful. It remained less clear after the High Court judgment in *Portsmouth*, whether the contract would be retained in-house for other reasons, for example because it changed its policy on its in-house services. If it could, then as Arrowsmith pointed out, despite the application of the Regulations, a contracting authority might be able to take redundancy costs into account when deciding on whether to contract out the work. However, this was not considered in the judgment.[25] Generally, after this judgment "The difficult question of the application of the procurement rules to in-house bids remain[ed] an open issue which [was] ripe for consideration by the European and national courts."[26]

iii. The Court of Appeal judgment

During the hearing of the appeal against the High Court judgment in the Court of Appeal, Portsmouth City Council submitted a new argument for Coles and Austin not being able to rely on the Works Directive. The Works Directive applied only to "public works contracts", which are defined as "contract for pecuniary consideration concluded in writing between a contractor (a natural or legal person) and an authority awarding contracts." Article 29 (9) Works Directive itself refers to "[t]he criteria on which the authori-

23. Arrowsmith, *ibid.*, at CS95.
24. Works Regulations 20 (8); Supply Regulations 21 (9); Services Regulations 21 (9).
25. Arrowsmith, "*Interpretation of the Procurement Directives and Regulations: a note on R. v. Portsmouth City Council, ex p. Bonaco Builders*", *supra* note 22, at CS96.
26. *Ibid*, at CS96.

ties awarding contracts shall base the award of contracts." This "killer argument"[27] led to the conclusion summarised by Leggat L.J. as follows:

> " [...] when awarding work to PSC the Council were not, and could not have been, awarding contracts properly so-called, because even if (which seems unlikely) PSC must be regarded as a 'natural or legal person', it was not possible for the Council to contract with its own department. Liberally though the European Court of Justice might be expected to construe the provision, it is difficult to see how (unless by analogy) a Council could be regarded as having with this department any 'contract for pecuniary consideration'."[28]

This was different to the approach to this matter in the 1991 Regulations. According to Regulation 5 the Regulations applied "whenever a contracting authority seeks offers in relation to a public works contract". Moreover, the Regulations expressly provided in Regulation 20 (8) that:

> "[f]or the purposes of this regulation an 'offer' includes a bid by one part of a contracting authority to carry out work or works for another part of the contracting authority when the former part is invited by the latter part to compete with the offers sought from other persons."

However, the 1991 Regulations had not yet implemented the Works Directive. The Court rejected the argument of Coles and Austin that the Regulation simply reproduced the express or implied effect of the Works Directive as part of the United Kingdom implementation process and held instead that:

> "[Regulation 20 (8)]] must be regarded as having been included by the draftsmen of the 1991 Regulations in order to make good an obvious lacuna in the Works Directive."

The same point had already been made in the similar case of *Cumbria Professional Care Ltd v. Cumbria County Council*[29] where Turner J. held with respect to the Services Directive:

> "Since as matter of law, the respondents cannot contract with themselves, the Directive cannot in my judgment, be called into play [...] A contract as recognised by domestic law, is not made when, as a result of an administrative decision a service provider, who happens to be in-house with the purchasing authority is selected to perform a function which the purchaser can lawfully award to itself."

27. Craig, *supra* note 21, at 107.
28. C.A. transcript, at p. 11A-C.
29. [1996] EWHC 63.

Leggat L. J. considered the same reasoning to apply in *Portsmouth*:

"[it is] inescapable that, when awarding work to PSC the Council were not entering into a public service contract within the meaning of the Works Directive, which could therefore have no application to the transaction."[30]

Hobhouse L.J. agreed on the following lines:

"Where a Local Authority, as did this County Council, decides to use its own direct labour department, it is deciding not to award a contract. Such a decision is something which falls outside the purview of the Directives although [...] it has been covered by the 1991 Regulations."[31]

Thorpe L.J. agreed. Consequently the Court of Appeal did not uphold the appeal. The Directives do not apply to a decision to keep a work in-house because this does not involve a contract.[32] Therefore it was lawful to award the contract to the in-house bidder.

iv. An assessment

The *Portsmouth* ruling was criticised in the academic literature of the time. Kunzlik questioned the fairness of the basic rule of the judgment, by which an authority can initiate a procurement procedure in which the in-house provider participates and then awards the contract to the latter without following the requirements of the procurement procedure.[33] Moreover, as can be seen from the discussion on CCT above, this unfairness can have a negative effect on competition for services for which an in-house provider exists. If the authority can 'pull the break' at almost any time of a procurement procedure, terminate the procedure and ask the in-house provider to do the work, private competitors might consider that too risky a framework to operate in. After all, there is no guarantee that the authority will not terminate the procedure, potentially wasting a great deal of time and effort of other tenderers. This 'pull the break' privilege of contracting authorities is different from their general 'in-house' privilege. In *Portsmouth*, the authority should have considered the redundancy costs at a much earlier stage, before wasting the time, money,

30. C.A. transcript, at p. 12B-C.
31. *Ibid.* at p. 19A-B.
32. Arrowsmith, *The Law of Public and Utilities Procurement*, *supra* note 18, at 394-395.
33. Kunzlik, "*Interpretation of the procurement Directives and Regulations*" (1997) 6 Public Procurement Law Review CS73-87, at CS85.

and effort of the applicants. It would not be unreasonable to expect the authority to compensate the other bidders for at least their bidding costs when using such an "unmeritorious defence".[34] Ron Craig points out that on the authority of Canadian case law the applicants could possibly have argued that the authority was in breach of a "tendering contract" in using secret and undisclosed contract award criteria to obtain compensation.[35] However, a comprehensive discussion of this idea would go beyond the aim of this chapter.

Furthermore, Kunzlik pointed out that a tenderer might already have complained about a breach of a Directive before the award to the in-house provider and that the *Portsmouth* judgment indicates that in such a case there would be no decision of an outstanding complaint since there would be no "public works contract".[36] This would be unsatisfactory since an applicant wishing to bring review proceedings could not do so with confidence "until the very end of the process, if and when the authority awarded a contract to a third party". This gap questions the effectiveness of public procurement remedies in such a case. However, this would not represent a violation of the effectiveness requirement of the public procurement remedies directives and their national implementations since these directives and their requirements apply only to 'contracts' to which the substantive procurement directives apply.

Moreover, the possibility to award the contract to the in-house provider in the course of an ongoing competitive procurement procedure without following any of the procedural requirements of the Directive does not comply with the principle of the equality of tenders.[37] However, as also pointed out by Kunzlik,[38] the notion "public works contract" defined the scope of the Directive and without such a 'contract' the Directive and thus its principle of equal treatment does not apply. Arguably, the same principle of equality in the EC Treaty equally requires a public works, services, or supplies contract to apply.

The Court of Appeal stated that as a matter of English law there could be no contract between an authority and its in-house provider. However, within

34. *Ibid.*
35. Craig, *supra* note 22, at 110 citing *Health Care Developers Incorporated v. The Queen in right of Newfoundland* (1996) 136 D.L.R. (4th) 609, Newfoundland Court of Appeal, discussed also by Craig in (1997) 16 A.C.L.R. 33, and *Procurement Law for Construction and Engineering Works and Services* (Blackwell Science: Oxford, 1998), at 279.
36. Kunzlik, *supra* note 33, at CS86.
37. *Ibid.*
38. Kunzlik, *supra* note 33, at footnote 42.

the field of application of EU public procurement law, the term must have an EU rather than a national meaning since otherwise the objective of the Directives to complete the internal (procurement) market could be undermined by many different national meanings of the essential term 'contract'.[39] However, as the problem did not even arise in the context of the implementing Regulations, this point is of "passing transitional importance." The aspect of more general and sustainable importance is the *Portsmouth* approach to interpret key terms in the Directives on the basis of their normal meaning according to English legal concepts. It has been suggested by Arrowsmith that "in determining when a contract exists for the purposes of the Community rules the courts are likely to look to substance of the transaction, and not whether it constitutes a contract under the domestic law of the relevant Member State, and thus it may be prepared to hold that certain transactions of this type are in fact subject to the Community rules".[40] Kunzlik pointed out that the Court of Appeal's approach in *Portsmouth* suggests that the English courts may "find it difficult to take this step".[41]

The interpretation that the Directives do not apply to a decision to keep a work or service in-house was adopted by the Court of Appeal for England and Wales in *Portsmouth* and in *Cumbria Professional Care*. This interpretation was later confirmed with application for the entire EU by the European Court of Justice in *Teckal*. *Teckal* clarifies that an in-house arrangement is not a contract for the purpose of the Directives. This rule applies even when, different to the ruling in *Portsmouth* for the United Kingdom, the national legal system does consider an in-house arrangement to be a contract.

b. The *Risk Management* Case 2008-2009

The recent case of *Risk Management Partners v Brent London Borough Council*[42] concerned an authority that had commenced a competitive procurement procedure. It later abandoned the process, and made a direct award to London Authorities Mutual Ltd (LAML). The latter is jointly owned by a number of London boroughs, including Brent. The claimant, Risk Management Partners Limited (RMPL), was a bidder in the abandoned process and

39. *Ibid.*, at CS86.

40. Arrowsmith, *The Law of Public and Utilities Procurement* (Sweet & Maxwell: London, 1st ed. 1996) at 439.

41. Kunzlik, *supra* note 33, at CS86.

42. *Risk Management Partners v Brent LBC* [2008] EWHC (Admin) per Burnton LJ. For annotations see: P. Henty in (2008) Public Procurement Law Review NA240-244.

applied for damages. It is the second of two judgments of 16th May 2008 which is of main interest for the purposes of this chapter.[43]

i. The High Court judgment

The main issue of general interest regarding the operation of in-house services considered by the High Court was whether the principles of *Teckal* were available under English law. Brent had argued that it did not need to comply with the Regulations as it satisfied the *Teckal* exemption due to the nature of its relationship with LAML. In contrast, the claimants RMPL had argued that when implementing Directive 2004/18/EC the United Kingdom regulator had deliberately excluded the exemption in *Teckal* and related other cases. While other provisions of the Regulations expressly referred to the Directive, there was no reference to the *Teckal* exemption. Regulation 30 Public Contracts Regulations 2006 contain an obligation of authorities to award contracts to the lowest or best offer. Regulation 30 (10) provides that an offer can include:

> "a bid by one part of a [...] authority [...] to another part of the [...] authority when the former part is invited by the latter part to compete with offers sought from other persons."

The claimants RMPL interpreted this as showing the intention of the United Kingdom regulator to extend the Regulations to situations where under the Directive the *Teckal* exemption would apply. When implementing exclusions in Directives, Member State legislators have the discretion not to implement them.

What followed from the Court was a detailed analysis of Directive 2004/18/EC which formed the basis of the Public Contracts Regulations and the relevant case law starting with *Teckal*[44] itself but also covering *Arnhem*,[45] *Stadt Halle*,[46] *ARGE*,[47] *Parking Brixen*,[48] *Carbotermo*,[49] and *ASEMFO*.[50]

43. [2008] EWHC 1094 (Admin). In the first judgment of 22 April 2008 [2009] EWHC 692 (Admin) it was held that Brent London Borough Council had no power to participate in London Authorities Mutual Limited, since neither section 111 of the Local Government Act 1972 nor the wellbeing power in section 2 of the Local Government Act 2000 gave that authority to the council. See: http://www.blackstonechambers.com/news/cases/risk_management.html.
44. Case C-107/98, *Teckal Srl* v *Comune di Viano* [1999] ECR I-8121.
45. Case C-360/96, *Gemeente Arnhem* v *BFI Holding BV* [1998] ECR I-6821.
46. Case C-26/03, *Stadt Halle and RPL Recyclingpark Lochau GmbH* v. *Arbeitsgemeinschaft Termische Restabfall-und Energieverwertungsanlage TREA Leuna* [2005] ECR I-1.

The High Court ruled that Regulation 30 does not show an intention of the United Kingdom legislator to extend the application of the Public Contracts Regulations to situations where *Teckal* would apply. This interpretation was also based on the Explanatory Memorandum of the Regulations prepared by the Office of Government Commerce. Burnton LJ ruled in particular:

"[...] I cannot see why the Government should have wanted to exclude the *Teckal* exemption from English law. There is nothing in the Explanatory Memorandum to indicate that it was intended to depart from the jurisprudence of the Court in this respect. It is noteworthy that paragraph (10) of Regulation 30 is limited in effect. It applies only to bids where one part of a contracting authority is invited by another to compete with offers sought from third parties. It has no application (not surprisingly) where a simple decision is made by a public authority to employ a part of it to provide services, when it has not gone out to tender. What is meant by "one part of a contracting authority" is not defined, but I do not see why a separate corporate entity satisfying the *Teckal* conditions should not be a part of a contracting authority for these purposes. If so, it is curious that the draftsman did not deal expressly with the exemption if he had intended to depart from it. Lastly, I do not see that excluding the exemption could be considered to be necessary super-equivalence."[51]

He concluded on this issue of interpretation that:

"[...] the term "contract" in the Regulations should be construed in the light of the expressed intention to implement the Directive, and as requiring two contracting parties that do not satisfy the *Teckal* conditions."[52]

Regulation 30 (1) applies only when the in-house division was invited to apply, not where it is decided to undertake a task in-house.

Burnton LJ then carefully applied *Teckal* to the case. Brent does not have to be the sole owner with a decisive control over LAML (ownership test). The LAML board is largely independent of its shareholders thereby reducing the ability of Brent to control it. Moreover, there was a delegation of LAML functions to a management company (dilution of control test.). The latter as-

47. Case C-94/99, *ARGE Gewässerschutz* v. *Bundesministerium für Land-und Forstwirtschaft* [2000] ECR I-11037
48. Case C-458/03, *Parking Brixen GmbH* v. *Gemeinde Brixen and Stadtwerke Brixen AG*, judgment of 13 October 2005, nyr.
49. Case C-340/04, *Carbotermo SpA* v. *Comune di Busto Arsizio* [2006] ECR I-4137.
50. Case C-295/05, *Asociacion Nacional de Empresas Forestales (ASEMFO)* v *Transformacion Agraria (Tragsa) and Administracion del Estado* [2007] ECR I-2999.
51. Paragraph 64 of the judgment.
52. Paragraph 65 of the judgment.

sessment involved in-depth review of the articles of association, policy documentation, and insurance policy. Due to the ownership of LAML and the dilution of control *Teckal* did not apply. The key passage[53] in the judgment is:

> "The general picture given by the documents to which I have referred is of a business the administration of which is relatively independent. Just as in *Stadt Halle* the fact that there was private participation in the ownership of the contractor was inconsistent with the *Teckal* exemption, and in *Carboteromo* the fact that the public authority's interest was held through a holding company was an indication that the *Teckal* exemption did not apply, so in my judgment the employment of a private company to manage LAML points against it. Moreover, and perhaps more importantly, there are contractual provisions that point to a degree of independence of decision that is inconsistent with the first condition. I refer in particular to Article 11 of the Articles of Association and to Rule 22 (1), under which a Participating Member will normally be excluded from the Board's consideration of its insurance claim. Similarly, the terms of the policies referred to in paragraph 77, are typical of a policy issued by a wholly independent insurer to its insured. They envisage a relationship (including disputes) between Brent and LAML that is inconsistent with *Teckal* [emphasis added]."

As the Court had found that Brent had not satisfied the *Teckal* control test, it did not proceed to consider the *Teckal* essential activities test.

ii. The Court of Appeal judgment

The High Court judgment outlined above was appealed by Brent, resulting in a Court of Appeal judgment on 9th June 2009.[54] Regarding the in-house issue of the case, Pill LJ first provided a partly even more detailed analysis of the *Teckal* case law of the Court of Justice. This included again, *Teckal,*[55] *Stadt Halle,*[56] *Parking Brixen,*[57] *Cabotermo,*[58] and *ASEMFO.*[59] Moreover, the analysis included Case C-220/06, *Asociación Profesional de Empresas de Reparto y Manipulado de Correspondencia* v. *Administración General del Estado*, decision of 18 December 2007[60] and Case C-371/05, *Commission* v.

53. See the article of Julia Rudin, http://www.sharpepritchard.co.uk/articles/risk-management-partners-limited-v-london-borough-of-brent, at page 4.
54. [2009] EWCA Civ 490; [2009] WLR (D) 179.
55. Paragraphs 64-69.
56. Paragraph 70.
57. Paragraph 71.
58. Paragraphs 75-79.
59. Paragraph 79.
60. [2007] ECR I-12175. The Court of Appeal dealt with the case under paragraph 82.

Italy, decision of 17th July 2008.[61] Finally, the judge included judgments decided after the High Court judgment in *Risk Management*, namely Case C-327/07, *Coditel Brabant* v. *Commune D'Uccle*, decision of 13th November 2008[62] and the advisory opinion of Advocate General Mazák in C-480/06, *Commission* v. *Germany*, delivered on 19th February 2009.[63] Pill LJ agreed with the High Court judgment of Burnton LJ outlined above. In paragraph 133 he summarises his assessment as follows:

"On the discrete issue whether the *Teckal* exemption applies in England and Wales [...], I note that the *Teckal* exemption is mentioned neither in the present Directive (which post-dated the *Teckal* decision) nor in the 2006 Regulations. *In my judgment, the intention of the Regulations was to implement the Directive as construed by the ECJ.* The terminology in the Regulations is similar to that in the Directive. It was plainly intended that the public procurement regime promoted by the Directive should be applied throughout the Union; recital 2 of the Directive speaks of the advisability of "provisions of community coordination of national procedures for the award of such contracts". It is not necessary to consider whether Regulations broadening the scope of the Directive would be lawful; in the absence of a clear intention to the contrary, it was in my view intended that the Regulations be construed in accordance with the jurisprudence of the ECJ. The expressions defined do not require a construction in national law different from that contemplated in the Directive [emphasis added]."

Similar to the High Court judgment Pill LJ applied the *Teckal* exemption to the facts of the case. He first considered the question whether there are contracts between the local authority and the entity concerned as it might appear from the wording of the first sentence of paragraph 50 of *Teckal*[64] that the very existence of a contract between the local authority and the entity is fatal to the application of the *Teckal* exemption. However, Pill LJ regarded that sentence only as one aspect of testing the relationship between the local authority and the entity concerned: "Paragraphs 48 to 51 of *Teckal*[65] must be

61. Not yet reported, available online in French at http://www.bailii.org/eu/cases/-EUECJ/2008/C37105.html. The Court of Appeal dealt with the case under paragraph 83.
62. Not yet reported. The Court of Appeal dealt with the case under paragraph 84.
63. Not yet reported. The Court of Appeal dealt with the advisory opinion under paragraph 90-91.
64. Paragraph 50 of the Teckal judgment reads:
"In that regard, in accordance with Article 1(a) of Directive 93/36, it is, in principle, sufficient if the contract was concluded between, on the one hand, a local authority and, on the other, a person legally distinct from that local authority. [...]"
65. Paragraphs 48 to 50 of the *Teckal* judgment read:

read together." While the contrast contemplated in paragraph 51 of *Teckal* was between contracts which are the equivalent of in-house departmental agreements, captive companies and their equivalent, and contracts where the local authority contracts with a person with independence from it and lacking the control it exercises over its own departments, he saw no merit in the argument that the *Teckal* exemption fails for want of a relevant contract:

> "Whatever its effect, the contract between the appellants and LAML was a contract as contemplated in paragraphs 48 to 51 of *Teckal*. The absence of a contract would normally indicate a departmental activity but, if there is a contract with the other entity, the *Teckal* principle may still extend to it."

On the question whether the first *Teckal* requirement was satisfied, Pill LJ ruled that an overall view of the arrangement between the authority or authorities and the other entity should be taken and the question should be whether there is control similar to that exercised over the authority's own departments. In the case at hand the local authorities are effectively the owners of LAML.[66]

Pill LJ then considered the dispute as to whether the relevant consideration is the power of the local authority over the legal entity on the basis of the documents or what would happen in practice. The present proceedings were brought before any settled practice between the local authorities and LAML had developed. In *Parking Brixen* the Court of Justice used the expression "in

"48. It is common ground in the present case that AGAC supplies products, namely fuel, to the Municipality of Viano in return for payment of a price.

49. As to whether there is a contract, the national court must determine whether there has been an agreement between two separate persons.

50. In that regard, in accordance with Article 1(a) of Directive 93/36, it is, in principle, sufficient if the contract was concluded between, on the one hand, a local authority and, on the other, a person legally distinct from that local authority. The position can be otherwise only in the case where the local authority exercises over the person concerned a control which is similar to that which it exercises over its own departments and, at the same time, that person carries out the essential part of its activities with the controlling local authority or authorities.

51. The answer to the question must therefore be that Directive 93/36 is applicable in the case where a contracting authority, such as a local authority, plans to conclude in writing, with an entity which is formally distinct from it and independent of it in regard to decision-making, a contract for pecuniary interest for the supply of products, whether or not that entity is itself a contracting authority."

As cited in Paragraph 66 of the Court of Appeal judgment.

66. Paragraph 127.

practice" and in *Carbotermo* the Advocate General required examination *in concreto*. In the judgment of Pill LJ the powers arising from the relevant documents provided the starting point for the analysis. However, it is permissible to consider the circumstances in which the arrangement will operate, including that LAML is an insurance company, in considering the powers of the authority or authorities over LAML and how they are likely to be exercised.[67] The guidance of the Court of Justice, for example, in *Parking Brixen*, paragraphs 67 to 72, and in *Carbotermo*, paragraphs 38 to 40, appears to the judge to assist the respondent LAML's case on the question of control. The burden of establishing control is on the appellants. In agreement with Burnton LJ in the High Court judgment, at paragraph 78, Pill LJ concludes that the relationship between the appellants and LAML is inconsistent with *Teckal*:

"While, in general meeting, a 75% membership of LAML may give directions to the Board, the powers of the Board are extensive. In exercising them, the directors of LAML, though the majority are appointed by Participating Members, owe duties to LAML and its needs. Those duties are owed by a director appointed by the appellants, even if that director is one of their senior officers. That is important in the context of insurance in which business must be conducted in accordance with the regulations of the Financial Services Authority and under its supervision and under the market agreed position as expressed by the Association of British Insurers."[68]

He continued:

"I note the power of the Board to terminate the membership of a Participating Member (article 11(b)) and the power to establish, collect, manage and redistribute both capital contributions and premiums of local authorities, a power delegated to the management company. In context, the power of a majority of participating members to call a general meeting, taken with the power to direct the Board by special resolution by a 75% majority, even taken with other factors relied on by the appellants, does not amount to control over LAML as contemplated in *Teckal*."[69]

Pill LJ concluded with the key passage regarding the control test of the *Teckal* judgment in this case:

"The intention to achieve the aim of operational independence is illustrated by the powers of the Board and the arrangements made with the management company and the terms of policies issued. I find it difficult to see how LAML can operate effectively unless its Board

67. Paragraph 128.
68. Paragraph 129.
69. Paragraph 130.

has considerable freedom to manage its insurance business. The nature of the business, and the possibly differing interests of different authorities and affiliates, are antithetic to the necessary local authority control."

Therefore the operational independence of LAML meant that Brent lacked the degree of control over it required by the *Teckal* exemption. Moore- Bick LJ and Hughes LJ delivered concurring judgments. The appeal of RMPL was dismissed in its entirety, not only but also with respect to the considerations on the in-house exemption of *Teckal* in the High Court judgment.

iii. Comments

The judgment is remarkable for three reasons. First, it shows that the question of in-house provision in the United Kingdom is now largely determined by the Directives and the case law following *Teckal*. While the question of whether the United Kingdom regulator had fully implemented the *Teckal* exemption was disputed by the parties, the High Court reluctantly[70] but rightly decided that the exemption had become part of the law of England, Wales, and Northern Ireland with the Public Sector Regulations 2006. This view was clearly confirmed by the Court of Appeal. The judgments are welcome in this respect as they ensure the effective application of an important aspect of Community law in this jurisdiction and enhance consistency with the other jurisdictions of the EU.

Second, the High Court and the Court of Appeal applied the *Teckal* exemption restrictively.[71] As pointed out in the annotations to the High Court judgment by one commentator, with respect to an entity owned by several authorities as in *Risk Management* it is unlikely that such an entity would not be run by an independent board as a multitude of owners could not each exercise sufficient control over the day-to-day running of the entity for the *Teckal* exemption to apply.[72] This would mean that in most cases an entity owned by several authorities would not be considered an in-house provider. It appears that the more complex the arrangements relating to a unit, the more difficult to satisfy the tests of the *Teckal* exemption. As another commentator pointed

70. Rudin, *supra* note 53, at 5.
71. Henty, *supra* note 42, at NA244; Heywood and Smith, Bevan Brittan LLP – Procurement Alert, 15th June 2009, on http://www.bevanbrittan.com/articles/Pages/-ProcurementAlertjune09.aspx (accessed 10th July 2009), last paragraph.
72. Taylor, "Court of Appeal and ECJ beg to differ on legality of shared service arrangements: Brent LNC v Risk Management Partners (the LAML case) and Commission v. Germany", on http://www.wragge.mobi/analysis_4652.asp (accessed 10th July 2009), at 3.

out, unless members of the local authority are running, managing, and thus controlling the unit themselves, the control test will not be satisfied.[73] There might be quite a few local authority companies across the United Kingdom who after *Risk Managment* might no longer be able to successfully rely on *Teckal*. Some commentators argue that local authorities will have to take great care when setting up new entities to ensure that they have sufficient control. They have to constrain the operational independence of the directors of these units to ensure their member's control, in particular when there are several authorities and their interests differ. Otherwise, they might be caught by the procurement rules.[74] The *Teckal* rule is an exemption. The European Court of Justice has always interpreted all exemptions narrowly and therefore the approach taken by the Court of Appeal should not come as a surprise.

Third, the burden of proof lies with the local authority seeking to rely on the exemption. This is in line with the established EU principle that the burden of proof for the existence of a situation justifying exemption lies with the one invoking it.

An interesting issue was raised by Gollancz[75] who contrasts the Court of Appeal's judgment in Risk Management with that of the Court of Justice in *Commission* v. *Germany* ('Stadtreinigung Hamburg').[76] As the latter case was decided in Luxembourg coincidently[77] on the same day, the judges in London could not take it into account. *Stadtreinigung Hamburg* concerned an arrangement between the City of Hamburg Waste Disposal Services and a number of other municipalities ('Landkreise') in neighbouring Lower Saxony making available waste disposal capacity to each other for a period of 20 years. The Court of Justice ruled that this arrangement was outside the public procurement rules because it represented in substance non-commercial internal administrative arrangement. Three principles emerge from the German case. First, co-operation between public bodies will not conflict with the public procurement rules and the internal market where it is exclusively designed to perform tasks in the public interest. Second, such co-operation will not be in conflict with these rules when the municipalities are simply using their own resources in co-operation with each other. Third and finally, an arrangement as in *Stadtreinigung Hamburg* does not represent a contract in the

73. Rudin, *supra* note 53, at 5.
74. Heywood and Smith, *supra* note 71. Taylor, *supra* note 72, at 4.
75. Gollancz, "Brent v. Risk Management – could it have been different?" on http://publicsector.practicallaw.com/blog/publicsector/plc/?p=157.
76. Case C-480/06, *Commission* v. *Germany*, judgment of 9th June 2009, nyr.
77. Taylor, *supra* note 72, at 4.

sense of the procurement directives but a non-commercial agreement to co-operate. There was no risk transfer or payment between the relevant municipalities, they were not contractually bound to perform and obligations, and only the operator who was not a party to the agreement received a reimbursement of fees.[78] Gollancz summarizes the Court of Justice judgment as

> "a common sense response to arrangements which could not reasonably be seen as coming within the procurement rules or undermining its objectives of the free movement of services and the opening up of competition between Member States."[79]

He then contrasts these facts and findings with those of *Risk Management*. With regards to the first public interest principle of *Stadtreinigung Hamburg*, he argues that while obtaining insurance is not in itself a public service it is necessary for local authorities to perform their functions as otherwise unacceptable risks for tax payers and third parties could arise. Thus Brent could have been performing a public interest task in establishing and insuring with LAML. With regards to the second own-resources principle of *Stadtreinigung Hamburg*, Gollancz points out that it would have been hard for the Court of Appeal to rule that LAML was only a body which facilitated co-operation between authorities using their own resources as the individual municipalities could not each have insured themselves. Thus the insurance cover of LAML for Brent was not a performance of a function of the latter using its own resources. With regards to the final non-commercial agreement principle of *Stadtreinigung Hamburg*, he argues that "normal contractual terms, as would be found in any insurance contract, governed the relationship between the members and the LAML".[80] Hence, due to the second and third principles, the Court of Appeal judgment in *Risk Management* is consistent with the Court of Justice judgment in *Stadtreinigung Hamburg*. Another commentator sees the discrepancy between the cases more critical:

> "Just as the ECJ was becoming increasingly tolerant to the pooling of public services, the Court of Appeal appears to have put on the brakes."[81]

Although he also acknowledges that *Stadtreinigung Hamburg* was more about central purchasing than shared services, he considers *Risk Management*

78. Gollancz, *supra* note 75.
79. *Ibid.*
80. Gollancz, *supra* note 75.
81. Taylor, *supra* note 72, at 4.

to be "quite fact specific" and possibly overturned when appealed. The higher United Kingdom Courts would get the opportunity to rule on similar cases in the light of *Stadtreinigung Hamburg*. This author concurs with this latter statement. However, in the light of the convincing analysis of Gollancz, he finds it less likely that the Court of Appeal judgment in *Risk Management* will be overturned on appeal based on the Court of Justice ruling in *Stadtreinigung Hamburg*. The earlier judgment complies with the entire *Teckal* case law, including the German case decided on the same day. Risk Management reflects the current law on in-house provision for England, Wales, and Northern Ireland.

6. Conclusions

This chapter provided an overview over the current legal situation of in-house providers in the law of the United Kingdom. After looking at how United Kingdom law dealt with in-house providers before its procurement law became largely determined by European Community rules, the paper considered the treatment of in-house providers in the statutory instruments implementing the Public Sector Directive 2004/18/EC in the United Kingdom, and with a number of relevant leading cases from the highest courts of the United Kingdom dealing with the in-house provision of services. The current law is largely meeting the requirements of European Community law on the matter.

7. Bibliography

Arrowsmith, Sue, "*Implementation of the New EC Procurement Directives and the Alcatel Ruling in England and Wales and Northern Ireland: a Review of the New Legislation and Guidance*" (2006) 15 Public Procurement Law Review 86

Arrowsmith, Sue, *The Law of Public and Utilities Procurement* (Sweet & Maxwell: London, 2nd ed. 2005)

Arrowsmith, "*Interpretation of the Procurement Directives and Regulations: a note on R. v. Portsmouth City Council, ex p. Bonaco Builders*" (1996) 5 Public Procurement Law Review CS90-96

Arrowsmith, Sue, *The Law of Public and Utilities Procurement* (Sweet & Maxwell: London, 1st ed. 1996)

Arrowsmith, Sue, "*Developments in Compulsory Competitive Tendering*" (1994) 3 Public Procurement Law Review CS153-172

Badcoe, Penny, "*The national procurement strategy for local government*" (2004) 12 Public Procurement Law Review NA181-192, at 182

Bullivant, Bill, "*Replacing compulsory competitive tendering with a duty of best value: a review of the Government's proposals*" (1997) 6 Public Procurement Law Review CS238-241.

Craig, Ron, "*Public works procurement: the Portsmouth case*" (1999) 15 Construction Law Journal 88-110

Craig, Ron, *Procurement Law for Construction and Engineering Works and Services* (Blackwell Science: Oxford, 1998)

Frederick, D., "*Why Compulsory Competitive Tendering for Local Government Services is not as Good as Privatisation*", Economic Notes No. 52, Libertarian Alliance, London, 1994, at http://www.libertarian.co.uk/-lapubs/econn/econn052.pdf

Gollancz, David "*Brent v. Risk Management – could it have been different*?" on http://publicsector.practicallaw.com/blog/publicsector/plc/?p=157 (accessed 9th July 2009)

Henty, Paul, *Annotations to Risk Management Partners v Brent LBC* in (2008) Public Procurement Law Review NA240-244

Heywood, Tim and Smith, Susie, Bevan Brittan LLP – Procurement Alert, 15th June 2009, on http://www.bevanbrittan.com/articles/Pages/ProcurementAlertjune09.aspx (accessed 10th July 2009)

Kunzlik, Peter, "*Interpretation of the procurement Directives and Regulations*" (1997) 6 Public Procurement Law Review CS73-87

Maughan, Alistair and Negishi, Masayuki, "*UK Procurement Law Digest: The "Teckal principle and in-house arrangements*", 17th |June 2009, on http://www.mofo.com/news/updates/bulletins/15727.html (accessed on 10th July 2009)

Rudin, Julia, "*Risk Management Partners Limited v. London Borough Council of Brent*" http://www.sharpepritchard.co.uk/articles/risk-management-partners-limited-v london-borough-of-brent (accessed 5th July 2009)

Taylor, Simon, "*Court of Appeal and ECJ beg to differ on legality of shared service arrangements: Brent LNC v Risk Management Partners (the LAML case) and Commission v. Germany*", on http://www.wragge.-mobi/analysis_4652.asp (accessed 10th July 2009).

List of Authors

Professor Roberto Caranta, University of Torino, Italy

Professor Fabrizio Cassella, University of Torino, Italy

Professor Martin Burgi, University of Bochum, Germany

Professor Mario Comba, University of Torino, Italy

Professor Julio González García, Complutense University of Madrid, Spain

Professor Marcin Spyra, Jagellonian University of Cracow, Poland

Professor Steen Treumer, University of Copenhagen, Denmark

Professor Martin Trybus, University of Birmingham, United Kingdom